Table of Contents

W9-BQS-344

Table of Contents

MATH
Level 1

Level 2

LANGUAGE ARTS

Level 1

Vocabulary: Synonyms

A **synonym** is a word that means the same, or nearly the same, as another word.
Example: quick and **fast**

Directions: Draw lines to match the words in Column A with their synonyms in Column B.

Column A	Column B
plain	unusual
career	vocation
rare	disappear
vanish	greedy
beautiful	finish
selfish	simple
complete	lovely

Directions: Choose a word from Column A or Column B to complete each sentence below.

1. Dad was very excited when he discovered the _____ coin for sale on the display counter.

2. My dog is a real magician; he can _____ into thin air when he sees me getting his bath ready!

3. Many of my classmates joined the discussion about _____ choices we had considered.

4. "You will need to _____ your report on ancient Greece before you sign up for computer time," said Mr. Rastetter.

5. Your _____ painting will be on display in the art show.

Synonym Search

Directions: Complete the puzzle using a synonym for each clue from the box.

Down:
1. shirt
2. kind
3. coat
4. forest
6. sleepy

Across:
1. skinny
3. hop
4. us
5. jacket
7. top

tired
jacket
top
woods
thin
we
shirt
coat
jump
nice

Vocabulary: Synonyms

| tired | greedy | easy | rough | minute | melted | friend | smart |

Directions: For each sentence, choose a word from the box that is a synonym for the bold word. Write the synonym above the word.

1. Boy, this road is really **bumpy**!

2. The operator said politely, "One **moment**, please."

3. My parents are usually **exhausted** when they get home from work.

4. "Don't be so **selfish**! Can't you share with us?" asked Rob.

5. That puzzle was actually quite **simple**.

6. "Who's your **buddy**?" Dad asked, as we walked onto the porch.

7. When it comes to animals, my Uncle Steve is quite **intelligent**.

8. The frozen treat **thawed** while I stood in line for the bus.

Vocabulary: Antonyms

An **antonym** is a word that means the opposite of another word.
Example: difficult and **easy**

Directions: Choose words from the box to complete the crossword puzzle.

friend	vanish	quit	safety	liquids	scatter	help	noisy

Across:

2. Opposite of **gather**
3. Opposite of **enemy**
4. Opposite of **prevent**
6. Opposite of **begin**
7. Opposite of **silent**

Down:

1. Opposite of **appear**
2. Opposite of **danger**
5. Opposite of **solids**

Antonyms

Directions: Complete the word pyramids using the antonym of the bold word in each sentence.

1. When I passed the test, it was the **saddest** day of my life.
2. I **dropped** the dishes on the way to the kitchen.
3. You may play after you **start** the dishes.
4. My sister is **little** compared to me.
5. He was **sad** because he won the prize.
6. How **short** was the snake we saw?

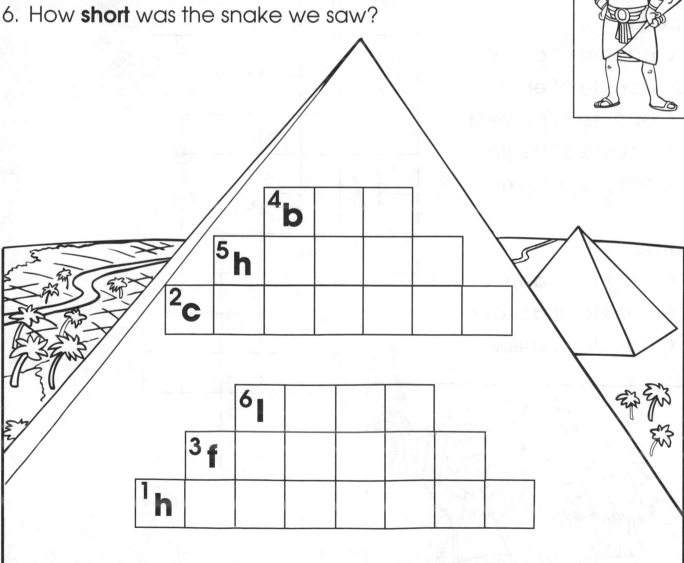

Homophones

Homophones are words that sound the same but have different spellings and meanings.

Directions: Complete each sentence using a word from the box.

blew	night	blue	knight	hour	in	ant	inn
our	aunt	meet	too	two	to	meat

1. A red _____ crawled up the wall.

2. It will be one _____ before we can go back home.

3. Will you _____ us later?

4. We plan to stay at an _____ during our trip.

5. The king had a _____ who fought bravely.

6. The wind _____ so hard that I almost lost my hat.

7. His jacket was _____.

8. My_____ plans to visit us this week.

9. I will come _____ when it gets too cold outside.

10. It was late at _____ when we finally got there.

11. _____ of us will go with you.

12. I will mail a note _____ someone at the bank.

Multiple-Meaning Words

Directions: Complete each sentence on pages 10 and 11 using one of the words below. Each word will be used only twice.

1. The kitten watched the _____ crawl slowly up the wall.

2. "You wouldn't _____ me, would you?" asked Dad.

3. Do you think Aunt Donna and Uncle Mike will come to my school _____ ?

4. He hit the ball so hard it broke the _____ .

5. "My favorite part of the story is when the princess goes to the _____ ," sighed Veronica.

6. My brother scored the first _____ in the game.

Multiple-Meaning Words

7. We will have to _____ quietly while the baby is sleeping.

8. Before we go to the store, I want to get some coins out of my _____.

9. The nature center will bring a live _____ for our class to see.

10. We sat on the_____ as we fished in the river.

11. The umpire decided the pitcher needed a new _____.

12. We will _____ in a race tomorrow.

13. "Can we please go to the _____ after I clean my room?" asked Jordan.

14. That boomerang can really_____!

15. Is it okay to _____ my bike here?

16. The baby goat, or _____, follows its mother everywhere.

Nouns

A noun names a person, place or thing.
Examples:

> **person** — sister, uncle, boy, woman
> **place** — building, city, park, street
> **thing** — workbook, cat, candle, bed

Directions: Circle the nouns in each sentence.
The first one has been done for you.

1. The (dog) ran into the (street.)

2. Please take this book to the librarian.

3. The red apples are in the kitchen.

4. That scarf belongs to the bus driver.

5. Get some blue paper from the office to make a card.

6. Look at the parachute!

7. Autumn leaves are beautiful.

8. The lion roared loudly at the visitors.

Directions: Write the nouns you circled in the correct group.

Persons	Places	Things	
librarian	street	dog	

Verbs

When a verb tells what one person or thing is doing now, it usually ends in **s**. **Example:** She **sings**.

When a verb is used with **you**, **I** or **we**, we do not add an **s**.

Example: I **sing**.

Directions: Write the correct verb in each sentence.

Example:

I ___write___ a newspaper about our street.   **writes, write**

1. My sister _____ me sometimes.   **helps, help**

2. She _____ the pictures.   **draw, draws**

3. We _____ them together.   **delivers, deliver**

4. I _____ the news about all the people.   **tell, tells**

5. Mr. Macon _____ the most beautiful flowers.   **grow, grows**

6. Mrs. Jones _____ to her plants.   **talks, talk**

7. Kevin Turner _____ his dog loose everyday.   **lets, let**

8. Little Mikey Smith _____ lost once a week.   **get, gets**

9. You may _____ I live on an interesting street.   **thinks, think**

10. We _____ it's the best street in town.   **say, says**

Irregular Verbs

Directions: Circle the verb that completes each sentence.

1. Scientists will try to (find, found) the cure.

2. Eric (brings, brought) his lunch to school yesterday.

3. Everyday, Betsy (sings, sang) all the way home.

4. Jason (breaks, broke) the vase last night.

5. The ice had (freezes, frozen) in the tray.

6. Mitzi has (swims, swum) in that pool before.

7. Now I (choose, chose) to exercise daily.

8. The teacher has (rings, rung) the bell.

9. The boss (speaks, spoke) to us yesterday.

10. She (says, said) it twice already.

Irregular Verbs

Irregular verbs are verbs that do not change from the present tense to the past tense in the regular way with **d** or **ed**.

Example: sing, **sang**

Directions: Read the sentence and underline the verbs. Choose the past-tense form from the box and write it next to the sentence.

blow — blew	fly — flew
come — came	give — gave
take — took	wear — wore
make — made	sing — sang
grow — grew	

Example:

Dad will <u>make</u> a cake tonight.   made

1. I will probably grow another inch this year. _____

2. I will blow out the candles. _____

3. Everyone will give me presents. _____

4. I will wear my favorite red shirt. _____

5. My cousins will come from out of town. _____

6. It will take them four hours. _____

7. My Aunt Betty will fly in from Cleveland. _____

8. She will sing me a song when she gets here. _____

Adjectives

Adjectives are words that tell more about nouns, such as a **happy** child, a **cold** day or a **hard** problem. Adjectives can tell how many (**one** airplane) or which one (**those** shoes).

Directions: The nouns are in bold letters. Circle the adjectives that describe the nouns.

Example: Some people have (unusual) **pets**.

1. Some people keep wild **animals**, like lions and bears.

2. These **pets** need special care.

3. These **animals** want to be free when they get older.

4. Even small **animals** can be difficult if they are wild.

5. Raccoons and squirrels are not tame **pets**.

6. Never touch a wild **animal** that may be sick.

Complete the story below by writing in your own adjectives. Use your imagination.

My Cat

My cat is a very_____ animal. She has _____

and _____ fur. Her favorite toy is a _____ ball.

She has _____ claws. She has a _____ tail.

She has a _____ face and _____ whiskers.

I think she is the _____ cat in the world!

And and But

We can use **and** or **but** to make one longer sentence from two short ones.

Directions: Use **and** or **but** to make two short sentences into a longer, more interesting one. Write the new sentence on the line below the two short sentences.

Example:

The skunk has black fur. The skunk has a white stripe.

The skunk has black fur and a white stripe.

1. The skunk has a small head. The skunk has small ears.

_____

2. The skunk has short legs. The skunk can move quickly.

_____

3. Skunks sleep in hollow trees. Skunks sleep underground.

_____

4. Skunks are chased by animals. Skunks do not run away.

_____

5. Skunks sleep during the day. Skunks hunt at night.

_____

Prepositions

Prepositions show relationships between the noun or pronoun and another noun in the sentence. The preposition comes before that noun.

Example: The <u>book</u> is on the table.

> ## Common Prepositions
>
> | above | behind | by | near | over |
> |---|---|---|---|---|
> | across | below | in | off | through |
> | around | beside | inside | on | under |

Directions: Circle the prepositions in each sentence.

1. The dog ran fast around the house.

2. The plates in the cupboard were clean.

3. Put the card inside the envelope.

4. The towel on the sink was wet.

5. I planted flowers in my garden.

6. My kite flew high above the trees.

7. The chair near the counter was sticky.

8. Under the ground, worms live in their homes.

9. I put the bow around the box.

10. Beside the pond, there was a playground.

Parts of Speech

Nouns, pronouns, verbs, adjectives, adverbs and prepositions are all **parts of speech**.

Directions: Label the words in each sentence with the correct part of speech.

Example:

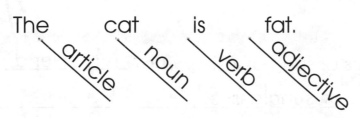

The   cat   is   fat.
article   noun   verb   adjective

1. My   cow   walks   in   the   barn.

2. Red   flowers   grow   in   the   garden.

3. The   large   dog   was   excited.

Subjects and Predicates

Directions: Write the words for the subject to answer the **who** or **what** questions. Write the words for the predicate to answer the **does**, **did**, **is** or **has** questions.

Example:

My friend has two pairs of sunglasses.   **who?** <u>My friend</u>

has? <u>has two pairs of sunglasses.</u>

1. John's dog went to school with him.   **what?** _____

   did? _____

2. The Eskimo traveled by dog sled.   **who?** _____

   did? _____

3. Alex slept in his treehouse last night.   **who?** _____

   did? _____

4. Cherry pie is my favorite kind of pie.   **what?** _____

   is? _____

5. The mail carrier brings the mail to the door.   **who?** _____

   does? _____

6. We have more than enough bricks to build the wall.   **who?** _____

   has? _____

7. The bird has a worm in its beak.   **what?** _____

   has? _____

Subjects and Predicates

The **subject** tells who or what the sentence is about. The **predicate** tells what the subject does, did, is doing or will do. A complete sentence must have a subject and a predicate.

Examples:

Subject	Predicate
Sharon	writes to her grandmother every week.
The horse	ran around the track quickly.
My mom's car	is bright green.
Denise	will be here after lunch.

Directions: Circle the subject of each sentence. Underline the predicate.

1. My sister is a very happy person.

2. I wish we had more holidays in the year.

3. Laura is one of the nicest girls in our class.

4. John is fun to have as a friend.

5. The rain nearly ruined our picnic!

6. My birthday present was exactly what I wanted.

7. Your bicycle is parked beside my skateboard.

8. The printer will need to be filled with paper before you use it.

9. Six dogs chased my cat home yesterday!

10. Anthony likes to read anything he can get his hands on.

Subjects and Predicates

A **sentence** is a group of words that expresses a complete thought. It must have at least one subject and one verb.

Examples:

   Sentence: John felt tired and went to bed early.
   Not a sentence: Went to bed early.

Directions: Write **S** if the group of words is a complete sentence. Write **NS** if the group of words is not a sentence.

_____ 1. Which one of you?

_____ 2. We're happy for the family.

_____ 3. We enjoyed the program very much.

_____ 4. Felt left out and lonely afterwards.

_____ 5. Everyone said it was the best party ever!

_____ 6. No one knows better than I what the problem is.

_____ 7. Seventeen of us!

_____ 8. Quickly, before they.

_____ 9. Squirrels are lively animals.

_____10. Not many people believe it really happened.

_____ 11. Certainly, we enjoyed ourselves.

Simple Subjects

A **simple subject** is the main noun or pronoun in the complete subject.

Directions: Draw a line between the subject and the predicate. Circle the simple subject.

Example: The black (bear) lives in the zoo.

1. Penguins look like they wear tuxedos.

2. The seal enjoys raw fish.

3. The monkeys like to swing on bars.

4. The beautiful peacock has colorful feathers.

5. Bats like dark places.

6. Some snakes eat small rodents.

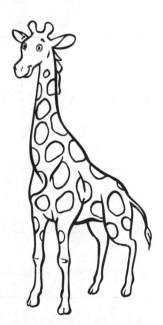

7. The orange and brown giraffes have long necks.

8. The baby zebra is close to his mother.

Compound Subjects

Compound subjects are two or more nouns that have the same predicate.

Directions: Combine the subjects to create one sentence with a compound subject.

Example: Jill can swing
Whitney can swing.
Luke can swing.

Jill, Whitney and Luke can swing.

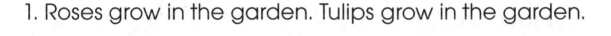

1. Roses grow in the garden. Tulips grow in the garden.

_____

2. Apples are fruit. Oranges are fruit. Bananas are fruit.

_____

3. Bears live in the zoo. Monkeys live in the zoo.

_____

4. Jackets keep us warm. Sweaters keep us warm.

_____

Simple Predicates

A **simple predicate** is the main verb or verbs in the complete predicate.

Directions: Draw a line between the complete subject and the complete predicate. Circle the simple predicate.

Example: The ripe apples (fell) to the ground.

1. The farmer scattered feed for the chickens.

2. The horses galloped wildly around the corral.

3. The baby chicks were staying warm by the light.

4. The tractor was bailing hay.

5. The silo was full of grain.

6. The cows were being milked.

7. The milk truck drove up to the barn.

8. The rooster woke everyone up.

Compound Predicates

Compound predicates have two or more verbs that have the same subject.

Directions: Combine the predicates to create one sentence with a compound predicate.

Example: We went to the zoo.
We watched the monkeys.
We went to the zoo and watched the monkeys.

1. Students read their books. Students do their work.

_____

2. Dogs can bark loudly. Dogs can do tricks.

_____

3. The football player caught the ball. The football player ran.

_____

4. My dad sawed wood. My dad stacked wood.

_____

5. My teddy bear is soft. My teddy bear likes to be hugged.

_____

Compound Predicates

Directions: Underline the simple predicates (verbs) in each predicate.

Example: The fans <u>clapped</u> and <u>cheered</u> at the game.

1. The coach talks and encourages the team.

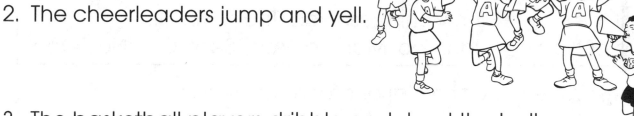

2. The cheerleaders jump and yell.

3. The basketball players dribble and shoot the ball.

4. The basketball bounces and hits the backboard.

5. The ball rolls around the rim and goes into the basket.

6. Everyone leaps up and cheers.

7. The team scores and wins!

Abbreviations

An **abbreviation** is the shortened form of a word. Most abbreviations begin with a capital letter and end with a period.

Mr.	Mister	St.	Street
Mrs.	Missus	Ave.	Avenue
Dr.	Doctor	Blvd.	Boulevard
A.M.	before noon	Rd.	Road
P.M.	after noon		

Days of the week: Sun. Mon. Tues. Wed. Thurs. Fri. Sat.
Months of the year: Jan. Feb. Mar. Apr. Aug. Sept. Oct. Nov. Dec.

Directions: Write the abbreviations for each word.

street _____   doctor _____   Tuesday _____

road _____   mister _____   avenue _____

missus _____   October _____   Friday _____

before noon _____   March _____   August _____

Directions: Write each sentence using abbreviations.

1. On Monday at 9:00 before noon, Mister Jones had a meeting.

_____

2. In December, Doctor Carlson saw Missus Zuckerman.

_____

3. One Tuesday in August, Mister Wood went to the park.

_____

Possessive Nouns

Possessive nouns tell who or what is the owner of something. With singular nouns, we use an apostrophe **before** the **s**. With plural nouns, we use an apostrophe **after** the **s**.

Example:

singular: one elephant

The **elephant's** dance was wonderful.

plural: more than one elephant

The **elephants'** dance was wonderful.

Directions: Put the apostrophe in the correct place in each bold word. Then write the word in the blank.

1. The **lions** cage was big. _____

2. The **bears** costumes were purple. _____

3. One **boys** laughter was very loud. _____

4. The **trainers** dogs were dancing about. _____

5. The **mans** popcorn was tasty and good. _____

6. **Marks** cotton candy was delicious. _____

7. A little **girls** balloon burst in the air. _____

8. The big **clowns** tricks were very funny. _____

9. **Lauras** sister clapped for the clowns. _____

10. The **womans** money was lost in the crowd. _____

11. **Kellys** mother picked her up early. _____

Punctuation: Quotation Marks

Use quotation marks (" ") before and after the exact words of a speaker.

Examples:

I asked Aunt Martha, "How do you feel?"

"I feel awful," Aunt Martha replied.

Do not put quotation marks around words that report what the speaker said.

Examples:

Aunt Martha said she felt awful.

I asked Aunt Martha how she felt.

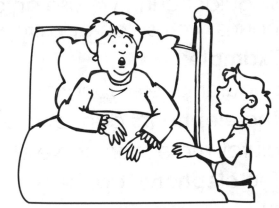

Directions: Write **C** if the sentence is punctuated correctly. Draw an **X** if the sentence is not punctuated correctly. The first one has been done for you.

__C__ 1. "I want it right now!" she demanded angrily.

_____ 2. "Do you want it now? I asked."

_____ 3. She said "she felt better" now.

_____ 4. Her exact words were, "I feel much better now!"

_____ 5. "I am so thrilled to be here!" he shouted.

_____ 6. "Yes, I will attend," she replied.

_____ 7. Elizabeth said "she was unhappy."

_____ 8. "I'm unhappy," Elizabeth reported.

_____ 9. "Did you know her mother?" I asked.

_____10. I asked "whether you knew her mother."

_____11. I wondered, "What will dessert be?"

_____12. "Which will it be, salt or pepper?" the waiter asked.

Review

Directions: Unscramble this sentence and write it on the line below.

1. have tails short bodies wide and pigs

_____

Directions: Put a question mark, a period or an exclamation point at the end of the following sentences:

1. Tiny pigs, called miniature pigs, weigh only 60 pounds

2. Pigs can weigh as much as 800 pounds

3. Wow

4. Do pigs have spots

Directions: Put the apostrophes in the sentences to replace a letter or to show ownership.

1. A pigs pen should have water in it.

2. Theyre really not animals that like mud.

3. Its an animal that needs water to keep cool.

4. Most farmers dont give them their own pools.

Directions: Put quotation marks in the sentences below.

1. You eat like a pig, said my Uncle Homer.

2. That is not an insult, I told him.

3. Pigs are really clean animals, I said.

LANGUAGE ARTS
Level 2

Vocabulary: Prefixes

A **prefix** is a syllable at the beginning of a word that changes its meaning.

Directions: Add a prefix to the beginning of each word in the box to make a word with the meaning given in each sentence below. The first one is done for you.

PREFIX	MEANING
bi	two or twice
en	to make
in	within
mis	wrong
non	not or without
pre	before
re	again
un	not

grown	write	information	large	cycle	usual	school	sense

1. Jimmy's foot hurt because his toenail was (growing within). __*ingrown*__

2. If you want to see what is in the background, you will have to (make bigger) the photograph. _____

3. I didn't do a very good job on my homework, so I will have to (write it again) it. _____

4. The newspaper article about the event has some (wrong facts). _____

5. I hope I get a (vehicle with two wheels) for my birthday. _____

6. The story he told was complete (words without meaning)! _____

7. Did you go to (school that comes before kindergarten) before you went to kindergarten? _____

8. The ability to read words upside down is most (not usual). _____

Vocabulary: Prefixes

Directions: Circle the correct word for each sentence.

1. You will need to _____ the directions before you complete this page.

   reset   reread   repair

2. Since she is allergic to milk products, she has to

   use _____ products.

   nondairy   nonsense   nonmetallic

3. That certainly was an _____ costume he selected for the Halloween party.

   untied   unusual   unable

4. The directions on the box said to _____ the oven before baking the brownies.

   preheat   preschool   prevent

5. "I'm sorry if I _____ you as to the cost of the trip," explained the travel agent.

   misdialed   misread   misinformed

6. You may use the overhead projector to _____ the picture so the whole class can see it.

   enlarge   enable   endanger

Vocabulary: Suffixes

A **suffix** is a syllable at the end of a word that changes its meaning. In most cases, when adding a suffix that begins with a vowel, drop the final **e** of the root word. For example, **fame** becomes **famous**. Also, change a final **y** in the root word to **i** before adding any suffix except **ing**. For example, **silly** becomes **silliness**.

Directions: Add a suffix to the end of each word in the box to make a word with the meaning given (in parentheses) in each sentence below. The first one is done for you.

SUFFIX	MEANING
ful	full of
ity	quality or degree
ive	have or tend to be
less	without or lacking
able	able to be
ness	state of
ment	act of
or	person that does something
ward	in the direction of

effect	like	thought	pay	beauty	thank	back	act	happy

1. Mike was (full of thanks) for a hot meal. _____thankful_____

2. I was (without thinking) for forgetting your birthday. _____

3. The mouse trap we put out doesn't seem to be (have an effect). _____

4. In spring, the flower garden is (full of beauty). _____

5. Sally is such a (able to be liked) girl! _____

6. Tim fell over (in the direction of the back) because he wasn't watching where he was going. _____

7. Jill's wedding day was one of great (the state of being happy). _____

8. The (person who performs) was very good in the play. _____

9. I have to make a (act of paying) for the stereo I bought. _____

Vocabulary: Suffixes

Directions: Read the story. Choose the correct word from the box to complete the sentences.

beautiful	colorful	payment	careless	director	agreement
breakable	careful	backward	basement	forward	firmness

Colleen and Marj carried the boxes down to the _____ apartment. "Be

_____ with those," cautioned Colleen's mother. "All the things in that box

are _____ ." As soon as the two girls helped carry all the boxes from the moving

van down the stairs, they would be able to go to school for the play tryouts. That was the

_____ made with Colleen's mother earlier that day.

"It won't do any good to get _____ with your work. Just keep at it and the

job will be done quickly," she spoke with a _____ in her voice.

"It's hard to see where I'm going when I walk _____ ," groaned Marj.

Colleen agreed to switch places, but they soon discovered that the last two boxes

were lightweight. Each girl had her own box to carry, so each of them got to walk looking

_____ . "These are so light," remarked Marj. "What's in them?"

"These have the _____ , _____ hats I was telling you about. We can take

them to the play tryouts with us," answered Colleen. "I bet we'll impress the

_____ . Even if we don't get parts in the play, I bet our hats will!"

Colleen's mother handed each of the girls a 5-dollar bill. "I really appreciate your help.

Will this be enough?"

"Thanks, Mom. You bet!" Colleen shouted as the girls ran down the sidewalk.

Vocabulary: Synonyms and Antonyms

Directions: Use the words in the box to write a synonym for each word below. Write it next to the S. Next to the A, write an antonym. The first one is done for you.

appear	proud	merry	straight	repair	plain
under	melted	unnecessary	late	new	smooth
embarrassed	gloomy	bent	break	fancy	above
icy	valuable	immediate	old	bumpy	vanish

1. crooked

   S: __bent__

   A: __straight__

2. frozen

   S: _____

   A: _____

3. instant

   S: _____

   A: _____

4. damage

   S: _____

   A: _____

5. important

   S: _____

   A: _____

6. ashamed

   S: _____

   A: _____

7. cheerful

   S: _____

   A: _____

8. elegant

   S: _____

   A: _____

9. rough

   S: _____

   A: _____

10. beneath

    S: _____

    A: _____

11. disappear

    S: _____

    A: _____

12. ancient

    S: _____

    A: _____

Vocabulary: Homophones

Homophones are two words that sound the same, have different meanings and are usually spelled differently.
Example: write and **right**

Directions: Write the correct homophone in each sentence below.

weight — how heavy something is
wait — to be patient

threw — tossed
through — passing between

steal — to take something that doesn't belong to you
steel — a heavy metal

1. The bands marched _____ the streets lined with many cheering people.

2. _____ for me by the flagpole.

3. One of our strict rules at school is: Never _____ from another person.

4. Could you estimate the _____ of this bowling ball?

5. The bleachers have _____ rods on both ends and in the middle.

6. He walked in the door and _____ his jacket down.

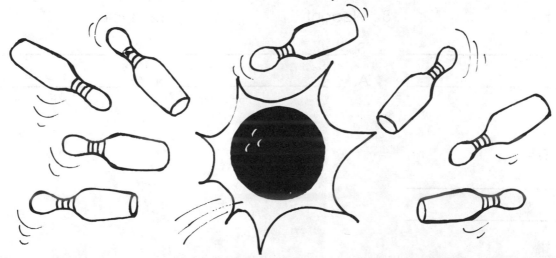

Vocabulary: Words That Sound Alike

Directions: Choose the correct word in parentheses to complete each sentence. The first one is done for you.

1. Jimmy was so _____**bored**_____ that he fell asleep. (board, bored)

2. We'll need a _____ and some nails to repair the fence. (board, bored)

3. Do you want _____ after dinner? (desert, dessert)

4. A _____ is hot and sandy. (desert, dessert)

5. The soldier had a _____ pinned to his uniform. (medal, metal)

6. Gold is a precious _____ . (medal, metal)

7. Don't _____ at your present before Christmas! (peak, peek)

8. They climbed to the _____ of the mountain. (peak, peek)

9. Jack had to repair the emergency _____ on his car. (brake, break)

10. Please be careful not to _____ my bicycle. (brake, break)

11. The race _____ was a very difficult one. (coarse, course)

12. We will need some _____ sandpaper to finish the job. (coarse, course)

Pronouns

A **pronoun** is a word that takes the place of a noun in a sentence.

Examples:

I, my, mine, me

we, our, ours, us

you, your, yours

he, his, him

she, her, hers

it, its

they, their, theirs, them

Directions: Underline the pronouns in each sentence.

1. Bring them to us as soon as you are finished.

2. She has been my best friend for many years.

3. They should be here soon.

4. We enjoyed our trip to the Mustard Museum.

5. Would you be able to help us with the project on Saturday?

6. Our homeroom teacher will not be here tomorrow.

7. My uncle said that he will be leaving soon for Australia.

8. Hurry! Could you please open the door for him?

9. She dropped her gloves when she got off the bus.

10. I can't figure out who the mystery writer is today.

Nouns and Pronouns

To make a story or report more interesting, pronouns can be substituted for "overused" nouns.

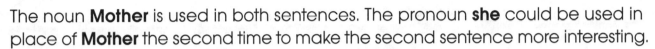

Example:

Mother made the beds. Then Mother started the laundry.

The noun **Mother** is used in both sentences. The pronoun **she** could be used in place of **Mother** the second time to make the second sentence more interesting.

Directions: Cross out nouns when they appear a second and/or third time. Write a pronoun that could be used instead. The first one is done for you.

we 1. My friends and I like to go ice skating in the winter. ~~My friends and I~~ usually fall down a lot, but ~~my friends and I~~ have fun!

_____ 2. All the children in the fourth-grade class next to us must have been having a party. All the children were very loud. All the children were happy it was Friday.

_____ 3. I try to help my father with work around the house on the weekends. My father works many hours during the week and would not be able to get everything done.

_____ 4. Can I share my birthday treat with the secretary and the principal? The secretary and the principal could probably use a snack right now!

_____ 5. I know Mr. Jones needs a copy of this history report. Please take it to Mr. Jones when you finish.

Pronoun Referents

A **pronoun referent** is the noun or nouns a
pronoun refers to.

Example:

Green beans, corn and potatoes are
my favorite vegetables. I could eat them for every meal.

The pronoun **them** refers to the nouns green beans, corn and potatoes.

Directions: Find the pronoun in each sentence, and write it in the blank below. Underline
the word the pronoun refers to. The first one is done for you.

1. The fruit trees look so beautiful in the spring when they are covered with blossoms.

   _____they_____

2. Tori is a high school cheerleader. She spends many hours at practice.

   _____

3. The football must have been slippery because of the rain. The quarterback could
   not hold on to it.

   _____

4. Aunt Donna needs a babysitter for her three year old tonight.

   _____

5. The art projects are on the table. Could you please put them on the top shelf along
   the wall?

   _____

Pronoun Referents

Directions: Read each sentence carefully. Draw a line
to connect each sentence to the correct pronoun.

1. All the teachers in our building said _____
   could use a day off!   him

2. The whole cast spent a lot of time in rehearsals for the school   it
   play. _____ should go very well.

3. My Uncle Mike is driving around in a very old car. I know   they
   _____ would like to buy a new one.

4. Mr. Barker is having some trouble programming that VCR.   she
   Can you help _____ ?

5. There are too many books on the shelf. I know I can't fit all of   them
   _____ into this small box.

6. Ms. Hart slipped on the bleachers at the football game. That's   he
   why _____ is using crutches.

Irregular Verbs: Past Tense

Irregular verbs change completely in the past tense. Unlike regular verbs, past-tense forms of irregular verbs are not formed by adding **ed**.

Example: The past tense of **go** is **went**.

Other verbs change some letters to form the past tense.
Example: The past tense of **break** is **broke**.

A **helping verb** helps to tell about the past. **Has, have** and **had** are helping verbs used with action verbs to show the action occurred in the past. The past-tense form of the irregular verb sometimes changes when a helping verb is added.

Present-Tense Irregular Verb	Past-Tense Irregular Verb	Past-Tense Irregular Verb With Helper
go	went	have/has/had gone
see	saw	have/has/had seen
do	did	have/has/had done
bring	brought	have/has/had brought
sing	sang	have/has/had sung
drive	drove	have/has/had driven
swim	swam	have/has/had swum
sleep	slept	have/has/had slept

Directions: Choose four words from the chart. Write one sentence using the past-tense form of the verb without a helping verb. Write another sentence using the past-tense form with a helping verb.

1. _____
   _____

2. _____
   _____

3. _____
   _____

4. _____
   _____

The Irregular Verb "Be"

Be is an irregular verb. The present-tense forms of **be** are **be**, **am**, **is** and **are**. The past-tense forms of **be** are **was** and **were**.

Directions: Write the correct form of **be** in the blanks. The first one has been done for you.

1. I _____am_____ so happy for you!

2. Jared _____ unfriendly yesterday.

3. English can _____ a lot of fun to learn.

4. They _____ among the nicest people I know.

5. They _____ late yesterday.

6. She promises she _____ going to arrive on time.

7. I _____ nervous right now about the test.

8. If you _____ satisfied now, so am I.

9. He _____ as nice to me last week as I had hoped.

10. He can _____ very gracious.

11. Would you _____ offended if I moved your desk?

12. He _____ watching at the window for me yesterday.

Verbs: "Was" and "Were"

Singular	Plural
I was	we were
you were	you were
he, she, it was	they were

Directions: Write the correct form of the verb in the blanks. Circle the subject of each sentence. The first one is done for you.

was   1. (He) was/were so happy that we all smiled, too.

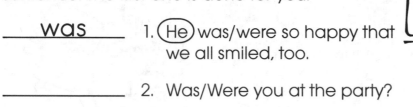

_____ 2. Was/Were you at the party?

_____ 3. She was/were going to the store.

_____ 4. He was/were always forgetting his hat.

_____ 5. Was/Were she there?

_____ 6. Was/Were you sure of your answers?

_____ 7. She was/were glad to help.

_____ 8. They was/were excited.

_____ 9. Exactly what was/were you planning to do?

_____ 10. It was/were wet outside.

_____ 11. They was/were scared by the noise.

_____ 12. Was/Were they expected before noon?

_____ 13. It was/were too early to get up!

_____ 14. She was/were always early.

_____ 15. You were/was the first person I asked.

Verbs: Present, Past and Future Tense

The **present tense** of a verb tells what is happening now.

Examples:

I **am** happy.
I **run** fast.

The **past tense** of a verb tells what has already happened.

Examples:

I **was** happy.
I **ran** fast.

The **future tense** of a verb refers to what is going to happen.
The word **will** usually comes before the future tense of a verb.

Examples:

I **will be** happy.
I **will run** fast.

Directions: The sentences below are in the present tense. Rewrite each sentence using the past and future tense of the verb. The first one is done for you.

1. I think of you as my best friend.
   <u>I thought of you as my best friend.</u>
   <u>I will think of you as my best friend.</u>

2. I hear you coming up the steps.

   _____

   _____

3. I rush every morning to get ready for school.

   _____

   _____

4. I bake brownies every Saturday.

   _____

   _____

Verbs: Present, Past and Future Tense

Directions: Read the following sentences. Write **PRES** if the sentence is in present tense. Write **PAST** if the sentence is in past tense. Write **FUT** if the sentence is in future tense. The first one is done for you.

FUT   1. I will be thrilled to accept the award.

_____ 2. Will you go with me to the dentist?

_____ 3. I thought he looked familiar!

_____ 4. They ate every single slice of pizza.

_____ 5. I run myself ragged sometimes.

_____ 6. Do you think this project is worthwhile?

_____ 7. No one has been able to repair the broken plate.

_____ 8. Thoughtful gifts are always appreciated.

_____ 9. I like the way he sang!

_____ 10. With a voice like that, he will go a long way.

_____ 11. It's my fondest hope that they visit soon.

_____ 12. I wanted that coat very much.

_____ 13. She'll be happy to take your place.

_____ 14. Everyone thinks the test will be a breeze.

_____ 15. Collecting stamps is her favorite hobby.

Adding "ed" to Make Verbs Past Tense

To make many verbs past tense, add **ed**.

Examples:

    cook + ed = cooked   wish + ed = wished   play + ed = played

When a verb ends in a **silent e**, drop the **e** and add **ed**.

Examples:

    hope + ed = hoped   hate + ed = hated

When a verb ends in **y** after a consonant, change the **y** to **i** and add **ed**.

Examples:

    hurry + ed = hurried   marry + ed = married

When a verb ends in a single consonant after a single short vowel, double the final consonant before adding **ed**.

Examples:

    stop + ed = stopped   hop + ed = hopped

Directions: Rewrite the present tense of the verb correctly. The first one is done for you.

1. call   called   11. reply _____

2. copy _____   12. top _____

3. frown _____   13. clean _____

4. smile _____   14. scream _____

5. live _____   15. clap _____

6. talk _____   16. mop _____

7. name _____   17. soap _____

8. list _____   18. choke _____

9. spy _____   19. scurry _____

10. phone _____   20. drop _____

Adjectives That Add "er"

The suffix **er** is often added to adjectives to compare two things.

Example:

My feet are **large**.

Your feet are **larger** than my feet.

When a one-syllable adjective ends in a single consonant and the vowel is short, double the final consonant before adding **er**. When a word ends in two or more consonants, add **er**.

Examples:

big — bigger (single consonant)

bold — bolder (two consonants)

When an adjective ends in **y**, change the **y** to **i** before adding **er**.

Examples:

easy — easier

greasy — greasier

breezy — breezier

Directions: Use the correct rule to add **er** to the words below. The first one is done for you.

1. fast _____faster_____   11. skinny _____
2. thin _____   12. fat _____
3. long _____   13. poor _____
4. few _____   14. juicy _____
5. ugly _____   15. early _____
6. silly _____   16. clean _____
7. busy _____   17. thick _____
8. grand _____   18. creamy _____
9. lean _____   19. deep _____
10. young _____   20. lazy _____

Adjectives That Add "est"

The suffix **est** is often added to adjectives to compare more than two things.

Example:

My glass is **full**.

Your glass is **fuller**.

His glass is **fullest**.

When a one-syllable adjective ends in a single consonant and the vowel sound is short, you usually double the final consonant before adding **est**.

Examples:

big — biggest (short vowel)

steep — steepest (long vowel)

When an adjective ends in **y**, change the **y** to **i** before adding **est**.

Example:

easy — easiest

Directions: Use the correct rule to add **est** to the words below.
The first one is done for you.

1. thin   thinnest

2. skinny _____

3. cheap _____

4. busy _____

5. loud _____

6. kind _____

7. dreamy _____

8. ugly _____

9. pretty _____

10. early _____

11. quick _____

12. trim _____

13. silly _____

14. tall _____

15. glum _____

16. red _____

17. happy _____

18. high _____

19. wet _____

20. clean _____

Adding "er" and "est" to Adjectives

Directions: Circle the correct adjective for each sentence. The first one is done for you.

1. Of all the students in the gym, her voice was (louder, (loudest)).

2. "I can tell you are (busier, busiest) than I am," he said to the librarian.

3. If you and Carl stand back to back, I can see which one is (taller, tallest).

4. She is the (kinder, kindest) teacher in the whole building.

5. Wow! That is the (bigger, biggest) pumpkin I have ever seen!

6. I believe your flashlight is (brighter, brightest) than mine.

7. "This is the (cleaner, cleanest) your room has been in a long time," Mother said.

8. The leaves on that plant are (prettier, prettiest) than the ones on the window sill.

Adjectives Preceded by "More"

Most adjectives of two or more syllables are preceded by the word **more** as a way to show comparison between two things.

Examples:

Correct: intelligent, more intelligent
Incorrect: intelligenter
Correct: famous, more famous
Incorrect: famouser

Directions: Write **more** before the adjectives that fit the rule. Draw an **X** in the blanks of the adjectives that do not fit the rule. To test yourself, say the words aloud using **more** and adding **er** to hear which way sounds correct. The first two have been done for you.

___X___	1. cheap	_____	11. awful
__more__	2. beautiful	_____	12. delicious
_____	3. quick	_____	13. embarrassing
_____	4. terrible	_____	14. nice
_____	5. difficult	_____	15. often
_____	6. interesting	_____	16. hard
_____	7. polite	_____	17. valuable
_____	8. cute	_____	18. close
_____	9. dark	_____	19. fast
_____	10. sad	_____	20. important

Adjectives Preceded by "Most"

Most adjectives of two or more syllables are preceded by the word **most** as a way to show comparison between more than two things.

Examples:

Correct: intelligent, most intelligent
Incorrect: intelligentest
Correct: famous, most famous
Incorrect: famousest

Directions: Read the following groups of sentences. In the last sentence for each group, write the adjective preceded by **most**. The first one is done for you.

1. My uncle is intelligent.
   My aunt is more intelligent.
   My cousin is the _____ most intelligent _____ .

2. I am thankful.
   My brother is more thankful.
   My parents are the _____ .

3. Your sister is polite.
   Your brother is more polite.
   You are the _____ .

4. The blouse was expensive.
   The sweater was more expensive.
   The coat was the _____ .

5. The class was fortunate.
   The teacher was more fortunate.
   The principal was the _____ .

6. The cookies were delicious.
   The cake was even more delicious.
   The brownies were the _____ .

7. The painting is elaborate.
   The sculpture is more elaborate.
   The finger painting is the _____ .

Adverbs

Adverbs are words that tell when, where or how.

Adverbs of time tell when.

Example:

The train left yesterday.

Yesterday is an adverb of time. It tells when the train left.

Adverbs of place tell where.

Example:

The girl walked away.

Away is an adverb of place. It tells where the girl walked.

Adverbs of manner tell how.

Example:

The boy walked quickly.

Quickly is an adverb of manner. It tells how the boy walked.

Directions: Write the adverb for each sentence in the first blank. In the second blank, write whether it is an adverb of time, place or manner. The first one is done for you.

1. The family ate downstairs. ___downstairs___ ___place___

2. The relatives laughed loudly. _____ _____

3. We will finish tomorrow. _____ _____

4. The snowstorm will stop soon. _____ _____

5. She sings beautifully! _____ _____

6. The baby slept soundly. _____ _____

7. The elevator stopped suddenly. _____ _____

8. Does the plane leave today? _____ _____

9. The phone call came yesterday. _____ _____

10. She ran outside. _____ _____

Adverbs of Time

Directions: Choose a word, or group of words, from the box to complete each sentence. Make sure the adverb you choose makes sense with the rest of the sentence.

in 2 weeks	last winter
next week	at the end of the day
soon	right now
2 days ago	tonight

1. We had a surprise birthday party for him _____ .

2. Our science projects are due _____ .

3. My best friend will be moving _____ .

4. Justin and Ronnie need our help _____ !

5. We will find out who the winners are _____ .

6. Can you take me to ball practice _____ ?

7. She said we will be getting a letter _____ .

8. Diane made the quilt _____ .

Adverbs of Place

Directions: Choose one word from the box to complete each sentence. Make sure the adverb you choose makes sense with the rest of the sentence.

inside	upstairs	below	everywhere
home	somewhere	outside	there

1. Each child took a new library book _____ .

2. We looked _____ for his jacket.

3. We will have recess _____ because it is raining.

4. From the top of the mountain, we could see the village far _____ .

5. My sister and I share a bedroom _____ .

6. The teacher warned the children, "You must play with the ball _____ ."

7. Mother said, "I know that recipe is _____ in this file box!"

8. You can put the chair _____ .

Adverbs of Manner

Directions: Choose a word from the box to complete each sentence. Make sure the adverb you choose makes sense with the rest of the sentence. One word will be used twice.

quickly	carefully	loudly	easily	carelessly	slowly

1. The scouts crossed the old bridge _____.

2. We watched the turtle move _____ across the yard.

3. Everyone completed the math test _____.

4. The quarterback scampered _____ down the sideline.

5. The mother _____ cleaned the child's sore knee.

6. The fire was caused by someone _____ tossing a match.

7. The alarm rang _____ while we were eating.

Adjectives and Adverbs

Directions: Write **ADJ** on the line if the bold word is an adjective. Write **ADV** if the bold word is an adverb. The first one is done for you.

_____ADV_____ 1. That road leads **nowhere**.

_____ 2. The squirrel was **nearby**.

_____ 3. Her **delicious** cookies were all eaten.

_____ 4. Everyone rushed **indoors**.

_____ 5. He **quickly** zipped his jacket.

_____ 6. She hummed a **popular** tune.

_____ 7. Her **sunny** smile warmed my heart.

_____ 8. I hung your coat **there**.

_____ 9. Bring that **here** this minute!

_____ 10. We all walked **back** to school.

_____ 11. The **skinniest** boy ate the most food!

_____ 12. She acts like a **famous** person.

_____ 13. The **silliest** jokes always make me laugh.

_____ 14. She must have parked her car **somewhere**!

_____ 15. Did you take the test **today**?

Review

Directions: Write the correct words to complete the sentences. Use the words on the presents at the bottom of the page.

1. The suffix _____ and the word _____ are used when comparing two things.

2. One example of an adverb of time is _____ .

3. When an adjective ends in a consonant _____ , you change the y to i before adding er or est.

4. An _____ is a word that tells when, where or how.

5. An example of an adverb of place is _____ .

6. The suffix _____ and the word _____ are used when comparing more than two things.

7. An _____ is a word that describes a noun.

8. An example of an adverb of manner is _____ .

adjective est softly adverb

er y

most there more tomorrow

Review

Directions: For the bold word in each sentence, write **N** for noun, **V** for verb, **ADJ** for adjective or **ADV** for adverb.

_____ 1. She is the **tallest** one outside.

_____ 2. **She** is the tallest one outside.

_____ 3. She **is** the tallest one outside.

_____ 4. She is the tallest one **outside**.

Directions: For the bold word in each sentence, write **P** for adverb of place, **T** for adverb of time or **M** for adverb of manner.

_____ 5. Your shoes are **downstairs**.

_____ 6. His response was **speedy**.

_____ 7. **Here** is my homework.

_____ 8. The present will be mailed **tomorrow**.

Directions: Add **er** and **est** or **more** and **most** to the words below to show comparison.

9. fat _____ _____

10. grateful _____ _____

11. serious _____ _____

12. easy _____ _____

Directions: For the bold word in each sentence, write **ADV** for adverb or **ADJ** for adjective.

_____ 13. **Grumpy** people are not pleasant.

_____ 14. Put the package **there**, please.

_____ 15. **Upstairs** is where I sleep.

_____ 16. **Warm** blankets feel toasty on cold nights.

Conjunctions

Directions: Choose the best conjunction from the box to combine the pairs of sentences. Then rewrite the sentences.

and	but	or	because	when	after	so

1. I like Leah. I like Ben.

_____

2. Should I eat the orange? Should I eat the apple?

_____

3. You will get a reward. You turned in the lost item.

_____

4. I really mean what I say! You had better listen!

_____

5. I like you. You're nice, friendly, helpful and kind.

_____

6. You can have dessert. You ate all your peas.

_____

7. I like your shirt better. You should decide for yourself.

_____

8. We walked out of the building. We heard the fire alarm.

_____

9. I like to sing folk songs. I like to play the guitar.

_____

Conjunctions

Words that join sentences or combine ideas like **and**, **but**, **or**, **because**, **when**, **after** and **so** are called **conjunctions**.

Examples:

I played the drums, **and** Sue played the clarinet.
She likes bananas, **but** I do not.
We could play music **or** just enjoy the silence.
I needed the book **because** I had to write a book report.
He gave me the book **when** I asked for it.
I asked her to eat lunch **after** she finished the test.
You wanted my bike **so** you could ride it.

Using different conjunctions can affect the meaning of a sentence.

Example:

He gave me the book **when** I asked for it.
He gave me the book **after** I asked for it.

Directions: Choose the best conjunction to combine the pairs of sentences. The first one is done for you.

1. I like my hair curly. Mom likes my hair straight.

<u>I like my hair curly, but Mom likes it straight.</u>

2. I can remember what she looks like. I can't remember her name.

_____

3. We will have to wash the dishes. We won't have clean plates for dinner.

_____

4. The yellow flowers are blooming. The red flowers are not.

_____

5. I like banana cream pie. I like chocolate donuts.

_____

Run-On Sentences

A **run-on sentence** occurs when two or more sentences are joined together without punctuation.

Examples:

> **Run-on sentence**: I lost my way once did you?
> **Two sentences with correct punctuation**: I lost my way once. Did you?
> **Run-on sentence**: I found the recipe it was not hard to follow.
> **Two sentences with correct punctuation**: I found the recipe. It was not hard to follow.

Directions: Rewrite the run-on sentences correctly with periods, exclamation points and question marks. The first one is done for you.

1. Did you take my umbrella I can't find it anywhere!

<u>Did you take my umbrella? I can't find it anywhere!</u>

2. How can you stand that noise I can't!

_____

3. The cookies are gone I see only crumbs.

_____

4. The dogs were barking they were hungry.

_____

5. She is quite ill please call a doctor immediately!

_____

6. The clouds came up we knew the storm would hit soon.

_____

7. You weren't home he stopped by this morning.

_____

Combining Sentences

Some simple sentences can be easily combined into one sentence.

Examples:

Simple sentences: The bird sang. The bird was tiny. The bird was in the tree.
Combined sentence: The tiny bird sang in the tree.

Directions: Combine each set of simple sentences into one sentence. The first one is done for you.

1. The big girls laughed. They were friendly. They helped the little girls.

The big, friendly girls laughed as they helped the little girls.

2. The dog was hungry. The dog whimpered. The dog looked at its bowl.

_____

3. Be quiet now. I want you to listen. You listen to my joke!

_____

4. I lost my pencil. My pencil was stubby. I lost it on the bus.

_____

5. I see my mother. My mother is walking. My mother is walking down the street.

_____

6. Do you like ice cream? Do you like hot dogs? Do you like mustard?

_____

7. Tell me you'll do it! Tell me you will! Tell me right now!

_____

Combining Sentences in Paragraph Form

A **paragraph** is a group of sentences that share the same idea.

Directions: Rewrite the paragraph by combining the simple sentences into larger sentences.

Jason awoke early. He threw off his covers. He ran to his window. He looked outside. He saw snow. It was white and fluffy. Jason thought of something. He thought of his sled. His sled was in the garage. He quickly ate breakfast. He dressed warmly. He got his sled. He went outside. He went to play in the snow.

_____

_____

_____

_____

_____

_____

_____

_____

_____

_____

Identifying the Parts of a Sentence

The **subject** tells who or what the sentence is about. The subject is always a noun or pronoun. A **noun** is a word that names a person, place or thing. A **pronoun** is a word that takes the place of a noun.

Example:

The handsome **boy** danced yesterday.
Boy is the subject. The sentence is about the boy.

A verb tells what something does or that something exists.

Example:

The handsome boy **danced** yesterday.
Danced is the verb. It shows action.

An adverb tells when, where or how something happened.

Example:

The handsome boy danced **yesterday**.
Yesterday is an adverb. It tells when the boy danced.

An adjective describes a noun.

Example:

The **handsome** boy danced yesterday.

Handsome is an adjective. It describes the noun **boy**.

Directions: Write **N** for noun, **V** for verb, **ADJ** for adjective or **ADV** for adverb for the bold word in each sentence.

_____ 1. She is an **excellent** singer.

_____ 2. The huge black **horse** easily won the race.

_____ 3. The **red-haired** girl was shy.

_____ 4. Joshua **quickly** finished his homework and went out to play.

_____ 5. **Carrots** are my least favorite vegetable.

_____ 6. Why should **I** always have to take out the trash?

_____ 7. That girl **ran** like the wind!

_____ 8. Elizabeth **told** her sister to pick her up at noon.

_____ 9. He was glad he had a **warm** coat to wear.

_____ 10. I live **nearby**.

Review

Directions: Circle the subjects.

1. Everyone felt the day had been a great success.

2. Christina and Andrea were both happy to take the day off.

3. No one really understood why he was crying.

4. Mr. Winston, Ms. Fuller and Ms. Landers took us on a field trip.

Directions: Underline the predicates.

5. Who can tell what will happen tomorrow?

6. Mark was a carpenter by trade and a talented painter, too.

7. The animals yelped and whined in their cages.

8. Airplane rides made her feel sick to her stomach.

Directions: Combine the sentences to make one sentence with a compound subject.

9. Elizabeth ate everything in sight. George ate everything in sight.

_____

10. Wishing something will happen won't make it so. Dreaming something will happen won't make it so.

_____

Directions: Combine the sentences to make one sentence with a compound predicate.

11. I jumped for joy. I hugged all my friends.

_____

12. She ran around the track before the race. She warmed up before the race.

_____

Direct Objects

A **direct object** is the word or words that come after a verb to complete its meaning. The direct object answers the question **whom** or **what**.

Examples:

>Aaron wrote a **letter**.
>**Letter** is the direct object. It tells what Aaron wrote.
>We heard **Tom**.
>**Tom** is the direct object. It tells whom we heard.

Directions: Identify the direct object in each sentence. Write it in the blank.

_____ 1. My mother called me.

_____ 2. The baby dropped it.

_____ 3. I met the mayor.

_____ 4. I like you!

_____ 5. No one visited them.

_____ 6. We all heard the cat.

_____ 7. Jessica saw the stars.

_____ 8. She needs a nap.

_____ 9. The dog chewed the bone.

_____ 10. He hugged the doll.

_____ 11. I sold the radio.

_____ 12. Douglas ate the banana.

_____ 13. We finally found the house.

Indirect Objects

An **indirect object** is the word or words that come between the verb and the direct object. Indirect objects tells **to whom** or **what** or **for whom** or **what** something is done.

Examples:

He read **me** a funny story.

Me is the indirect object. It tells to whom something (reading a story) was done.

She told her **mother** the truth.

Mother is the indirect object. It tells to whom something (telling the truth) was done.

Directions: Identify the indirect object in each sentence. Write it in the blank.

1. The coach gave Bill a trophy. _____

2. He cooked me a wonderful meal. _____

3. She told Maria her secret. _____

4. Someone gave my mother a gift. _____

5. The class gave the principal a new flag for the cafeteria. _____

6. The restaurant pays the waiter a good salary. _____

7. You should tell your dad the truth. _____

8. She sent her son a plane ticket. _____

9. The waiter served the patron a salad. _____

10. Grandma gave the baby a kiss. _____

11. I sold Steve some cookies. _____

12. He told us six jokes. _____

13. She brought the boy a sucker. _____

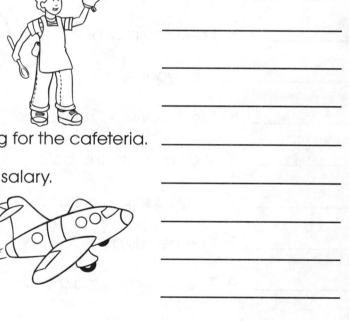

Direct and Indirect Objects

Example: Sharon told <u>Jennifer</u> a funny (story.)

Jennifer is the indirect object. It tells **to whom** Sharon told the story. Story is the direct object. It tells **what** Sharon told.

Directions: Circle the direct object in each sentence. Underline the indirect object.

1. The teacher gave the class a test.

2. Josh brought Elizabeth the book.

3. Someone left the cat a present.

4. The poet read David all his poems.

5. My big brother handed me the ticket.

6. Luke told everyone the secret.

7. Jason handed his dad the newspaper.

8. Mother bought Jack a suitcase.

9. They cooked us an excellent dinner.

10. I loaned Jonathan my bike.

11. She threw him a curve ball.

12. You tell Dad the truth!

Punctuation: Commas

Use a comma to separate words in a series. A comma is used after each word in a series but is not needed before the last word. Both ways are correct. In your own writing, be consistent about which style you use.

Examples:

We ate apples, oranges, and pears.
We ate apples, oranges and pears.

Always use a comma between the name of a city and a state.

Example:

She lives in Fresno, California.
He lives in Wilmington, Delaware.

Directions: Write **C** if the sentence is punctuated correctly. Draw an **X** if the sentence is not punctuated correctly. The first one is done for you.

X   1. She ordered shoes, dresses and shirts to be sent to her home in Oakland California.

_____ 2. No one knew her pets' names were Fido, Spot and Tiger.

_____ 3. He likes green beans lima beans, and corn on the cob.

_____ 4. Typing paper, pens and pencils are all needed for school.

_____ 5. Send your letters to her in College Park, Maryland.

_____ 6. Send your letter to her in Reno, Nevada.

_____ 7. Before he lived in New York, City he lived in San Diego, California.

_____ 8. She mailed postcards, and letters to him in Lexington, Kentucky.

_____ 9. Teacups, saucers, napkins, and silverware were piled high.

_____ 10. Can someone give me a ride to Indianapolis, Indiana?

Punctuation: Commas

Use a comma to separate the number of the day of a month and the year. Do not use a comma to separate the month and year if no day is given.

Examples:

June 14, 1999

June 1999

Use a comma after **yes** or **no** when it is the first word in a sentence.

Examples:

Yes, I will do it right now.

No, I don't want any.

Directions: Write **C** if the sentence is punctuated correctly. Draw an **X** if the sentence is not punctuated correctly. The first one is done for you.

__C__ 1. No, I don't plan to attend.

_____ 2. I told them, oh yes, I would go.

_____ 3. Her birthday is March 13, 1995.

_____ 4. He was born in May, 1997.

_____ 5. Yes, of course I like you!

_____ 6. No I will not be there.

_____ 7. They left for vacation on February, 14.

_____ 8. No, today is Monday.

_____ 9. The program was first shown on August 12, 1991.

_____ 10. In September, 2007 how old will you be?

_____ 11. He turned 12 years old on November, 13.

_____ 12. I said no, I will not come no matter what!

_____ 13. Yes, she is a friend of mine.

_____ 14. His birthday is June 12, 1992, and mine is June 12, 1993.

_____ 15. No I would not like more dessert.

"Good" and "Well"

Use the word **good** to describe a noun. Good is an adjective.

Example: She is a **good** teacher.

Use the word **well** to tell or ask how something is done or to describe someone's health. Well is an adverb. It describes a verb.

Example: She is not feeling **well**.

Directions: Write **good** or **well** in the blanks to complete the sentences correctly. The first one is done for you.

good 1. Our team could use a good/well captain.

_____ 2. The puny kitten doesn't look good/well.

_____ 3. He did his job so good/well that everyone praised him.

_____ 4. Whining isn't a good/well habit.

_____ 5. I might just as good/well do it myself.

_____ 6. She was one of the most good/well- liked girls at school.

_____ 7. I did the book report as good/well as I could.

_____ 8. The television works very good/well.

_____ 9. You did a good/well job repairing the TV!

_____ 10. Thanks for a job good/well done!

_____ 11. You did a good/well job fixing the computer.

_____ 12. You had better treat your friends good/well.

_____ 13. Can your grandmother hear good/well?

_____ 14. Your brother will be good/well soon.

"Your" and "You're"

The word **your** shows possession.

Examples:

Is that **your** book?

I visited **your** class.

The word **you're** is a contraction for **you are**. A **contraction** is two words joined together as one. An apostrophe shows where letters have been left out.

Examples:

You're doing well on that painting.

If you're going to pass the test, you should study.

Directions: Write **your** or **you're** on the blanks to complete the sentences correctly. The first one is done for you.

<u>You're</u>   1. Your/You're the best friend I have!

_____ 2. Your/You're going to drop that!

_____ 3. Your/You're brother came to see me.

_____ 4. Is that your/you're cat?

_____ 5. If your/you're going, you'd better hurry!

_____ 6. Why are your/you're fingers so red?

_____ 7. It's none of your/you're business!

_____ 8. Your/You're bike's front tire is low.

_____ 9. Your/You're kidding!

_____ 10. Have it your/you're way.

_____ 11. I thought your/you're report was great!

_____ 12. He thinks your/you're wonderful!

_____ 13. What is your/you're first choice?

_____ 14. What's your/you're opinion?

_____ 15. If your/you're going, so am I!

_____ 16. Your/You're welcome.

"Its" and "It's"

The word **its** shows ownership.

Examples:

    Its leaves have all turned green.
    Its paw was injured.

The word **it's** is a contraction for **it is**.

Examples:

    It's better to be early than late.
    It's not fair!

Directions: Write **its** or **it's** to complete the sentences correctly.
The first one is done for you.

___It's___   1. Its/It's never too late for ice cream!

_____   2. Its/It's eyes are already open.

_____   3. Its/It's your turn to wash the dishes!

_____   4. Its/It's cage was left open.

_____   5. Its/It's engine was beyond repair.

_____   6. Its/It's teeth were long and pointed.

_____   7. Did you see its/it's hind legs?

_____   8. Why do you think its/it's mine?

_____   9. Do you think its/it's the right color?

_____   10. Don't pet its/it's fur too hard!

_____   11. Its/It's from my Uncle Harry.

_____   12. Can you tell its/it's a surprise?

_____   13. Is its/it's stall always this clean?

_____   14. Its/It's not time to eat yet.

_____   15. She says its/it's working now.

Punctuation: Commas

Use a comma to separate the number of the day of a month and the year. Do not use a comma to separate the month and year if no day is given.

Examples:

June 14, 1999

June 1999

Use a comma after **yes** or **no** when it is the first word in a sentence.

Examples:

Yes, I will do it right now.

No, I don't want any.

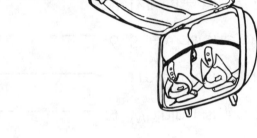

Directions: Write **C** if the sentence is punctuated correctly. Draw an **X** if the sentence is not punctuated correctly. The first one is done for you.

C ___ 1. No, I don't plan to attend.

___ 2. I told them, oh yes, I would go.

___ 3. Her birthday is March 13, 1995.

___ 4. He was born in May, 1997.

___ 5. Yes, of course I like you!

___ 6. No I will not be there.

___ 7. They left for vacation on February, 14.

___ 8. No, today is Monday.

___ 9. The program was first shown on August 12, 1991.

___ 10. In September, 2007 how old will you be?

___ 11. He turned 12 years old on November, 13.

___ 12. I said no, I will not come no matter what!

___ 13. Yes, she is a friend of mine.

___ 14. His birthday is June 12, 1992, and mine is June 12, 1993.

___ 15. No I would not like more dessert.

"Good" and "Well"

Use the word **good** to describe a noun. Good is an adjective.

Example: She is a **good** teacher.

Use the word **well** to tell or ask how something is done or to describe someone's health. Well is an adverb. It describes a verb.

Example: She is not feeling **well**.

Directions: Write **good** or **well** in the blanks to complete the sentences correctly. The first one is done for you.

good   1. Our team could use a good/well captain.

_____ 2. The puny kitten doesn't look good/well.

_____ 3. He did his job so good/well that everyone praised him.

_____ 4. Whining isn't a good/well habit.

_____ 5. I might just as good/well do it myself.

_____ 6. She was one of the most good/well- liked girls at school.

_____ 7. I did the book report as good/well as I could.

_____ 8. The television works very good/well.

_____ 9. You did a good/well job repairing the TV!

_____ 10. Thanks for a job good/well done!

_____ 11. You did a good/well job fixing the computer.

_____ 12. You had better treat your friends good/well.

_____ 13. Can your grandmother hear good/well?

_____ 14. Your brother will be good/well soon.

"Your" and "You're"

The word **your** shows possession.

Examples:

Is that **your** book?

I visited **your** class.

The word **you're** is a contraction for **you are**. A **contraction** is two words joined together as one. An apostrophe shows where letters have been left out.

Examples:

You're doing well on that painting.

If you're going to pass the test, you should study.

Directions: Write **your** or **you're** on the blanks to complete the sentences correctly. The first one is done for you.

You're 1. Your/You're the best friend I have!

_____ 2. Your/You're going to drop that!

_____ 3. Your/You're brother came to see me.

_____ 4. Is that your/you're car?

_____ 5. If your/you're going, you'd better hurry!

_____ 6. Why are your/you're fingers so red?

_____ 7. It's none of your/you're business!

_____ 8. Your/You're bike's front tire is low.

_____ 9. Your/You're kidding!

_____ 10. Have it your/you're way.

_____ 11. I thought your/you're report was great!

_____ 12. He thinks your/you're wonderful!

_____ 13. What is your/you're first choice?

_____ 14. What's your/you're opinion?

_____ 15. If your/you're going, so am I!

_____ 16. Your/You're welcome.

"Its" and "It's"

The word **its** shows ownership.

Examples:

Its leaves have all turned green.

Its paw was injured.

The word **it's** is a contraction for **it is**.

Examples:

It's better to be early than late.

It's not fair!

Directions: Write **its** or **it's** to complete the sentences correctly.
The first one is done for you.

It's

1. ____ Its/it's never too late for ice cream!
2. ____ Its/it's eyes are already open.
3. ____ Its/it's your turn to wash the dishes!
4. ____ Its/it's cage was left open.
5. ____ Its/it's engine was beyond repair.
6. ____ Its/it's teeth were long and pointed.
7. ____ Did you see its/it's hind legs?
8. ____ Why do you think its/it's mine?
9. ____ Do you think its/it's the right color?
10. ____ Don't pet its/it's fur too hard!
11. ____ Its/it's from my Uncle Harry.
12. ____ Can you tell its/it's a surprise?
13. ____ Is its/it's stall always this clean?
14. ____ Its/it's not time to eat yet.
15. ____ She says its/it's working now.

"Can" and "May"

The word **can** means **am able to** or **to be able to**.

Examples:

I **can** do that for you.
Can you do that for me?

The word **may** means **be allowed to** or **permitted to**. **May** is used to ask or give permission. **May** can also mean **might** or **perhaps**.

Examples:

May I be excused?
You **may** sit here.

Directions: Write **can** or **may** on the blanks to complete the sentences correctly. The first one is done for you.

_____ May _____ 1. Can/May I help you?
_____ 2. He's smart. He can/may do it himself.
_____ 3. When can/may I have my dessert?
_____ 4. I can/may tell you exactly what she said.
_____ 5. He can/may speak French fluently.
_____ 6. You can/may use my pencil.
_____ 7. I can/may be allowed to attend the concert.
_____ 8. It's bright. I can/may see you!
_____ 9. Can/May my friend stay for dinner?
_____ 10. You can/may leave when your report is finished.
_____ 11. I can/may see your point!
_____ 12. She can/may dance well.
_____ 13. Can/May you hear the dog barking?
_____ 14. Can/May you help me button this sweater?
_____ 15. Mother, can/may I go to the movies?

"Sit" and "Set"

The word **sit** means **to rest**.

Examples:

Please **sit** here!

Will you **sit** by me?

The word **set** means **to put** or **place something**.

Examples:

Set your purse there.

Set the dishes on the table.

Directions: Write **sit** or **set** to complete the sentences correctly. The first one is done for you.

_____sit_____ 1. Would you please sit/set down here?

_____ 2. You can sit/set the groceries there.

_____ 3. She sit/set her suitcase in the closet.

_____ 4. He sit/set his watch for half past three.

_____ 5. She's a person who can't sit/set still.

_____ 6. Sit/Set the baby on the couch beside me.

_____ 7. Where did you sit/set your new shoes?

_____ 8. They decided to sit/set together during the movie.

_____ 9. Let me sit/set you straight on that!

_____ 10. Instead of swimming, he decided to sit/set in the water.

_____ 11. He sit/set the greasy pan in the sink.

_____ 12. She sit/set the file folder on her desk.

_____ 13. Don't ever sit/set on the refrigerator!

_____ 14. She sit/set the candles on the cake.

_____ 15. Get ready! Get sit/set! Go!

"They're," "Their," "There"

The word **they're** is a contraction for **they are**.

Examples:

They're our very best friends!

Ask them if **they're** coming over tomorrow.

The word **their** shows ownership.

Examples:

Their dog is friendly.

It's **their** bicycle.

The word **there** shows place or direction.

Examples:

Look over **there**.

There it is.

Directions: Write **they're**, **their** or **there** to complete the sentences correctly.
The first one is done for you.

1. <u>There</u> They're/Their/There is the sweater I want!

2. _____ Do you believe they're/their/there stories?

3. _____ Be they're/their/there by one o'clock.

4. _____ Were you they're/their/there last night?

5. _____ I know they're/their/there going to attend.

6. _____ Have you met they're/their/there mother?

7. _____ I can go they're/their/there with you.

8. _____ Do you like they're/their/there new car?

9. _____ They're/Their/There friendly to everyone.

10. _____ Did she say they're/their/there ready to go?

11. _____ She said she'd walk by they're/their/there house.

12. _____ Is anyone they're/their/there?

13. _____ I put it right over they're/their/there!

"This" and "These"

The word **this** is an adjective that refers to things that are near. **This** always describes a singular noun. Singular means one.

Example:

I'll buy **this** coat.

(Coat is singular.)

The word **these** is also an adjective that refers to things that are near. **These** always describes a plural noun. A plural noun refers to more than one thing.

Example:

I will buy **these** flowers.

(Flowers is a plural noun.)

Directions: Write **this** or **these** to complete the sentences correctly. The first one is done for you.

these 1. I will take this/these cookies with me.

_____ 2. Do you want this/these seeds?

_____ 3. Did you try this/these nuts?

_____ 4. Do it this/these way!

_____ 5. What do you know about this/these situation?

_____ 6. Did you open this/these doors?

_____ 7. Did you open this/these window?

_____ 8. What is the meaning of this/these letters?

_____ 9. Will you carry this/these books for me?

_____ 10. This/These pans are hot!

_____ 11. Do you think this/these light is too bright?

_____ 12. Are this/these boots yours?

_____ 13. Do you like this/these rainy weather?

Review

Directions: Complete the sentences by writing the correct words in the blanks.

_____ 1. You have a good/well attitude.

_____ 2. The teacher was not feeling good/well.

_____ 3. She sang extremely good/well.

_____ 4. Everyone said Josh was a good/well boy.

_____ 5. Your/You're going to be sorry for that!

_____ 6. Tell her your/you're serious.

_____ 7. Your/You're report was wonderful!

_____ 8. Your/You're the best person for the job.

_____ 9. Do you think its/it's going to have babies?

_____ 10. Its/It's back paw had a thorn in it.

_____ 11. Its/It's fun to make new friends.

_____ 12. Is its/it's mother always nearby?

_____ 13. How can/may I help you?

_____ 14. You can/may come in now.

_____ 15. Can/May you lift this for me?

_____ 16. She can/may sing soprano.

_____ 17. I'll wait for you to sit/set down first.

_____ 18. We sit/set our dirty boots outside.

_____ 19. It's they're/their/there turn to choose.

_____ 20. They're/Their/There is your answer!

_____ 21. They say they're/their/there coming.

_____ 22. I must have this/these one!

_____ 23. I saw this/these gloves at the store.

_____ 24. He said this/these were his.

Review

Directions: Write the correct answers in the blanks using the words in the box.

good	well	your	you're	its
it's	can	may	sit	set
they're	there	their	this	these

1. _____ is an adjective that refers to a particular thing.

2. Use _____ to tell or ask how something is done or to describe someone's health.

3. _____ is a contraction for it is.

4. _____ describes a plural noun and refers to particular things.

5. _____ means to rest.

6. _____ means am able to or to be able to.

7. _____ is a contraction for they are.

8. _____ , _____ and _____ show ownership or possession.

9. Use _____ to ask politely to be permitted to do something.

10. _____ is a contraction for you are.

11. _____ means to place or put.

12. _____ describes a noun.

13. Use _____ to show direction or placement.

READING
Level 1

Poetry: Cinquains

A **cinquain** is a type of poetry. The form is:

Noun
Adjective, adjective
Verb + ing, verb + ing, verb + ing
Four-word phrase
Synonym for noun in line 1.

Example:

Books
Creative, fun
Reading, choosing, looking
I love to read!
Novels

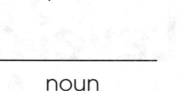

Directions: Write your own cinquain!

_____
noun

_____, _____
adjective   adjective

_____, _____, _____
verb + ing   verb + ing   verb + ing

_____
four-word phrase

_____
synonym for noun in first line

Idioms

Idioms are a colorful way of saying something ordinary. The words in idioms do not mean exactly what they say.

Directions: Read the idioms listed below. Draw a picture of the literal meaning. Then match the idiom to its correct meaning.

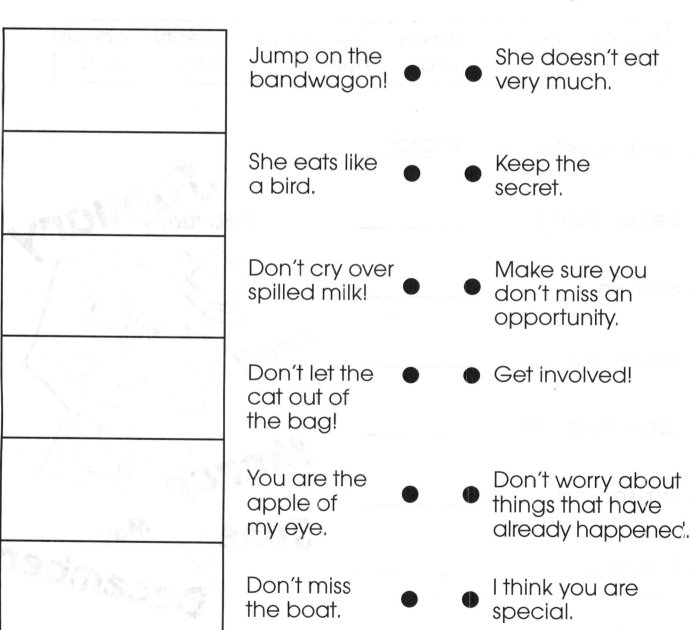

Jump on the bandwagon! ●   ● She doesn't eat very much.

She eats like a bird. ●   ● Keep the secret.

Don't cry over spilled milk! ●   ● Make sure you don't miss an opportunity.

Don't let the cat out of the bag! ●   ● Get involved!

You are the apple of my eye. ●   ● Don't worry about things that have already happened.

Don't miss the boat. ●   ● I think you are special.

Sequencing

Directions: Read each story. Circle the sentence that tells what might happen next.

1. Sam and Judy picked up their books and left the house. They walked to the bus stop. They got on a big yellow bus.

   What will Sam and Judy do next?

   They will go to school.

   They will visit their grandmother.

   They will go to the store.

2. Maggie and Matt were playing in the snow. They made a snow-man with a black hat and a red scarf. Then the sun came out.

   What might happen next?

   It will snow again.

   They will play in the sandbox.

   The snowman will melt.

3. Megan put on a big floppy hat and funny clothes. She put green make-up on her face.

   What will Megan do next?

   She will go to school.

   She will go to a costume party.

   She will go to bed.

4. Mike was eating a hot dog. Suddenly, he smelled smoke. He turned and saw a fire on the stove.

   What will Mike do next?

   He will watch the fire.

   He will call for help.

   He will finish his hot dog.

Sequencing

Directions: Number these sentences from 1 to 8 to show the correct order of the story.

_____ Jack's father called the family doctor.

_____ Jack felt much better as his parents drove him home.

_____ Jack woke up in the middle of the night with a terrible pain in his stomach.

_____ The doctor told Jack's father to take Jack to the hospital.

_____ Jack called his parents to come help him.

_____ At the hospital, the doctors examined Jack. They said the problem was not serious. They told Jack's parents that he could go home.

_____ Jack's mother took his temperature. He had a fever of 103 degrees.

_____ On the way to the hospital, Jack rested in the backseat. He was worried.

Sequencing

Directions: Read each story. Circle the phrase that tells what happened before.

1. Beth is very happy now that she has someone to play with. She hopes that her new sister will grow up quickly!

   A few days ago . . .

   Beth was sick.

   Beth's mother had a baby.

   Beth got a new puppy.

2. Sara tried to mend the tear. She used a needle and thread to sew up the hole.

   While playing, Sara had . . .

   broken her bicycle.

   lost her watch.

   torn her shirt.

3. The movers took John's bike off the truck and put it in the garage. Next, they moved his bed into his new bedroom.

   John's family . . .

   bought a new house.

   went on vacation.

   bought a new truck.

4. Katie picked out a book about dinosaurs. Jim, who likes sports, chose two books about baseball.

   Katie and Jim . . .

   went to the library.

   went to the playground.

   went to the grocery store.

Following Directions

Directions: Learning to follow directions is very important. Use the map to find your way to different houses.

1. Color the start house yellow.
2. Go north 2 houses, and east two houses.
3. Go north 2 houses, and west 4 houses.
4. Color the house green.

5. Start at the yellow house.
6. Go east 1 house, and north 3 houses.
7. Go west 3 houses, and south 3 houses.
8. Color the house blue.

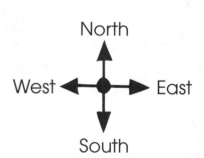

Following Directions

Directions: Read each sentence and do what it says to do.

1. Count the syllables in each word. Write the number on the line by the word.
2. Draw a line between the two words in each compound word.
3. Draw a circle around each name of a month.
4. Draw a box around each food word.
5. Draw an **X** on each noise word.
6. Draw a line under each day of the week.
7. Write the three words from the list you did not use. Draw a picture of each of those words.

_____ April	_____ vegetable	_____ tablecloth
_____ bang	_____ June	_____ meat
_____ sidewalk	_____ Saturday	_____ crash
_____ astronaut	_____ March	_____ jingle
_____ moon	_____ cardboard	_____ rocket
_____ Friday	_____ fruit	_____ Monday

Following Directions

Directions: Look at the calendar page. Read each sentence and do what it says to do.

__ __ b r __ __ r y						
Sunday	Mon_____	Tuesday	_____	Th ___ day	Friday	Saturday
1	2	3			6	
8	9	10	11	12		14
15				19	20	21
	23					28

1. Guess the month. It is a winter month, and it is the month with the fewest days. Write the missing letters in the name on the top line.
2. Write the missing numbers for the dates.
3. Write the name of the missing day where it belongs.
4. Write the missing letters in the names of two days.
5. Circle the dates that will be Saturdays.
6. The 2nd is Groundhog Day. Draw a brown **X** in that square.
7. The 12th is Abraham Lincoln's birthday. Draw a black top hat in that square.
8. The 14th is Valentine's Day. Draw a red heart in that square.
9. George Washington's birthday is on the 22nd. Draw a red cherry in that square.

Classification

Classification is grouping similar things into one category.

A title can tell a lot about a book. Read the following book titles.

Directions: Write each title in the correct category below. One title does not fit into any of the categories.

The Case of the Missing Key	*How Raccoon Got His Mask*	*Your Heart*
Guide to Computers	*Haunted House Tale*	*Where's Susie?*
The Brain: Nerve Central	*Turtle's Trip*	*The Hidden Passage*
Nutrition Network	*No Bones About It*	*Reptiles of the Desert*
Tommy, the Seeing-Eye Dog	*The Secret Letter*	*The Amazing Body*

Health

_____
_____
_____
_____
_____

Animals

_____
_____
_____
_____
_____

Mysteries

_____
_____
_____
_____
_____

Which title is left? _____

In what section of the library might it be? _____

Webs

Webs are another way to classify information. Look at the groups below.

Directions: Add more words in each group.

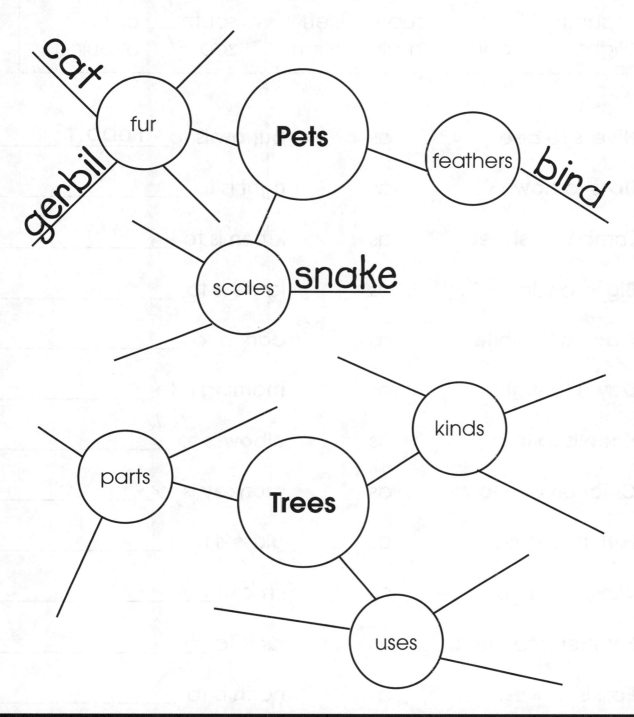

Completing Analogies

Directions: Complete each analogy using a word from the box. The first one is done for you.

rabbit	fish	cup	left	south	cat
light	bear	small	arm	zoo	evening

1. **Hive** is to **bee**   as   **burrow** is to __rabbit__.

2. **Up** is to **down**   as   **right** is to _____.

3. **Lamb** is to **sheep**   as   **kitten** is to _____.

4. **Big** is to **little**   as   **large** is to _____.

5. **Black** is to **white**   as   **dark** is to _____.

6. **Day** is to **night**   as   **morning** is to _____.

7. **Knee** is to **leg**   as   **elbow** is to _____.

8. **Chicken** is to **farm**   as   **monkey** is to _____.

9. **Fork** is to **spoon**   as   **glass** is to _____.

10. **Wing** is to **bird**   as   **fin** is to _____.

11. **Feather** is to **duck**   as   **fur** is to _____.

12. **East** is to **west**   as   **north** is to _____.

Completing Analogies

Directions: Complete each analogy using a word from the box. The first one is done for you.

finish	less	pony	oven	finger	big
week	hour	cat	weak	under	little

1. **Second** is to **minute**   as   **minute** is to ___hour___ .

2. **Fast** is to **slow**   as   **big** is to _____ .

3. **Child** is to **adult**   as   **kitten** is to _____ .

4. **Puppy** is to **kitten**   as   **calf** is to _____ .

5. **Less** is to **more**   as   **little** is to _____ .

6. **Freeze** is to **freezer**   as   **bake** is to _____ .

7. **Late** is to **early**   as   **more** is to _____ .

8. **First** is to **last**   as   **start** is to _____ .

9. **In** is to **out**   as   **over** is to _____ .

10. **Hard** is to **soft**   as   **strong** is to _____ .

11. **Earring** is to **ear**   as   **ring** is to _____ .

12. **Hour** is to **day**   as   **day** is to _____ .

Main Idea

The **main idea** of a story is what the story is mostly about.

Directions: Read the story. Then answer the questions.

A tree is more than the enormous plant you see growing in your yard. A large part of the tree grows under the ground. This part is called the roots. If the tree is very big and very old, the roots may stretch down 100 feet!

The roots hold the tree in the ground. The roots do another important job for the tree. They gather minerals and water from the soil to feed the tree so it will grow. Most land plants, including trees, could not live without roots to support and feed them.

1. The main idea of this story is:

   The roots of a tree are underground.
   The roots do important jobs for the tree.

2. Where are the roots of a tree? _____

Circle the correct answer.

3. The roots help to hold the tree up.   True   False

4. Name two things the roots collect from the soil for the tree.

   1) _____   2) _____

Parts of a Paragraph

A **paragraph** is a group of sentences that all tell about the same thing. Most paragraphs have three parts: a **beginning**, a **middle** and an **end**.

Directions: Write **beginning**, **middle** or **end** next to each sentence in the scrambled paragraphs below. There can be more than one middle sentence.

Example:

_____middle_____ We took the tire off the car.

___beginning___ On the way to Aunt Louise's, we had a flat tire.

____middle____ We patched the hole in the tire.

_____end_____ We put the tire on and started driving again.

_____ I took all the ingredients out of the cupboard.

_____ One morning, I decided to bake a pumpkin pie.

_____ I forgot to add the pumpkin!

_____ I mixed the ingredients together, but something was missing.

_____ The sun was very hot and our throats were dry.

_____ We finally decided to turn back.

_____ We started our hike very early in the morning.

_____ It kept getting hotter as we walked.

Topic Sentences

A **topic sentence** is usually the first sentence in a paragraph. It tells what the story will be about.

Directions: Read the following sentences. Circle the topic sentence that should go first in the paragraph that follows.

Rainbows have seven colors.

There's a pot of gold.

I like rainbows.

The colors are red, orange, yellow, green, blue, indigo and violet. Red forms the outer edge, with violet on the inside of the rainbow.

He cut down a cherry tree.

His wife was named Martha.

George Washington was a good president.

He helped our country get started. He chose intelligent leaders to help him run the country.

Mark Twain was a great author.

Mark Twain was unhappy sometimes.

Mark Twain was born in Missouri.

One of his most famous books is *Huckleberry Finn*. He wrote many other great books.

Cause and Effect

Directions: Draw a line to match each phrase to form a logical cause and effect sentence.

1. Dad gets paid today, so	because she is sick.
2. When the electricity went out,	we're going out for dinner.
3. Courtney can't spend the night	so she bought a new sweater.
4. Our front window shattered	we grabbed the flashlights.
5. Sophie got $10.00 for her birthday,	when the baseball hit it.

Directions: Read each sentence beginning. Choose an ending from the box that makes sense. Write the correct letter on the line.

1. Her arm was in a cast, because ____

2. They are building a new house on our street, so ____

3. Since I'd always wanted a puppy, ____

4. I had to renew my library book, ____

5. My parents' anniversary is tomorrow, ____

> A. we all went down to watch.
> B. so my sister and I bought them some flowers.
> C. since I hadn't finished it.
> D. she fell when she was skating.
> E. Mom gave me one for my birthday.

Noting Details

Directions: Read the story. Then answer the questions.

Thomas Edison was one of America's greatest inventors. An **inventor** thinks up new machines and new ways of doing things. Edison was born in Milan, Ohio in 1847. He went to school for only three months. His teacher thought he was not very smart because he asked so many questions.

Edison liked to experiment. He had many wonderful ideas. He invented the light bulb and the phonograph (record player).

Thomas Edison died in 1931, but we still use many of his inventions today.

1. What is an inventor?

_____

2. Where was Thomas Edison born?

_____

3. How long did he go to school?

_____

4. What are two of Edison's inventions?

_____

Reading Comprehension

Directions: Read the story. Then answer the questions.

Have you ever seen a tree that has been cut down? If so, you may have seen many circles in the trunk. These are called the **annual rings**. You can tell how old a tree is by counting these rings.

Trees have these rings because they grow a new layer of wood every year. The new layer grows right below the bark. In a year when there is a lot of rain and sunlight, the tree grows faster; the annual ring that year will be thick. When there is not much rain or sunlight, the tree grows slower and the ring is thin.

Circle the correct answer.

1. The annual ring of a tree tells how big the tree is.

   True   False

2. Each year, a new layer of wood grows on top of the bark.

   True   False

3. In a year with lots of rain and sunlight, the annual ring will be thick.

   True   False

4. Trees grow faster when there is more rain and sunlight.

   True   False

5. How old was the tree on this page? _____

Comprehension: Mary Lou Retton

Mary Lou Retton became the first U.S. woman to win Olympic gold in gymnastics. She accomplished this at the 1984 Olympics held in Los Angeles, when she was 16 years old. "Small but mighty" would certainly describe this gymnast.

She was the youngest of five children—all good athletes. She grew up in Fairmont, West Virginia, and began her gymnastic training at the age of 7.

Most women gymnasts are graceful, but Mary Lou helped open up the field of gymnastics to strong, athletic women. Mary Lou was 4 feet 10 inches tall and weighed a mere 95 pounds!

Directions: Answer these questions about Mary Lou Retton.

1. Circle the main idea:

   Mary Lou loved performing.

   Mary Lou is a famous Olympic gymnast.

2. She was born in _____.

3. At what age did she begin her gymnastics training?

   _____

4. Mary Lou won a gold medal when she was _____ years old.

Reading Comprehension

Directions: Read the story. Then answer the questions.

What is a **robot**? Does a robot do any of your work for you?

A robot is any machine that can do work without a person being needed to run it all the time. A dishwasher is a kind of robot. A clock radio is a robot, too. They may not look like the robots you see on television or read about in books, but they are.

Robots are controlled by computers. There are robots to do many useful jobs, such as flying airplanes and building cars. Many factories use robots to do simple jobs, such as picking up objects and putting them in place. These are jobs that people find boring. A robot can do them over and over without becoming tired or bored.

1. What is a robot? _____

_____.

2. Name two uses for robots.

    1) _____ 2) _____

3. What controls a robot? _____

_____.

Types of Books

A **fiction** book is a book about things that are made up or not true. Fantasy books are fiction. A **nonfiction** book is about things that have really happened. Books can be classified into more types:

Mystery — books that have clues that lead to solving a problem or mystery

Biography — book about a real person's life

Poetry — a collection of poems, which may or may not rhyme

Fantasy — books about things that cannot really happen

Sports — books about different sports or sport figures

Travel — books about going to other places

Directions: Write mystery, biography, poetry, fantasy, sports or travel next to each title.

The Life of Helen Keller _____

Let's Go to Mexico! _____

The Case of the Missing Doll _____

How to Play Golf _____

Turtle Soup and Other Poems _____

Fred's Flying Saucer _____

Reading for Information: Dictionaries

Dictionaries contain meanings and pronunciations of words. The words in a dictionary are listed in alphabetical order. Guide words appear at the top of each dictionary page. They help us know at a glance what words are on each page.

Directions: Place the words in alphabetical order.

apple	dog	crab	ear
book	atlas	cake	frog
egg	drip	coat	crib

Dictionary Skills: Entry Words

Words in a dictionary are called **entries**. Some entries have more than one meaning. Dictionaries number each meaning.

Directions: Read the entry word below and its different meanings. Then answer the questions.

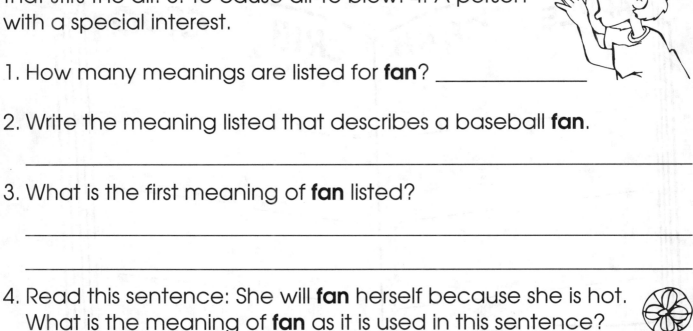

fan 1. An instrument shaped like a semicircle that is waved by hand. 2. An instrument with rotating blades that stirs the air. 3. To cause air to blow. 4. A person with a special interest.

1. How many meanings are listed for **fan**? _____

2. Write the meaning listed that describes a baseball **fan**.

_____

3. What is the first meaning of **fan** listed?

_____

_____

4. Read this sentence: She will **fan** herself because she is hot. What is the meaning of **fan** as it is used in this sentence?

_____

_____

5. Read the second meaning of **fan**. Write a sentence using that meaning of **fan**.

_____

_____

Reading for Information: The Food Pyramid

Eating foods that are good for you is very important for you to stay healthy.

Directions: List different foods or draw pictures to go in each group.

Food Pyramid (per day)

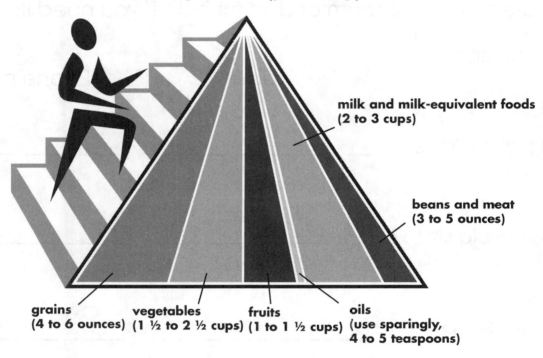

milk and milk-equivalent foods
(2 to 3 cups)

beans and meat
(3 to 5 ounces)

grains
(4 to 6 ounces)

vegetables
(1 ½ to 2 ½ cups)

fruits
(1 to 1 ½ cups)

oils
(use sparingly,
4 to 5 teaspoons)

Circle the correct answers.

1. You should eat as many sweets as possible.   True   False

2. You should eat 4-6 ounces of the grain   True   False
   group per day.

3. You should eat more than 5 ounces of meat   True   False
   per day.

4. What is your favorite food? _____

Reading for Information

Telephone books contain information about people's addresses and phone numbers. They also list business addresses and phone numbers. The information in a telephone book is listed in alphabetical order.

Directions: Use your telephone book to find the following places in your area. Ask your mom or dad for help if you need it.

Can you find . . .

	Name	Phone number

. . . a pizza place? _____ _____

. . . a bicycle store? _____ _____

. . . a pet shop? _____ _____

. . . a toy store? _____ _____

. . . a water park? _____ _____

What other telephone numbers would you like to have?

_____

Reading for Information: Newspapers

A newspaper has many parts. Some of the parts of a newspaper are:

- banner — the name of the paper
- lead story — the top news item
- caption — sentences under the picture which give information about the picture
- sports — scores and information on current sports events
- comics — drawings that tell funny stories
- editorial — an article by the editor expressing an opinion about something
- ads — paid advertisements
- weather — information about the weather
- advice column — letters from readers asking for help with a problem
- movie guides — a list of movies and movie times
- obituary — information about people who have died

Directions: Match the newspaper sections below with their definitions.

banner	an article by the editor
lead story	sentences under pictures
caption	movies and movie times
editorial	the name of the paper
movies	information about people who have died
obituary	the top news item

Newspaper Writing

Directions: Use the front page below to create a newspaper story about Cinderella.

♥ _____ ♥
(banner)

Glass Slipper Found!
(lead story)

_____
_____
_____
_____
_____

Evil Stepmothers: What do you think?
(editorial)

_____
_____
_____
_____

Today's Weather:

_____
_____
_____

Draw a picture

(caption) _____
_____

Classified Ads: Wanted!

_____
_____
_____

Advice:
Dear Fairy Godmother,
   I want to go to the ball, and my stepmother won't let me go. What should I do?

_____
_____
_____

Newspaper Writing

A good news story gives us important information. It answers the questions:

WHO?   WHY?   WHAT?

WHERE?   HOW?   WHEN?

Directions: Think about the story "Little Red Riding Hood." Answer the following questions about the story.

Who are the characters?_____

_____

What is the story about? _____

_____

Why does Red go to Granny's house?_____

_____

Where does the story take place? _____

_____

When did she go to Granny's house? _____

_____

Where did the Wolf greet Red?_____

_____

Letter Writing

Letters have five parts: the **heading**, the **greeting**, the **body**, the **closing** and the **signature**.

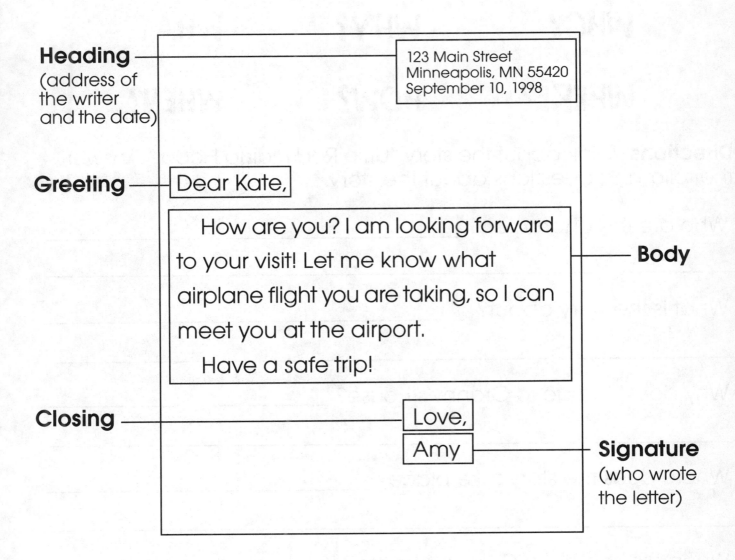

Heading
(address of
the writer
and the date)

123 Main Street
Minneapolis, MN 55420
September 10, 1998

Greeting

Dear Kate,

How are you? I am looking forward to your visit! Let me know what airplane flight you are taking, so I can meet you at the airport.

Have a safe trip!

Body

Closing

Love,

Amy

Signature
(who wrote
the letter)

Letter Writing

Directions: Write a friendly letter below. Be sure to include a heading, greeting, body, closing and signature.

_____

_____

_____

(heading)

_____ ,

(greeting)

_____

_____

(body)

_____

_____

_____

_____ , (closing)

_____ (signature)

READING
Level 2

Writing Question Sentences

Directions: Rewrite each sentence to make it a question. The first one is done for you. In some cases, the form of the verb must be changed.

1. She slept soundly all day.

_____

2. The cookies are hot.

_____

3. He put the cake in the oven.

_____

4. She lives in the green house.

_____

5. He understood my directions.

_____

6. Jessica ran faster than anyone.

_____

7. The bus was gone before he arrived.

_____

8. His car is yellow.

_____

9. Elizabeth wants some more beans.

_____

Exclamations

Exclamation points are used for sentences that express strong feelings. These sentences can have one or two words or be very long.

Example: Wait! or **Don't forget to call!**

Directions: Add an exclamation point at the end of sentences that express strong feelings. Add a period at the end of the statements.

1. My parents and I were watching television

2. The snow began falling around noon

3. Wow

4. The snow was really coming down

5. We turned the television off and looked out the window

6. The snow looked like a white blanket

7. How beautiful

8. We decided to put on our coats and go outside

9. Hurry

10. Get your sled

11. All the people on the street came out to see the snow

12. How wonderful

13. The children began making a snowman

14. What a great day

Everything for Math and Reading Grade 4

Making Sense of Sentences

A **statement** is a sentence that tells something. It ends with a period (.).

Example: Columbus is the capital of Ohio.

A **question** is a sentence that asks something. It ends with a question mark (?).

Example: Do you like waffles?

An **exclamation** is a sentence that shows strong feeling.
It ends with an exclamation mark (!).

Example: You're the best friend in the world!

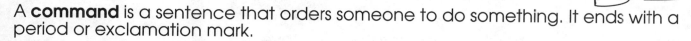

A **command** is a sentence that orders someone to do something. It ends with a period or exclamation mark.

Example: Shut the door. Watch out for that trunk!

A **request** is a sentence that asks someone to do something. It ends with a period or question mark.

Example: Please shut the door.

Directions: Write **S** if the sentence makes a statement, **Q** if it asks a question, **E** if it is an exclamation, **C** if it issues a command or **R** if it makes a request. Punctuate each sentence correctly.

____ 1. Please open your mouth

____ 2. Will you be going to the party

____ 3. That's hot

____ 4. Give me the car keys right now

____ 5. Do you think she will run fast

____ 6. It's cold today

____ 7. You're incredible

____ 8. Run for your life

____ 9. Is today the deadline

____ 10. I turned in my paper early

____ 11. Call the doctor immediately

____ 12. Turn around and touch your toes

____ 13. Be at my house at noon tomorrow

____ 14. Give me a clue

____ 15. Can you give me a clue

____ 16. Please wipe your face

____ 17. It's time for me to go home

____ 18. No one believed what she said

____ 19. Are you interested

____ 20. He's badly hurt

Reading Skills: Classifying

Classifying is placing similar things into categories.

Directions: Classify each group by crossing out the word that does not belong.

1. factory   hotel   lodge   pattern

2. Thursday   September   December   October

3. cottage   hut   carpenter   castle

4. cupboard   orchard   refrigerator   stove

5. Christmas   Thanksgiving   Easter   spring

6. brass   copper   coal   tin

7. stomach   breathe   liver   brain

8. teacher   mother   dentist   office

9. musket   faucet   bathtub   sink

10. basement   attic   kitchen   neighborhood

Reading Skills: Classifying

Directions: Read the title of each TV show. Write the correct number to tell what kind of show it is.

| 1 — Cooking | 3 — Sports | 5 — Humor |
| 2 — Nature | 4 — Mystery | 6 — Famous People |

_____ *The Secret of the Lost Locket*

_____ *Learn Tennis With the Pros*

_____ *Birds in the Wild*

_____ *The Life of George Washington*

_____ *Great Recipes From Around the World*

_____ *A Laugh a Minute*

Directions: Read the description of each TV show. Write the number of each show above in the blank.

_____ The years before he became the first president of the United States are examined.

_____ Featured: eagles and owls

_____ Clues lead Detective Logan to a cemetery in his search for the missing necklace.

_____ Famous players give tips on buying a racket.

_____ Six ways to cook chicken

_____ Cartoon characters in short stories

Reading Skills: Classifying

Directions: Complete each idea by crossing out the word or phrase that does not belong.

1. If the main idea is **things that are green**, I don't need:

   the sun   apples   grass   leaves in summer

2. If the idea is **musical instruments**, I don't need a:

   piano   trombone   beach ball   tuba

3. If the idea is **months of the year**, I don't need:

   Friday   January   July   October

4. If the idea is **colors on the U.S. flag**, I don't need:

   white   blue   black   red

5. If the idea is **types of weather,** I don't need:

   sleet   stormy   roses   sunny

6. If the idea is **fruits**, I don't need:

   kiwi   orange   spinach   banana

7. If the idea is **U.S. presidents**, I don't need:

   Lincoln   Jordan   Washington   Adams

8. If the idea is **flowers**, I don't need:

   oak   daisy   tulip   daffodil

9. If the idea is **sports**, I don't need:

   pears   soccer   wrestling   baseball

Reading Skills: Sequencing

Directions: Read each set of events. Then number them in the correct order.

_____ Get dressed for school and hurry downstairs for breakfast.

_____ Roll over, sleepy-eyed, and turn off the alarm clock.

_____ Meet your friends at the corner to walk to school.

_____ The fourth-grade class walked quietly to a safe area away from the building.

_____ The teacher reminded the last student to shut the classroom door.

_____ The loud clanging of the fire alarm startled everyone in the room.

_____ Barb's dad watched from the seat of the tractor as the boys and girls climbed into the wagon.

_____ By the time they returned to the barn, there wasn't much straw left.

_____ As the wagon bumped along the trail, the boys and girls sang songs they learned in music class.

_____ The referee blew his whistle and held up the hand of the winner of the match.

_____ Each wrestler worked hard, trying to out-maneuver his opponent.

_____ The referee said, "Shake hands, boys, and wrestle a fair match."

Reading Skills: Sequencing

Directions: In each group below, one event in the sequence is missing. Write the correct sentence from the box where it belongs.

> - Paul put his bait on the hook and cast out into the pond.
> - "Sorry," he said, "but the TV repairman can't get here until Friday."
> - Everyone pitched in and helped.
> - Corey put the ladder up against the trunk of the tree.

1. "All the housework has to be done before anyone goes to the game," said Mom.

2. _____

3. We all agreed that "many hands make light work."

1. _____

2. It wasn't long until he felt a tug on the line, and we watched the bobber go under.

3. He was the only one to go home with something other than bait!

1. The little girl cried as she stood looking up into the maple tree.

2. Between her tears, she managed to say, "My kitten is up in the tree and can't get down."

3. _____

1. Dad hung up the phone and turned to look at us.

2. _____

3. "This would be a good time to get out those old board games in the hall closet," he said.

Reading Skills: Sequencing

Directions: Read about how a tadpole becomes a frog. Then number the stages in order below.

Frogs and toads belong to a group of animals called amphibians (am-FIB-ee-ans). This means "living a double life." Frogs and toads live a "double life" because they live part of their lives in water and part on land. They are able to do this because their bodies change as they grow. This series of changes is called metamorphosis (met-a-MORE-fa-sis).

A mother frog lays her eggs in water, then leaves them on their own to grow. The eggs contain cells—the tiny "building blocks" of all living things—that multiply and grow. Soon the cells grow into a swimming tadpole. Tadpoles breathe through gills—small holes in their sides—like fish do. They spend all of their time in the water.

The tadpole changes as it grows. Back legs slowly form. Front legs begin inside the tadpole under the gill holes. They pop out when they are fully developed. At the same time, lungs, which a frog uses to breathe instead of gills, are almost ready to be used.

As the tadpole reaches the last days of its life in the water, its tail disappears. It is ready for life on land. It has become a frog.

_____ The front legs pop out. The lungs are ready to use for breathing.

_____ The cells in the egg multiply and grow.

_____ The tadpole has become a frog.

_____ Back legs slowly form.

_____ Soon the cells grow into a swimming tadpole.

_____ Front legs develop inside the tadpole.

_____ The tadpole's tail disappears.

_____ A mother frog lays her eggs in water.

Following Directions: A Rocket Launcher

Directions: Read about how to make a rocket launcher. Then number the steps in order below. Have an adult help you.

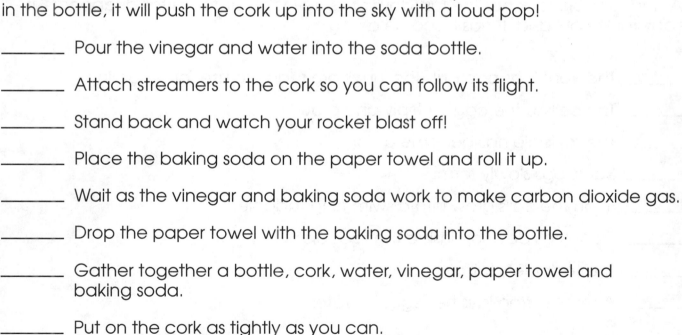

You can do this in your own backyard. To make this rocket launcher, you need an empty 1-quart soda bottle, cork, paper towel, 1/2 cup water, 1/2 cup vinegar and 1 teaspoon baking soda. You may want to add some streamers.

If you attach tissue paper streamers to the cork or rocket with a thumbtack, this helps you follow the rocket more easily during its flight.

Pour the water and vinegar into the launcher—the bottle. Cut the paper towel into a 4-inch square. Place the baking soda in the middle of the paper towel. Roll up the towel and twist the ends so the baking soda will stay inside.

Outside, you will need plenty of room for the rocket to fly. Drop the paper towel and baking soda into the bottle. Put the cork on as tightly as you can.

When the liquid soaks through the paper towel, the baking soda and vinegar work together to make a gas called carbon dioxide. As the carbon dioxide builds up in the bottle, it will push the cork up into the sky with a loud pop!

_____ Pour the vinegar and water into the soda bottle.

_____ Attach streamers to the cork so you can follow its flight.

_____ Stand back and watch your rocket blast off!

_____ Place the baking soda on the paper towel and roll it up.

_____ Wait as the vinegar and baking soda work to make carbon dioxide gas.

_____ Drop the paper towel with the baking soda into the bottle.

_____ Gather together a bottle, cork, water, vinegar, paper towel and baking soda.

_____ Put on the cork as tightly as you can.

Compare and Contrast

To **compare** means to discuss how things are similar. To contrast means to discuss how things are different.

Directions: Compare and contrast how people grow gardens. Write at least two answers for each question.

Many people in the country have large gardens. They have a lot of space, so they can plant many kinds of vegetables and flowers. Since the gardens are usually quite large, they use a wheelbarrow to carry the tools they need. Sometimes, they even have to carry water or use a garden hose.

People who live in the city do not always have enough room for a garden. Many people in big cities live in apartment buildings. They can put in a window box or use part of their balcony space to grow things. Most of the time, the only garden tools they need are a hand trowel to loosen the dirt and a watering can to make sure the plant gets enough water.

1. Compare gardening in the country with gardening in the city

_____

_____

2. Contrast gardening in the country with gardening in the city

_____

_____

Compare and Contrast: Venn Diagram

Directions: List the similarities and differences you find below on a chart called a **Venn diagram**. This kind of chart shows comparisons and contrasts.

Butterflies and moths belong to the same group of insects. They both have two pairs of wings. Their wings are covered with tiny scales. Both butterflies and moths undergo metamorphosis, or a change, in their lives. They begin their lives as caterpillars.

Butterflies and moths are different in some ways. Butterflies usually fly during the day, but moths generally fly at night. Most butterflies have slender, hairless bodies; most moths have plump, furry bodies. When butterflies land, they hold their wings together straight over their bodies. When moths land, they spread their wings out flat.

1. List three ways that butterflies and moths are alike.

   _____

   _____

   _____

2. List three ways that butterflies and moths are different.

   _____

   _____

   _____

3. Combine your answers from questions 1 and 2 into a Venn diagram. Write the differences in the circle labeled for each insect. Write the similarities in the intersecting part.

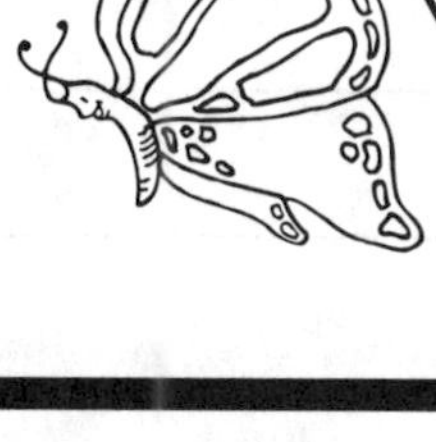

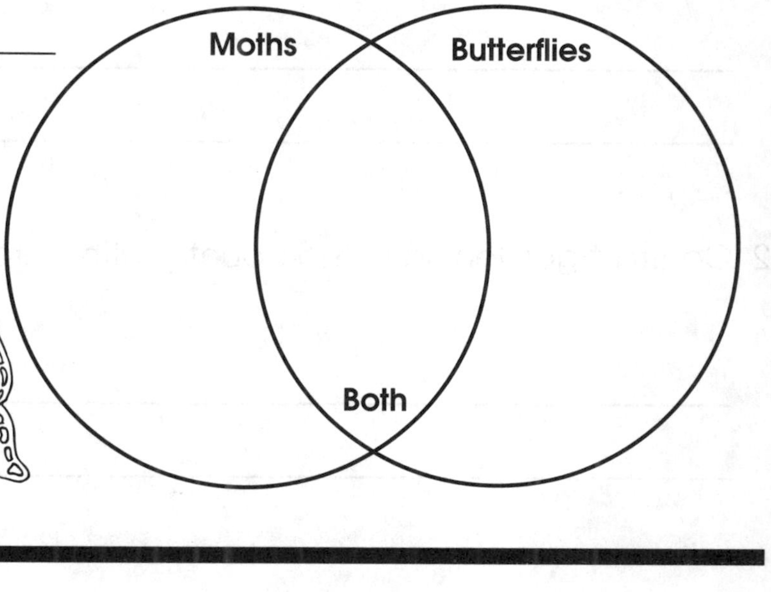

   Moths   Butterflies

   Both

Reading Skills: Analogies

An **analogy** is a way of comparing things to show how they are similar.

Directions: Read the sentences below. Determine how the first pair of words is related. Complete the second pair that relates in the same way. The first one is done for you.

cut	carry	ran	arm	listen
paint	lie	children	50	out
puppy	summer	hot	water	egg

1. Pencil is to write as brush is to _____paint_____ .

2. Foot is to leg as hand is to _____ .

3. Crayons are to draw as scissors are to _____ .

4. Leg is to walk as arm is to _____ .

5. Baby is to babies as child is to _____ .

6. Eye is to look as ear is to _____ .

7. Chair is to sit as bed is to _____ .

8. 600 is to 300 as 100 is to _____ .

9. White is to black as in is to _____ .

10. Ice skate is to winter as swim is to _____ .

11. Switch is to light as faucet is to _____ .

12. Fly is to flew as run is to _____ .

13. Cow is to milk as chicken is to _____ .

14. Cool is to cold as warm is to _____ .

15. Cat is to kitten as dog is to _____ .

Analogies

An **analogy** indicates how different items go together or are similar in some way.

Examples:
    Petal is to flower as leaf is to tree.
    Book is to library as food is to grocery.

The examples show how the second set of objects is related to the first set. A petal is part of a flower, and a leaf is part of a tree. A book can be found in a library, and food can be found in a grocery store.

Directions: Fill in the blanks to complete the analogies. The first one is done for you.

1. Cup is to saucer as glass is to _____coaster_____.

2. Paris is to France as London is to _____.

3. Clothes are to hangers as _____ are to boxes.

4. California is to _____ as Ohio is to Lake Erie.

5. _____ is to table as blanket is to bed.

6. Pencil is to paper as _____ is to canvas.

7. Cow is to _____ as child is to house.

8. State is to country as _____ is to state.

9. Governor is to state as _____ is to country.

10. _____ is to ocean as sand is to desert.

11. Engine is to car as hard drive is to _____ .

12. Beginning is to _____ as stop is to end.

Directions: Write three analogies of your own.

_____

_____

_____

Reading Skills: Main Idea in Sentences

The **main idea** is the most important idea, or main point, in a sentence, paragraph or story.

Directions: Circle the main idea for each sentence.

1. Emily knew she would be late if she watched the end of the TV show.
   a. Emily likes watching TV.
   b. Emily is always running late.
   c. If Emily didn't leave, she would be late.

2. The dog was too strong and pulled Jason across the park on his leash.
   a. The dog is stronger than Jason.
   b. Jason is not very strong.
   c. Jason took the dog for a walk.

3. Jennifer took the book home so she could read it over and over.
   a. Jennifer loves to read.
   b. Jennifer loves the book.
   c. Jennifer is a good reader.

4. Jerome threw the baseball so hard it broke the window.
   a. Jerome throws baseballs very hard.
   b. Jerome was mad at the window.
   c. Jerome can't throw very straight.

5. Lori came home and decided to clean the kitchen for her parents.
   a. Lori is a very nice person.
   b. Lori did a favor for her parents.
   c. Lori likes to cook.

6. It was raining so hard that it was hard to see the road through the windshield.
   a. It always rains hard in April.
   b. The rain blurred our vision.
   c. It's hard to drive in the rain.

Main Idea

Directions: Read each main idea sentence on pages 140 and 141. Then read the detail sentences following each main idea. Draw a ✓ on the line in front of each detail that supports the main idea.

Example: Niagara Falls is a favorite vacation spot.

✓   There are so many cars and buses that it is hard to get around.

____   My little brother gets sick when we go camping.

✓   You can see people there from all over the world.

1. Hummingbirds are interesting birds to watch.

____   They look like tiny helicopters as they move around the flowers.

____   One second they are "drinking" from the flower; the next, they are gone!

____   It is important to provide birdseed in the winter for our feathered friends.

2. Boys and girls look forward to Valentine's Day parties at school.

____   For days, children try to choose the perfect valentine for each friend.

____   The school program is next Tuesday night.

____   Just thinking about frosted, heart-shaped cookies makes me hungry!

Main Idea

3. In-line skating has become a very popular activity.

   ____ Bicycles today are made in many different styles.

   ____ It is hard to spend even an hour at a park without seeing children and adults skating.

   ____ The stores are full of many kinds and colors of in-line skates.

4. It has been a busy summer!

   ____ Dad built a new deck off the back of our house, and everyone helped.

   ____ Our next-door neighbor needed my help to watch her three-year-old twins.

   ____ We will visit my relatives on the East coast for Christmas this year.

Main Idea: Snow Fun

The **main idea** of a story or report is a sentence that summarizes the most important point. If a story or report is only one paragraph in length, then the main idea is usually stated in the first sentence (topic sentence). If it is longer than one paragraph, then the main idea is a general sentence including all the important points of the story or report.

Directions: Read the story. Then draw an **X** in the blank for the main idea.

> After a big snowfall, my friends and I enjoy playing in the snow. We bundle up in snow clothes at our homes, then meet with sleds at the hill by my house.
>
> One by one, we take turns sledding down the hill to see who will go the farthest and the fastest. Sometimes we have a contest to see whose sled will reach the fence at the foot of the hill first.
>
> When we tire of sledding, we may build a snowman or snowforts. Sometimes we have a friendly snowball fight.
>
> The end of our snow fun comes too quickly, and we head home to warm houses, dry clothes and hot chocolate.

1. What is the main idea?

_____ Playing in the snow with friends is an enjoyable activity.

_____ Sledding in the snow is fast and fun.

The first option is correct. The paragraphs discuss the enjoyable things friends do on a snowy day.

The second option is not correct because the entire story is not about sledding. Only the second paragraph discusses sledding. The other paragraphs discuss the additional ways friends have fun in the snow.

2. Write a paragraph about what you like to do on snowy days. Remember to make the first sentence your main idea.

_____

_____

_____

Reading Skills: Main Idea in Paragraphs

Directions: Read each paragraph below. Then circle the sentence that tells the main idea.

It looked as if our class field day would have to be cancelled due to the weather. We tried not to show our disappointment, but Mr. Wade knew that it was hard to keep our minds on the math lesson. We noticed that even he had been sneaking glances out the window. All morning the classroom had been buzzing with plans. Each team met to plan team strategies for winning the events. Then, it happened! Clouds began to cover the sky, and soon the thunder and lightning confirmed what we were afraid of—field day cancelled. Mr. Wade explained that we could still keep our same teams. We could put all of our plans into motion, but we would have to get busy and come up with some inside games and competitions. I guess the day would not be a total disaster!

a. Many storms occur in the late afternoon.

b. Our class field day had to be cancelled due to the weather.

c. Each team came up with its own strategies.

Allison and Emma had to work quietly and quickly to get Mom's birthday cake baked before she got home from work. Each of the girls had certain jobs to do—Allison set the oven temperature and got the cake pans prepared, while Emma got out all the ingredients. As they stirred and mixed, the two girls talked about the surprise party Dad had planned for Mom. Even Dad didn't know that the girls were baking this special cake. The cake was delicious. "It shows you what teamwork can do!" said the girls in unison.

a. Dad worked with the girls to bake the cake.

b. Mom's favorite frosting is chocolate cream.

c. Allison and Emma baked a birthday cake for Mom.

Main Idea

The **main idea** of a paragraph is the most important point. Often, the first sentence in a paragraph tells the main idea. Most of the other sentences are details that support the main idea.

Directions: One of the sentences in each paragraph below does not belong in the story. Circle the sentence that does not support the main idea.

My family and I went to the zoo last Saturday. It was a beautiful day. The tigers napped in the sun. I guess they liked the warm sunshine as much as we did! Mom and Dad laughed at the baby monkeys. They said the monkeys reminded them of how we act. My sister said the bald eagle reminded her of Dad! I know I'll remember that trip to the zoo for a long time. My cousin is coming to visit the weekend before school starts.

Thanksgiving was a special holiday in our classroom. Each child dressed up as either a Pilgrim or a Native American. My baby sister learned to walk last week. We prepared food for our "feast" on the last day of school before the holiday. We all helped shake the jar full of cream to make real butter. Our teacher cooked applesauce. It smelled delicious!

Reading Skills: Context Clues

When you read, you may confuse words that look alike. You can tell when you read a word incorrectly because it doesn't make sense. You can tell from the **context** (the other words in the sentence or the sentences before or after) what the word should be. These **context clues** can help you figure out the meaning of a word by relating it to other words in the sentence.

Directions: Circle the correct word for each sentence below. Use the context to help you.

1. We knew we were in trouble as soon as we heard the crash. The baseball had gone (through, thought) the picture window!

2. She was not able to answer my question because her (month, mouth) was full of pizza.

3. Asia is the largest continent in the (world, word).

4. I'm not sure I heard the teacher correctly. Did he say what I (through, thought) he said?

5. I was not with them on vacation so I don't know a (think, thing) about what happened.

6. My favorite (month, mouth) of the year is July because I love fireworks and parades!

7. You will do better on your book report if you (think, thing) about what you are going to say.

Reading Skills: Context Clues

Directions: In each sentence below, circle the correct meaning for the nonsense word.

1. Be careful when you put that plate back on the shelf—it is **quibbable**.

    flexible   colorful   breakable

2. What is your favorite kind of **tonn**, pears or bananas?

    fruit   salad   purple

3. The **dinlay** outside this morning was very chilly; I needed my sweater.

    tree   vegetable   temperature

4. The whole class enjoyed the **weat**. They wanted to see it again next Friday.

    colorful   plant   video

5. Ashley's mother brought in a **zundy** she made by hand.

    temperature   quilt   plant

6. "Why don't you sit over here, Ronnie? That **sloey**

    is not very comfortable," said Mr. Gross.

    chair   car   cat

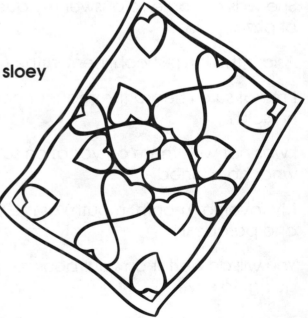

Reading Skills: Context Clues

Directions: Use context clues to help you choose the correct word for each sentence below.

selected	match	scarecrow

Diane and Donna are twin sisters. The clothes they wear nearly always

_____ . At school one day, Donna's teacher _____ one

of the students to dress up as a scarecrow for the fall harvest play. She chose Donna.

Everyone was quite surprised the night of the play. Donna was not the only

_____ . Diane looked the part, too!

problem	driver	intersection

Dad sometimes works very late. This caused a _____ on his way

home last night. As he was approaching an _____near our home,

he started to fall asleep! The whole family was very glad that the _____

in the car behind Dad honked his car horn to wake him up.

cancel	decision	storm

"It looks very much like it could _____ tonight," said Brent. Rob replied,

"Are you saying we should _____ our game?" "Let's not make a

_____ just yet," answered Brent.

Reading Skills: Context Clues

Directions: Read each sentence carefully and circle the word that makes sense.

1. We didn't (except, expect) you to arrive so early.

2. "I can't hear a (word, world) you are saying. Wait until I turn down the stereo," said Val.

3. I couldn't sleep last night because of the (noise, nose) from the apartment below us.

4. Did Peggy say (weather, whether) or not we needed our binoculars for the game?

5. He broke his (noise, nose) when he fell off the bicycle.

6. All the students (except, expect) the four in the front row are excused to leave.

7. The teacher said we should have good (whether, weather) for our field trip.

Directions: Choose a word pair from the sentences above to write two sentences of your own.

1. _____

   _____

2. _____

   _____

Reading Skills: Context Clues

Directions: Use context clues to figure out the bold word in each sentence below.

1. The teacher wanted all of us to put the names of the students in our class in two **columns**. It was a big help when I saw how she started each list on the board.

2. "I'm glad to see such a **variety** of art projects at the display," said the principal. "I was afraid that many of the projects would be the same."

3. My father used to work for a huge **corporation** in Florida. Since we moved to Virginia, his job is with a smaller company.

4. It would be hard to come up with a **singular** reason for the football team's success. There are so many good things happening that could explain it.

Directions: Draw a line to match the word on the left with its definition on the right.

variety	one
corporation	a large business
columns	vertical listings
singular	many different kinds

Reading Skills: Context Clues

Directions: Read the story. Match each bold word with its definition below.

Where the northern shores of North America meet the Arctic Ocean, the winters are very long and cold. No plants or crops will grow there. This is the land of the **Eskimo**.

Eskimos have figured out ways to live in the snow and ice. They sometimes live in **igloos**, which are made of snow. It is really very comfortable inside! An oil lamp provides light and warmth.

Often, you will find a big, furry **husky** sleeping in the long tunnel that leads to the igloo. Huskies are very important to Eskimos because they pull their sleds and help with hunting. Eskimos are excellent hunters. Many, many years ago, they learned to make **harpoons** and spears to help them hunt their food.

Eskimos get much of their food from the sea, especially fish, seals and whales. Often, an Eskimo will go out in a **kayak** to fish. Only one Eskimo fits inside, and he drives it with a paddle. The waves may turn the kayak upside down, but the Eskimo does not fall out. He is so skillful with a paddle that he quickly is right side up again.

A _____ is a large, strong dog.

An _____ is a member of the race of people who live on the Arctic coasts of North America.

_____ are houses made of packed snow.

A _____ is a one-person canoe made of animal skins.

_____ are spears with a long rope attached. They are used for spearing whales and other large sea animals.

Making Deductions

Making a deduction means using reasoning to arrive at a conclusion.

Directions: Read each group of sentences carefully. Then write your deduction.

1. Bob is tall. Jim is taller than Bob. Lee is taller than Jim. Who is the tallest?

   _____

2. Brett was happy. Jenny was happier than Brett. Roger was happier than Jenny. Who was the happiest?

   _____

3. An orange weighs a lot. A grapefruit weighs more than an orange. A watermelon weighs more than a grapefruit. What weighs the most?

   _____

4. Mark shot many baskets. Ted shot more baskets than Mark. Ed shot fewer than Mark. Who shot the most baskets?

   _____

5. Mandy liked the movie. Teresa liked the movie more than Mandy. Liz liked the movie more than Teresa. Who liked the movie the least?

   _____

6. Jane danced fast. Duane danced faster than Jane. Luann danced slower than Jane. Who danced the fastest?

   _____

7. The balloon floated high. The bubble went higher than the balloon. The airplane was higher than the bubble. What was the highest?

   _____

8. The kitten was small. The bird was smaller than the kitten. The mouse was smaller than the bird. Which was the largest?

   _____

Making Deductions: A Mystery

Ann's dog, Holly, has disappeared. Help Ann and her friends find Holly.

Directions: Look at the picture of Ann's house. Then read the clues. Write the person's name on the line in the room where he/she was.

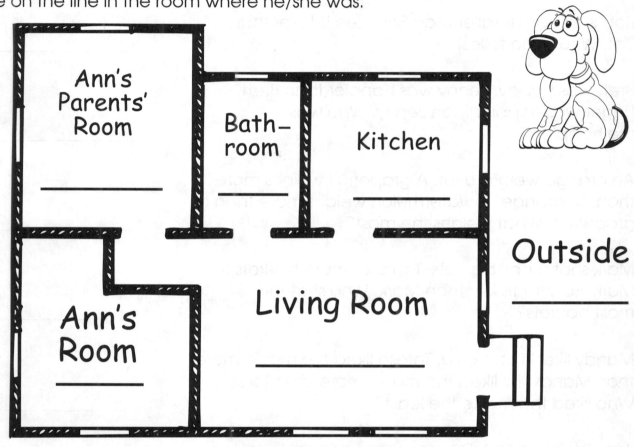

1. Holly is not under Ann's bed. Ann was in her room, and she did not see Holly go there.
2. Holly is not outside, because Paul was in the yard and did not see her.
3. Ann's mother was in the kitchen. Holly is not there.
4. Ann's father was in a room next to the kitchen. He was not in the bathroom. He did not see Holly either.
5. Holly never goes in the bathroom. She is afraid of the water.
6. Holly cannot leave the yard. There is a fence around it.

Where is Holly? _____

Drawing Conclusions

Drawing a conclusion means to use clues to make a final decision about something. To draw a conclusion, you must read carefully.

Directions: Read each story carefully. Use the clues given to draw a conclusion about the story.

The boy and girl took turns pushing the shopping cart. They went up and down the aisles. Each time they stopped the cart, they would look at things on the shelf and decide what they needed. Jody asked her older brother, "Will I need a box of 48 crayons in Mrs. Charles' class?"

"Yes, I think so," he answered. Then he turned to their mother and said, "I need some new notebooks. Can I get some?"

1. Where are they? _____

2. What are they doing there? _____

3. How do you know? Write at least two clue words that helped you.

_____

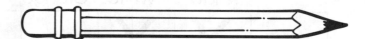

Eric and Randy held on tight. They looked around them and saw that they were not the only ones holding on. The car moved slowly upward. As they turned and looked over the side, they noticed that the people far below them seemed to be getting smaller and smaller. "Hey, Eric, did I tell you this is my first time on one of these?" asked Randy. As they started down the hill at a frightening speed, Randy screamed, "And it may be my last!"

1. Where are they? _____

2. How do you know? Write at least two clue words that helped you.

_____

Logic

Logic means to use deductive reasoning to solve a problem.

Maya, Paul, Traci, Kim and Scott went to the park on Saturday. Each child wore a different color t-shirt.

Directions: Read the clues. Fill out the chart to discover who wore what. Use an **X** to mark a "no" and a • to mark a "yes." The first clue is done for you.

1. Maya did not wear a yellow or white t-shirt.

2. Paul wore an orange t-shirt.

3. A boy wore a white t-shirt.

4. The girl who wore the yellow t-shirt was not Kim.

5. Scott did not wear a blue t-shirt.

6. Maya hates the color green.

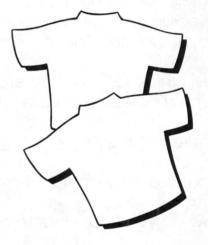

	Yellow	White	Orange	Blue	Green
Maya	X	X			
Paul					
Traci					
Kim					
Scott					

Comprehension: Kareem Abdul-Jabbar

Kareem Abdul-Jabbar grew up to be more than 7 feet tall! Kareem's father and mother were both very tall. When he was 9 years old, Kareem was already 5 feet 4 inches tall. Kareem was raised in New York City. He went to Power Memorial High School and played basketball on that team. He went to college at UCLA. He played basketball in college, too. At UCLA, Kareem's team lost only two games in 3 years! After college, Kareem made his living playing basketball.

Directions: Answer these questions about Kareem Abdul-Jabbar.

1. Who is the story about?

_____

2. For what is this athlete famous?

_____

3. When did Kareem reach the height of 5 feet 4 inches?

_____

4. Where did Kareem go to college?

_____

5. Why did Kareem grow so tall?

_____

_____

6. How did Kareem make his living?

_____

_____

Recognizing Details: Using Chopsticks

Directions: Read about chopsticks. Then answer the questions.

Asian people have eaten their food with chopsticks for many years. Chopsticks are two thin pieces of wood that are almost pointed on one end.

Chopsticks were used in China thousands of years ago. Ivory, gold or silver chopsticks were used for special occasions. People who used chopsticks to eat were considered very smart!

Today, some American people like to use chopsticks! But using chopsticks is not easy. Both chopsticks are held in one hand. A person holds one chopstick between the thumb and third finger. This chopstick is not supposed to move. The first and second fingers help move the other chopstick.

Chopsticks are an old custom with people from Asian countries such as China, Japan and Korea, but these people use forks and knives, too!

1. Who used chopsticks first? _____

2. What are chopsticks? _____

_____

3. When did the Chinese start using chopsticks? _____

4. Where are chopsticks also used today? _____

_____

5. Why is it hard to use chopsticks? _____

_____

6. How do chopsticks work? _____

_____

7. What do you think would happen if you tried to eat with chopsticks? _____

_____

_____

Reading Comprehension: Helen Keller

A B C D E F G H I J K L M

N O P Q R S T U V W X Y Z

When Helen Keller was a child, she often behaved in a wild way. She was very bright and strong, but she could not tell people what she was thinking or feeling. And she didn't know how others thought or felt. Helen was blind and deaf.

Helen was born with normal hearing and sight, but this changed when she was 1 year old. She had a serious illness with a very high fever. After that, Helen was never able to see or hear again.

As a child, Helen was angry and lonely. But when she was 6 years old, her parents got a teacher for her. They brought a young woman named Anne Sullivan to stay at their house and help Helen. After much hard work, Helen began to learn sign language. Anne taught Helen many important things, such as how to behave like other children. Because Helen was so smart, she learned things very quickly. She learned how to read Braille. By the time she was 8 years old, she was becoming very famous. People were amazed at what she could do.

Helen continued to learn. She even learned how to speak. When she was 20 years old, she went to college. Helen did so well in college that a magazine paid her to write the story of her life. After college, she earned money by writing and giving speeches. She traveled all around the world. She worked to get special schools and libraries for the blind and deaf. She wrote many books, including one about her teacher, Anne Sullivan.

Here is how "Helen" is written in Braille:

Directions: Answer these questions about Helen Keller.

1. What caused Helen to be blind and deaf? _____

_____

2. What happy thing happened when Helen was 6 years old? _____

_____

3. What was her teacher's name? _____

Reading Comprehension: Hummingbirds

Hummingbirds are very small birds. This tiny bird is quite an acrobat. Only a few birds, such as kingfishers and sunbirds, can hover, which means to stay in one place in the air. But no other bird can match the flying skills of the hummingbird. The hummingbird can hover, fly backward and fly upside down!

Hummingbirds got their name because their wings move very quickly when they fly. This causes a humming sound. Their wings move so fast that you can't see them at all. This takes a lot of energy. These little birds must have food about every 20 minutes to have enough strength to fly. Their favorite foods are insects and nectar. Nectar is the sweet water deep inside a flower. Hummingbirds use their long, thin bills to drink from flowers. When a hummingbird sips nectar, it hovers in front of a flower. It never touches the flower with its wings or feet.

Besides being the best at flying, the hummingbird is also one of the prettiest birds. Of all the birds in the world, the hummingbird's colors are among the brightest. Some are bright green with red and white markings. Some are purple. One kind of hummingbird can change its color from reddish-brown to purple to red!

The hummingbird's nest is special, too. It looks like a tiny cup. The inside of the nest is very soft. This is because one of the things the mother bird uses to build the nest is the silk from a spider's web.

Directions: Answer these questions about hummingbirds.

1. How did hummingbirds get their name? _____

   _____

2. What does **hover** mean? _____

3. How often do hummingbirds need to eat? _____

4. Name two things that hummingbirds eat. _____

5. What is one of the things a mother hummingbird uses to build her nest?

   _____

Reading Comprehension: Bats

Bats are the only mammals that can fly. They have wings made of thin skin stretched between long fingers. Bats can fly amazing distances. Some small bats have been known to fly more than 25 miles in one night.

Most bats eat insects or fruit. But some eat only fish, others only blood and still others the nectar and pollen of flowers that bloom at night. Bats are active only at night. They sleep during the day in caves or other dark places. At rest, they always hang with their heads down.

You may have heard the expression "blind as a bat." But bats are not blind. They don't, however, use their eyes to guide their flight or to find the insects they eat. A bat makes a high-pitched squeak, then waits for the echo to return to it. This echo tells it how far away an object is. This is often called the bat's sonar system. Using this system, a bat can fly through a dark cave without bumping into anything. Hundreds of bats can fly about in the dark without ever running into each other. They do not get confused by the squeaks of the other bats. They always recognize their own echoes.

Directions: Answer these questions about bats.

1. Bats are the only mammals that

    ☐ eat insects.　　☐ fly.　　☐ live in caves.

2. Most bats eat

    ☐ plants.　　☐ other animals.　　☐ fruits and insects.

3. Bats always sleep

    ☐ with their heads down.　　☐ lying down.　　☐ during the night.

4. Bats are blind.　　　　　　　　　　　　True　　　　False

5. Bats use a built-in sonar system to guide them.　　True　　　　False

6. Bats are confused by the squeaks of other bats.　　True　　　　False

Review: Venn Diagram

Directions: Make a Venn diagram comparing hummingbirds (see page 158) and bats (see page 159). Use page 136 to help you. Write at least three characteristics for each section of the diagram.

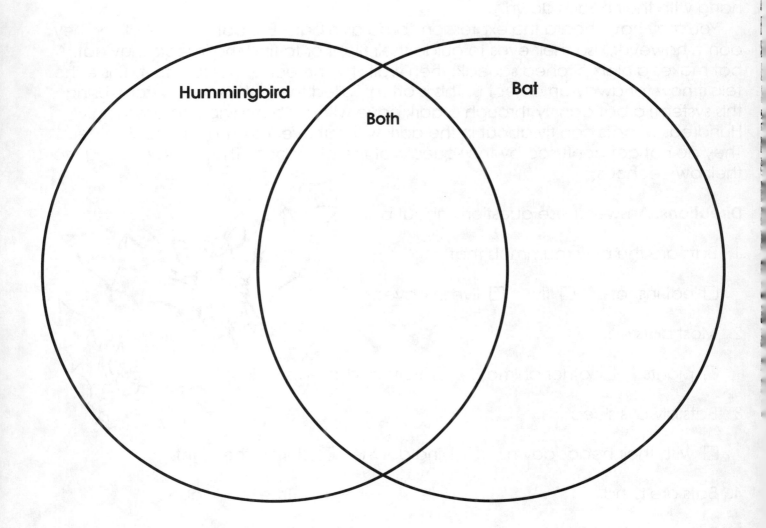

Hummingbird

Both

Bat

Reading Skills: Fact and Opinion

A **fact** is a statement that can be proven true. An **opinion** is a statement that tells how someone feels or what he/she thinks about something or someone.

Example:
> **Fact:** Ms. Davis is the new principal at Hayes Elementary.
> **Opinion:** Ms. Davis is the nicest principal we ever had.

Directions: Read each pair of sentences below. One is a fact; one is an opinion. Write **F** before the fact and **O** before the opinion.

_____ 1. Soccer is the best sport at our school.

_____ More students at our school play soccer than any other sport.

_____ 2. Grandmother Hall lives in Clarksburg.

_____ Grandmother Hall makes the best chocolate-chip cookies!

_____ 3. The county fair gate opens at 10:00 a.m.

_____ We're going to have a great time at the fair.

_____ 4. The drive along the river is very scenic.

_____ It is a 5-mile drive along the river.

_____ 5. Computers make our work much easier.

_____ We have four computers in our classroom.

_____ 6. *The Cinnamon Lake Mysteries* is a very good series.

_____ Our library has several copies of *The Cinnamon Lake Mysteries.*

_____ 7. Jerry falls asleep in class every day!

_____ Jerry is so tired, he can't stay awake.

_____ 8. That car is too old to make it across the country.

_____ That car was built in 1964.

Fact and Opinion

Directions: Write **F** before the facts and **O** before the opinions.

_____ 1. Our school football team had a winning season this year.

_____ 2. Mom's spaghetti is the best in the world!

_____ 3. Autumn is the nicest season of the year.

_____ 4. Mrs. Burns took her class on a field trip last Thursday.

_____ 5. The library always puts 30 books in our classroom book collection.

_____ 6. They should put only books about horses in the collection.

_____ 7. Our new art teacher is very strict.

_____ 8. Everyone should keep take-home papers in a folder so they don't have to look for them when it is time to go home.

_____ 9. The bus to the mall goes right by her house at 7:45 a.m.

_____10. Our new superintendent, Mr. Willeke, is very nice.

Fact and Opinion

Directions: Each fact sentence below has a "partner" opinion sentence in the box. Match "partners" by writing the correct sentences on the lines.

Maps can be very difficult to figure out.	Those brownies tasted awful!
The bridesmaids' dresses turned out beautiful!	Each child in here needs a computer.
You make the best cherry pie.	She is the best artist in the class.
If I can't go to the party, I will be really upset.	That car is so old, it looks like it will fall apart.

1. Paige helped her mother bake brownies last night.

   _____

2. Katherine made all the drawings for the book.

   _____

3. That cherry tree is full of cherries.

   _____

4. We have four computers in the classroom.

   _____

5. Mom made dresses for all of my bridesmaids.

   _____

6. If I can't go to the party, I won't be able to give her the present.

   _____

7. The car is old and rusty.

   _____

8. However he looked at it, he still couldn't figure out the map.

   _____

Facts and Opinions

Facts are statements or events that have happened and can be proven to be true.

Example: George Washington was the first president of the United States. This statement is a fact. It can be proven to be true by researching the history of our country.

Opinions are statements that express how someone thinks or feels.

Example: George Washington was the greatest president the United States has ever had.

This statement is an opinion. Many people agree that George Washington was a great president, but not everyone agrees he was the greatest president. In some people's opinion, Abraham Lincoln was our greatest president.

Directions: Read each sentence. Write **F** for fact or **O** for opinion.

_____ 1. There is three feet of snow on the ground.

_____ 2. A lot of snow makes the winter enjoyable.

_____ 3. Chris has a better swing set than Mary.

_____ 4. Both Chris and Mary have swing sets.

_____ 5. California is a state.

_____ 6. California is the best state in the west.

Directions: Write three facts and three opinions.

Facts:

1) _____

2) _____

3) _____

Opinions:

1) _____

2) _____

3) _____

Review

Directions: Read the paragraph. Then circle the sentence that tells the main idea.

Justin and Mina did everything together. They rode their bikes to school together, ate their lunches together, did their homework together, and even spent their weekends together playing baseball and video games. Even though Justin and Mina sometimes argued about silly things, they still loved being together. Sometimes the arguments were even fun, because then they got to make up! People often thought they were brother and sister because they sounded alike and even looked alike! Justin and Mina promised they would be friends forever.

a. Justin and Mina did everything together.

b. Justin and Mina like riding bikes.

c. Justin and Mina like to argue.

Directions: Write **F** before the facts and **O** before the opinions.

_____ 1. Justin loved to ride his bike.

_____ 2. Mina promised they would always be friends.

_____ 3. Justin and Mina should never argue.

_____ 4. Justin's dog needed to be washed.

_____ 5. That car is only big enough for three people!

_____ 6. The laundry basket is in the corner of the basement.

_____ 7. That laundry needs to be done today.

_____ 8. Brownies are my favorite snack.

_____ 9. She made chocolate cake for Mom's birthday.

_____ 10. I came all the way from Texas to see you.

Fiction and Nonfiction

Fiction writing is a story that has been invented. The story might be about things that could really happen (realistic) or about things that couldn't possibly happen (fantasy). **Nonfiction** writing is based on facts. It usually gives information about people, places or things. A person can often tell while reading whether a story or book is fiction or nonfiction.

Directions: Read the paragraphs below and on page 167. Determine whether each paragraph is fiction or nonfiction. Circle the letter **F** for fiction or the letter **N** for nonfiction.

"Do not be afraid, little flowers," said the oak. "Close your yellow eyes in sleep and trust in me. You have made me glad many a time with your sweetness. Now, I will take care that the winter shall do you no harm." **F N**

The whole team watched as the ball soared over the outfield fence. The game was over! It was hard to walk off the field and face parents, friends and each other. It had been a long season. Now, they would have to settle for second place. **F N**

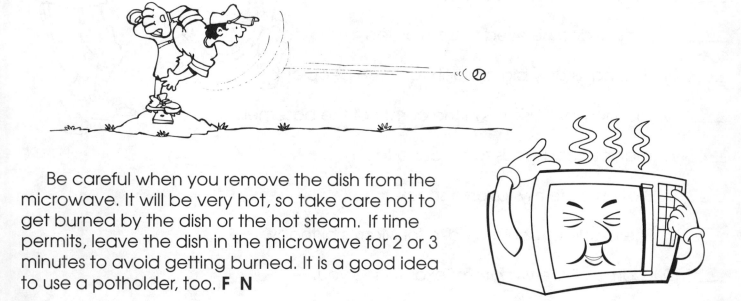

Be careful when you remove the dish from the microwave. It will be very hot, so take care not to get burned by the dish or the hot steam. If time permits, leave the dish in the microwave for 2 or 3 minutes to avoid getting burned. It is a good idea to use a potholder, too. **F N**

Fiction and Nonfiction

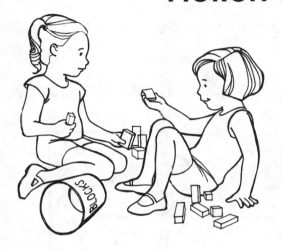

Megan and Mariah skipped out to the playground. They enjoyed playing together at recess. Today, it was Mariah's turn to choose what they would do first. To Megan's surprise, Mariah asked, "What do you want to do, Megan? I'm going to let you pick since it's your birthday!" **F N**

It is easy to tell an insect from a spider. An insect has three body parts and six legs. A spider has eight legs and no wings. Of course, if you see the creature spinning a web, you will know what it is. An insect wouldn't want to get too close to the web or it would be stuck. It might become dinner! **F N**

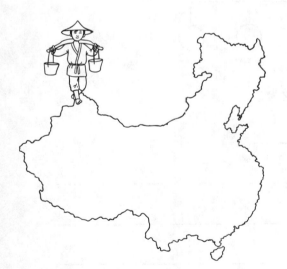

My name is Lee Chang, and I live in a country that you call China. My home is on the other side of the world from yours. When the sun is rising in my country, it is setting in yours. When it is day at your home, it is night at mine. **F N**

Henry washed the dog's foot in cold water from the brook. The dog lay very still, for he knew that the boy was trying to help him. **F N**

Reading a Diagram

A **family tree** is a diagram of a person's family and ancestors. Peter made a family tree as part of a school project.

Directions: Look at Peter's family tree, then answer the questions about his family.

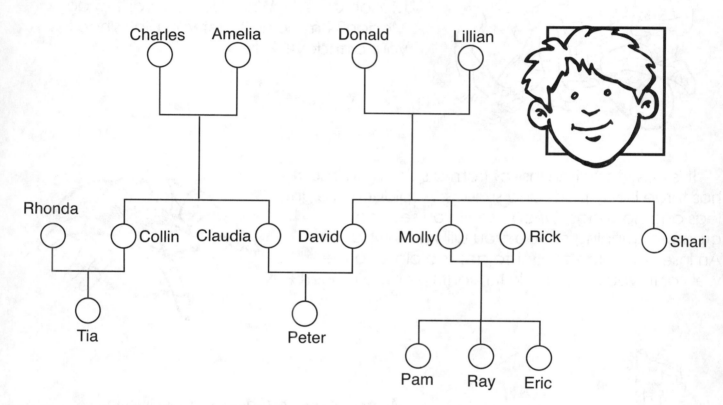

1. How many brothers and sisters does Peter have?

   brothers _____ sisters _____

2. Is Peter's mother an only child? _____

3. Who are Peter's uncles? _____

4. How many cousins does Peter have? _____

5. Who is Claudia's mother? _____

6. Who is Claudia's husband? _____

Reading Skills: Advertisements

Stores pay for advertisements, or ads, to let people know what is being sold. You see ads in newspapers and magazines, and on television and radio.

Directions: Use the following newspaper ad to answer the questions.

Home Cooking Restaurant

Open Easter Sunday 10:30 a.m. to 8:00 p.m.

Special Easter Menu
- Roast Turkey $10.50
- Baked Ham $12.00
- Roast Leg of Lamb $15.50

Many other dishes available, including veal, chicken, seafood and pasta.

Call for reservations 555–6241

Home Cooking Restaurant
1485 City Street

1. The restaurant is advertising special holiday meals. What holiday are they for?

_____

2. What is the most expensive meal listed on the menu?

_____

3. What hours will the restaurant be open on Easter?

_____

Reading Skills: Bus Schedules

Schedules are important to our daily lives. Your parents' jobs, school, even watching television—all are based on schedules. When you travel, you probably follow a schedule, too. Most forms of public transportation, such as subways, buses and trains, run on schedules. These "timetables" tell passengers when they will leave each stop or station.

Directions: Use the following city bus schedule to answer the questions.

No. 2 Cross-Town Bus Schedule			
State St. at Park Way	Oak St. at Green Ave.	Fourth St. at Ninth Ave.	Buyall Shopping Center
5:00 a.m.	5:14 a.m.	5:23 a.m.	5:30 a.m.
6:38	6:52	7:01	7:08
7:50	8:05	8:14	8:21
9:04	9:18	9:27	9:34
10:15	10:29	10:38	10:47
12:20 p.m.	12:34 p.m.	12:43 p.m.	12:50 p.m.
1:46	2:00	2:09	2:16
3:30	3:44	3:53	4:00
5:20	5:34	5:43	5:50
6:02	6:16	6:25	6:32

1. The first bus of the day leaves the State St./Park Way stop at 5 a.m. What time does the last bus of the day leave this stop? _____

2. The bus that leaves the Oak St./Green Ave. stop at 8:05 a.m. leaves the Buyall Shopping Center at what time? _____

3. What time does the first afternoon bus leave the Fourth St./Ninth Ave. stop? _____

4. How many buses each day run between the State St./Park Way stop and the Buyall Shopping Center? _____

Reading Skills: Labels

Directions: It is good to know how to read the label of a medicine bottle. Read the label to answer the questions.

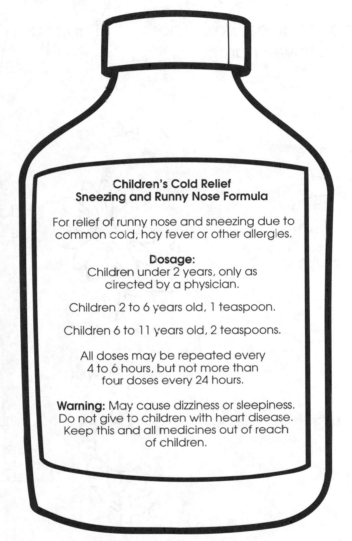

**Children's Cold Relief
Sneezing and Runny Nose Formula**

For relief of runny nose and sneezing due to common cold, hay fever or other allergies.

Dosage:
Children under 2 years, only as cirected by a physician.

Children 2 to 6 years old, 1 teaspoon.

Children 6 to 11 years old, 2 teaspoons.

All doses may be repeated every 4 to 6 hours, but not more than four doses every 24 hours.

Warning: May cause dizziness or sleepiness. Do not give to children with heart disease. Keep this and all medicines out of reach of children.

1. How much medicine should a 5-year-old take? _____

2. How often can this medicine be taken? _____

3. How do you know how much medicine to give a 1-year-old? _____

4. Who should not take this medicine? _____

Dictionary Skills: Guide Words

Guide words are the first and last words on a dictionary page. They are listed at the top of each page. All words on that page come between those two words.

Directions: Circle the pair of guide words that would appear on the same page as the flower name.

Dictionary

1. rose

rain — refuse
rock — rode
roar — ruler

4. daisy

bait — bar
dad — deck
dare — delight

2. tulip

tube — tug
track — twin
two — us

5. sunflower

slip — space
some — sun
such — swim

3. violet

vase — vent
vine — visit
visit — voice

6. lily

lamb — late
light — like
lift — line

Library Skills: Finding Books

Fiction books in a library are filed in alphabetical order using the author's last name.

Example: Ezra Jack Keats would be Keats, Ezra Jack and found under K.

Nonfiction books are grouped by subject. All books about snakes are grouped together, and all books about space are grouped together.

Directions: Practice filing books in alphabetical order. Number the authors' names in alphabetical order.

___ Rand, Ayn

___ Burton, Virginia Lee

___ Keats, Ezra Jack

___ Rey, H.A.

___ Irving, Washington

___ Lionni, Leo

___ Potter, Beatrix

___ Blume, Judy

Library Skills: Alphabetical Order

Ms. Ling, the school librarian, needs help shelving books. Fiction titles are arranged in alphabetical order by the author's last name. Ms. Ling has done the first set for you.

__3__ Silverstein, Shel   __1__ Bridwell, Norman   __2__ Farley, Walter

Directions: Number the following groups of authors in alphabetical order.

_____ Bemelmans, Ludwig   _____ Perkins, Al

_____ Stein, R.L.   _____ Dobbs, Rose

_____ Sawyer, Ruth   _____ Baldwin, James

_____ Baum, L. Frank   _____ Kipling, Rudyard

The content of some books is also arranged alphabetically.

Directions: Circle the books that are arranged in alphabetical order.

T.V. guide   dictionary   encyclopedia   novel

almanac   science book   Yellow Pages   catalog

Write the books you circled in alphabetical order.

1._____

2._____

3._____

Reference Books

Reference books are books that tell basic facts. They usually cannot be checked out from the library. Dictionaries and encyclopedias are reference books. A dictionary tells you about words. Encyclopedias give you other information, such as when the president was born, what the Civil War was and where Eskimos live. Encyclopedias usually come in sets of more than 20 books. Information is listed in alphabetical order, just like words are listed in the dictionary. There are other kinds of reference books, too, like books of maps called atlases. Reference books are not usually read from cover to cover.

Directions: Draw a line from each sentence to the correct type of book. The first one is done for you.

DICTIONARY

1. I can tell you the definition of **divide**. ————

2. I can tell you when George Washington was born.

3. I can give you the correct spelling for many words.

4. I can tell you where Native Americans live.

5. I can tell you the names of many butterflies.

6. I can tell you what **modern** means.

7. I can give you the history of dinosaurs.

8. If you have to write a paper about Eskimos, I can help you.

Periodicals

Libraries also have **periodicals** such as magazines and newspapers. They are called **periodicals** because they are printed regularly within a set period of time. There are many kinds of magazines. Some discuss the news. Some cover fitness, cats or other topics of special interest. Almost every city or town has a newspaper. Newspapers usually are printed daily, weekly or even monthly. Newspapers cover what is happening in your town and in the world. They usually include sections on sports and entertainment. They present a lot of information.

Directions: Follow the instructions.

1. Choose an interesting magazine.

   What is the name of the magazine? _____

   List the titles of three articles in the magazine.

   _____

   _____

   _____

2. Now, look at a newspaper.

   What is the name of the newspaper? _____

   The title of a newspaper story is called a headline.

   What are some of the headlines in your local

   newspaper?

   _____

   _____

   _____

References

Paul and Maria want to learn about the Moon. They go to the library. Where should they look while they are there?

Directions: Answer the questions to help Paul and Maria find information about the Moon.

1. Should they look in the children's section or in the adult's section? _____

2. Should they look for a fiction book or a nonfiction book? _____

3. Who at the library can help them? _____

4. What reference books should they look at? _____

5. Where can they find information that may have been in the news? _____

6. What word would they look up in the encyclopedia to get the information they need? _____

Proofreading

Proofreading means searching for and correcting errors by carefully reading and rereading what has been written. Use the proofreading marks below when correcting your writing or someone else's.

To insert a word or a punctuation mark that has been left out, use a caret ∧.

Example: We∧to the dance together.
         went

To show that a letter should be capitalized, put three lines under it.

Example: Mrs. jones drove us to school.

To show that a capital letter should be a small or lowercase, draw a diagonal line through it.

Example: Mrs. Jones Drove us to school.

To show that a word is spelled incorrectly, draw a horizontal line through it and write the correct spelling above it.

Example: The ~~wolres~~ is an amazing animal.
             walrus

Directions: Proofread the two paragraphs using the proofreading marks you learned. The author's last name, Towne, is spelled correctly.

The Modern ark

My book report is on the modern ark by Cecilia Fitzsimmons. The book tells abut 80 of worlds endangered animals. The book also an arc and animals inside for kids put together.

Their House

there house is a Great book! The arthur's name is Mary Towne. they're house tells about a girl name Molly. Molly's Family bys an old house from some people named warren. Then there big problems begin!

Proofreading

Directions: Proofread the paragraphs, using the proofreading marks you learned. There are seven capitalization errors, three missing words and eleven errors in spelling or word usage.

Key West

key West has been tropical paradise ever since Ponce de Leon first saw the set of islands called the keys in 1513. Two famus streets in Key West are named duval and whitehead. You will find the city semetery on Francis Street. The tombstones are funny!

The message on one is, "I told you I was sick!" On sailor's tombston is this mesage his widow: "At lease I no where to find him now."

The cemetery is on 21 akres in the midle of town. The most famous home in key west is that of the authur, Ernest Hemingway. Heminway's home was at 907 whitehead Street. He lived their for 30 years.

Proofreading

Directions: Proofread the sentences. Write **C** if the sentence has no errors. Draw an **X** if the sentence contains missing words or other errors. The first one is done for you.

__C__ 1. The new Ship Wreck Museum in Key West is exciting!

_____ 2. Another thing I liked was the litehouse.

_____ 3. Do you remember Hemingway's address in Key West?

_____ 4. The Key West semetery is on 21 acres of ground.

_____ 5. Ponce de eon discovered Key West.

_____ 6. The cemetery in Key West is on Francis Street.

_____ 7. My favorete tombstone was the sailor's.

_____ 8. His wife wrote the words on it. Remember?

_____ 9. The words said, "at least I know where to find him now!"

_____ 10. That sailor must have been away at sea all the time.

_____ 11. The troley ride around Key West is very interesting.

_____ 12. Do you why it is called Key West?

_____ 13. Can you imagine a lighthouse in the middle of your town?

_____ 14. It's interesting to no that Key West is our southernmost city.

_____ 15. Besides Harry Truman and Hemingway, did other famous people live there?

Review

Directions: Use the correct proofreading marks to show the two capitalization errors in each sentence.

1. Mrs. edwards drove us to edison Elementary School.

2. Who can Say what john's real problem was?

3. Did You tell dr. Lynn we would be there at noon?

4. My Aunt Nellie was there and so was aunt susan.

Directions: Use the correct proofreading mark to insert the missing word or letter in each sentence.

5. He promised me he be there on time!

6. Who tell me the answer to the first problem?

7. What his nickname when he was a baby?

8. Did he tell you same thing?

Directions: Use the correct proofreading mark, then correct the misspelled or misused word in each sentence.

9. I wondered if the princepal knew what had happened?

10. I herd her whole family was there!

11. Our team easley beat the other team.

12. Don't laugh to hard at those silly jokes!

MATH

Level 1

Place Value

The place value of a digit, or numeral, is shown by where it is in the number. For example, in the number 1,234, 1 has the place value of thousands, 2 is hundreds, 3 is tens and 4 is ones.

Hundred Thousands	Ten Thousands	Thousands	Hundreds	Tens	Ones
9	4	3	8	5	2

943,852

Directions: Match the numbers in Column A with the words in Column B.

A	B
62,453	two hundred thousands
7,641	three thousands
486,113	four hundred thousands
11,277	eight hundreds
813,463	seven tens
594,483	five ones
254,089	six hundreds
79,841	nine ten thousands
27,115	five tens

Place Value

Place value is the value of a digit, or numeral, shown by where it is in the number. For example, in 1,234, 1 has the place value of thousands, 2 is hundreds, 3 is tens and 4 is ones.

Directions: Write the numbers in the correct boxes to find how far the car has traveled.

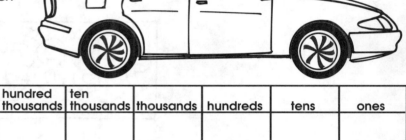

one thousand

six hundreds

eight ones

nine ten thousands

four tens

two millions

five hundred thousands

millions	hundred thousands	ten thousands	thousands	hundreds	tens	ones

How many miles has the car traveled?_____

Directions: In the number . . .

    2,386   _____   is in the ones place.

    4,957   _____   is in the hundreds place.

   102,432   _____   is in the ten thousands place.

   489,753   _____   is in the thousands place.

 1,743,998   _____   is in the millions place.

 9,301,671   _____   is in the hundred thousands place.

 7,521,834   _____   is in the tens place.

Addition: Regrouping

Addition means "putting together" or adding two or more numbers to find the sum. For example, 3 + 5 = 8. To regroup is to use ten ones to form one ten, ten tens to form one 100, and so on.

Directions: Add using regrouping.

Example:

Add the ones.	Add the tens with regrouping.
88 +21 9	88 +21 109

37 +72	56 +67	51 +88	37 +55	70 +68

93 +54	47 +82	81 +77	23 +92	36 +71

92 + 13 = _____   73 + 83 = _____   54 + 61 = _____

The Blues scored 63 points. The Reds scored 44 points.
How many points were scored in all?

_____

Subtraction: Regrouping

Subtraction means "taking away" or subtracting one number from another to find the difference. For example, 10 - 3 = 7. To regroup is to use one ten to form ten ones, one 100 to form ten tens, and so on.

Directions: Study the example. Subtract using regrouping.

Example:

$$
\begin{array}{rcl}
32 & = & 2 \text{ tens} + 12 \text{ ones} \\
-13 & = & 1 \text{ ten} + \underline{3 \text{ ones}} \\
19 & = & 1 \text{ ten} + 9 \text{ ones}
\end{array}
$$

33	86	92	71
-28	-59	-37	-48

63	45	31	55
-47	-18	-22	-39

82 - 69 = _____   73 - 36 = _____

The Yankees won 85 games.
The Cubs won 69 games.
How many more games
did the Yankees win? _____

Problem Solving: Addition, Subtraction

Directions: Read and solve each problem. The first one is done for you.

The clown started the day with 200 balloons. He gave away 128 of them. Some broke. At the end of the day he had 18 balloons left. How many of the balloons broke?   **54**

On Monday, there were 925 tickets sold to adults and 1,412 tickets sold to children. How many more children attended the fair than adults?   _____

At one game booth, prizes were given out for scoring 500 points in three attempts. Sally scored 178 points on her first attempt, 149 points on her second attempt and 233 points on her third attempt. Did Sally win a prize?   _____

The prize-winning steer weighed 2,348 pounds. The runner-up steer weighed 2,179 pounds. How much more did the prize steer weigh?   _____

There were 3,418 people at the fair on Tuesday, and 2,294 people on Wednesday. What was the total number of people there for the two days?   _____

Multiples

Directions: Draw a red circle around the numbers that can be divided by 2. We say these are multiples of 2.
Draw a blue **X** on the multiples of 3.
Draw a green square around the multiples of 5.
Draw a yellow triangle around the multiples of 10.

1	2	3	4	5	6	7	8	9	10
11	12	13	14	15	16	17	18	19	20
21	22	23	24	25	26	27	28	29	30
31	32	33	34	35	36	37	38	39	40
41	42	43	44	45	46	47	48	49	50
51	52	53	54	55	56	57	58	59	60
61	62	63	64	65	66	67	68	69	70
71	72	73	74	75	76	77	78	79	80
81	82	83	84	85	86	87	88	89	90
91	92	93	94	95	96	97	98	99	100

Look at your chart. Common multiples are those which are shared. You have marked them in more than one way/color. What numbers are common? _____

Multiplication

Factors are the numbers multiplied together in a multiplication problem. The answer is called the product. If you change the order of the factors, the product stays the same.

Example:

There are 4 groups of fish.
There are 3 fish in each group.
How many fish are there in all?

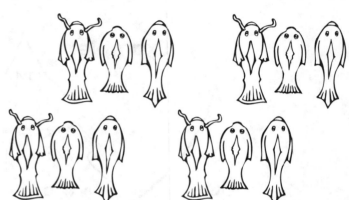

$$4 \ \times \ 3 \ = 12$$
factor x factor = product

Directions: Draw 3 groups of 4 fish.

$$3 \times 4 = 12$$

Compare your drawing and answer with the example. What did you notice?

Directions: Fill in the missing numbers. Multiply.

5 x 4 = _____   3 x 6 = _____   4 x 2 = _____

4 x 5 = _____   6 x 3 = _____   2 x 4 = _____

3	7	2	9	8	4
x7	x3	x9	x2	x4	x8

5	2	6	3	5	6
x2	x5	x3	x6	x6	x5

Factor Trees

Factors are the smaller numbers multiplied together to make a larger number. Factor trees are one way to find all the factors of a number.

Directions: Complete each factor tree

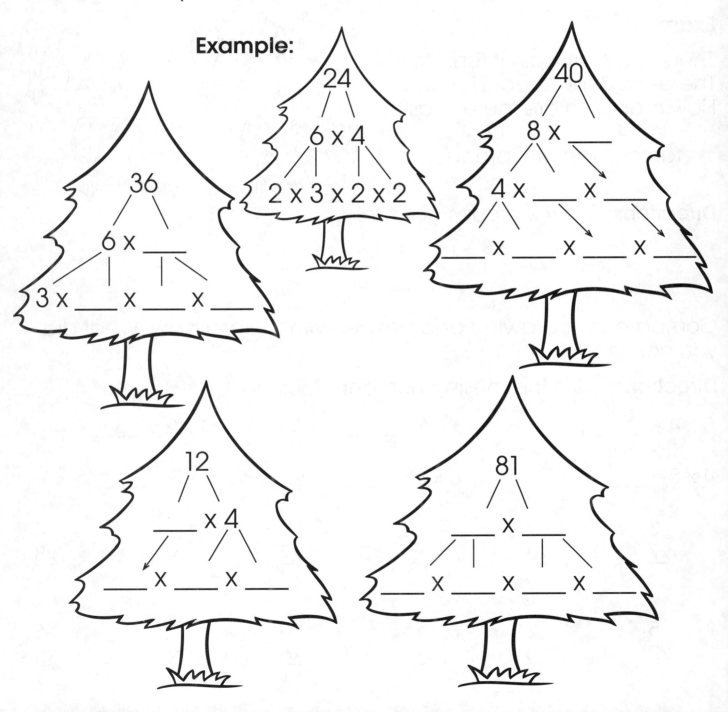

Example:

24
6 x 4
2 x 3 x 2 x 2

36
6 x ___
3 x ___ x ___ x ___

40
8 x ___
4 x ___ x ___
___ x ___ x ___

12
___ x 4
___ x ___ x ___

81
___ x ___
___ x ___ x ___ x ___

Division

Division is a way to find out how many times one number is contained in another number. The ∏ sign means "divided by." Another way to divide is to use $\lceil$. The dividend is the larger number that is divided by the smaller number, or divisor. The answer of a division problem is called the quotient.

Directions: Study the example. Divide.

Example:

$$20 \underset{\text{dividend}}{\uparrow} \quad \prod \quad \underset{\text{divisor}}{\underset{\uparrow}{4}} \quad = \quad \underset{\text{quotient}}{\underset{\uparrow}{5}}$$

$$\begin{array}{c} \text{quotient} \\ \uparrow \\ 5 \\ \underset{\text{divisor}}{\underset{\uparrow}{4}} \overline{\smash{\big)}\, \underset{\text{dividend}}{\underset{\uparrow}{20}}} \end{array}$$

35 ∏ 7 = _____   7)‾35   42 ∏ 6 = _____   6)‾42

2)‾12   3)‾18   4)‾36   5)‾50

6)‾24   7)‾21   8)‾32   9)‾27

36 ∏ 6 = _____   28 ∏ 4 = _____   15 ∏ 5 = _____   12 ∏ 2 = _____

A tree farm has 36 trees. There are 4 rows of trees. How many trees are there in each row?   _____

Division: Zero And One

Directions: Study the rules of division and the examples. Divide, then write the number of the rule you used to solve each problem.

Examples:

Rule 1: $1\overline{)5}$ with quotient 5 — Any number divided by 1 is that number.

Rule 2: $5\overline{)5}$ with quotient 1 — Any number except 0 divided by itself is 1.

Rule 3: $7\overline{)0}$ with quotient 0 — Zero divided by any number is zero.

Rule 4: $0\overline{)7}$ — You cannot divide by zero.

$1\overline{)6}$ Rule ____ $4 \div 1 =$ ____   Rule ____

$7\overline{)7}$ Rule ____ $9 \div 9 =$ ____   Rule ____

$9\overline{)0}$ Rule ____ $7 \div 1 =$ ____   Rule ____

$1\overline{)4}$ Rule ____ $6 \div 0 =$ ____   Rule ____

Divisibility Rules

A number is divisible... by 2 if the last digit is 0 or even (2, 4, 6, 8).
by 3 if the sum of all digits is divisible by 3.
by 4 if the last two digits are divisible by 4.
by 5 if the last digit is a 0 or 5.
by 10 if the last digit is 0.

Example: 250 is divisible by   2, 5, 10

Directions: Tell what numbers each of these numbers is divisible by.

3,732 _____   439 _____

50 _____   444 _____

7,960 _____   8,212 _____

104,924 _____   2,345 _____

Division: Remainders

Division is a way to find out how many times one number is contained in another number. For example, 28 ∏ 4 = 7 means that there are seven groups of four in 28. The dividend is the larger number that is divided by the smaller number, or divisor. The quotient is the answer in a division problem. The remainder is the amount left over. The remainder is always less than the divisor.

Directions: Study the example. Find each quotient and remainder.

Example:

There are 11 dog biscuits.
Put them in groups of 3.
There are 2 left over.

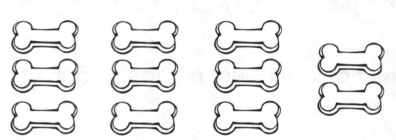

$$\begin{array}{r} 3 \\ 3\overline{)11} \\ -9 \\ \overline{2} \end{array} \text{remainder}$$

$$3\ r\ 2$$
$$3\overline{)11}$$

Remember: The remainder must be less than the **divisor!**

$$3\overline{)13} \qquad 4\overline{)17} \qquad 6\overline{)32} \qquad 5\overline{)26}$$

9 ∏ 4 = _____   12 ∏ 5 = _____   26 ∏ 4 = _____   49 ∏ 9 = _____

The pet store has 7 cats.
Two cats go in each
cage. How many cats
are left over?

_____

Problem Solving: Multiplication, Division

Directions: Read and solve each problem.

Jeff and Terry are planting a garden. They plant 3 rows of green beans with 8 plants in each row. How many green bean plants are there in the garden? _____

There are 45 tomato plants in the garden. There are 5 rows of them. How many tomato plants are in each row? _____

The children have 12 plants each of lettuce, broccoli and spinach. How many plants are there in all? _____

Jeff planted 3 times as many cucumber plants as Terry. He planted 15 of them. How many did Terry plant? _____

Terry planted 12 pepper plants. He planted twice as many green pepper plants as red pepper plants. How many green pepper plants are there? _____

How many red pepper plants? _____

Coordinates

Directions: Locate the points on the grid and color in each box.

What animal did you form?_____

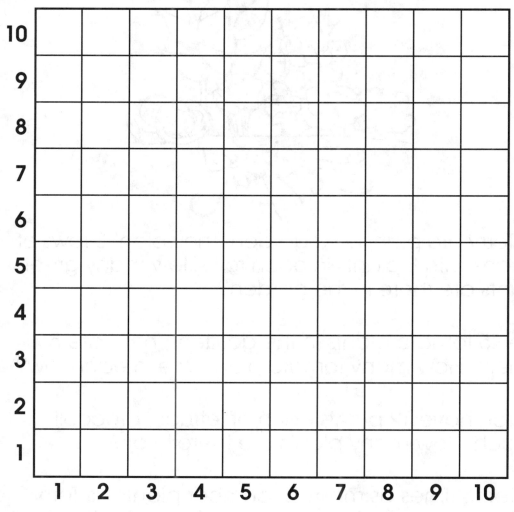

(across, up)

(4, 7)	(4, 1)	(7, 1)	(3, 5)	(2, 8)	(8, 6)	(4, 8)	(3, 7)
(5, 4)	(6, 5)	(5, 5)	(6, 6)	(7, 3)	(8, 5)	(10, 5)	(4, 3)
(7, 6)	(4, 6)	(1, 8)	(6, 4)	(7, 2)	(4, 5)	(9, 6)	(4, 9)
(3, 6)	(7, 5)	(5, 6)	(4, 2)	(4, 4)	(7, 4)	(2, 7)	(3, 8)

Fraction Pieces

Directions: Cut apart the fraction pieces below. Use them to help you work with fractions. Store the fraction sets in separate plastic bags.

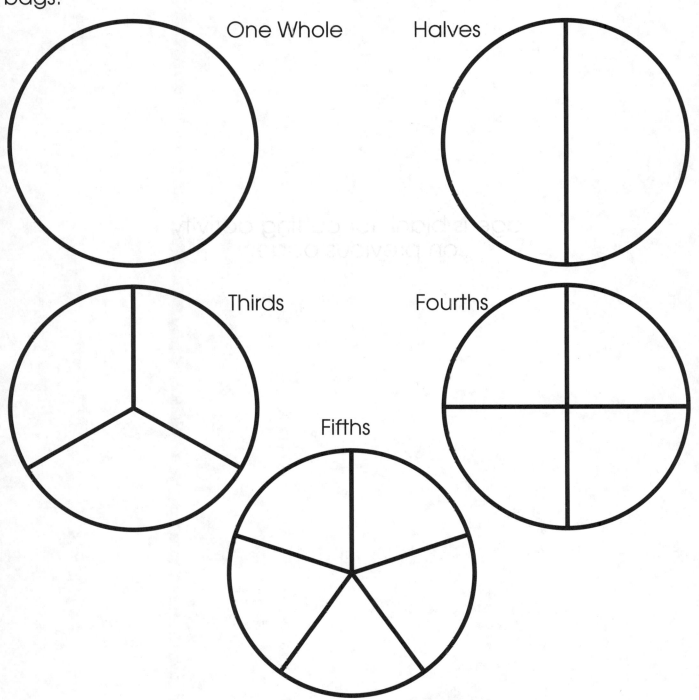

One Whole Halves

Thirds Fourths

Fifths

Page is blank for cutting activity
on previous page.

Fraction Pieces

Directions: Cut apart the fraction pieces below. Use them to help you work with fractions. Store the fraction sets in separate plastic bags.

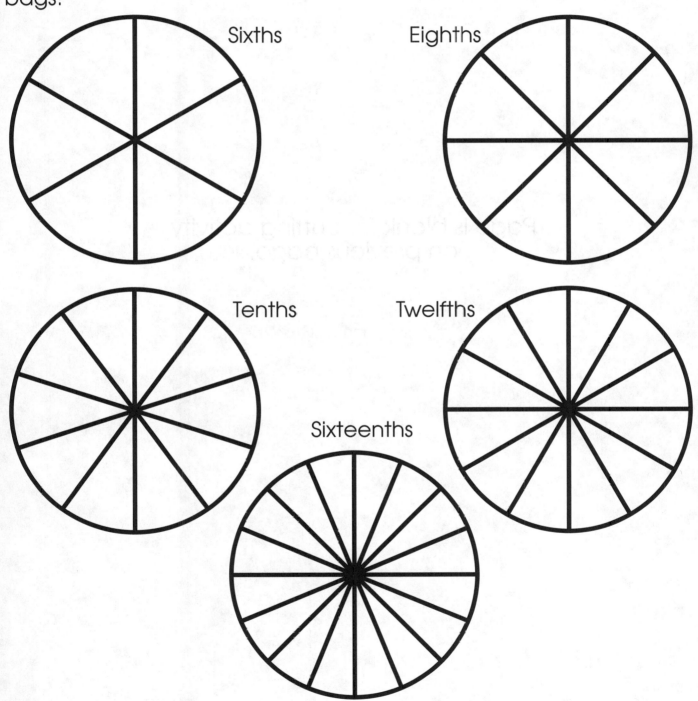

Sixths

Eighths

Tenths

Twelfths

Sixteenths

Page is blank for cutting activity
on previous page.

Fractions

A **fraction** is a number that names part of a whole, such as $\frac{1}{2}$ or $\frac{1}{3}$.

A fraction is made up of two numbers—the **numerator** (top number) and the **denominator** (bottom number). The larger the denominator, the smaller each of the equal parts. $\frac{1}{16}$ is smaller than $\frac{1}{2}$.

Directions: Study the fractions below.

1 whole.

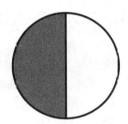

2 equal parts or halves

One-half of the circle is shaded.　$\frac{1}{2}$

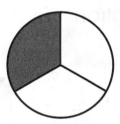

3 equal parts or thirds

One-third of the circle is shaded.　$\frac{1}{3}$

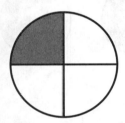

4 equal parts or halves

One-fourth of the circle is shaded.　$\frac{1}{4}$

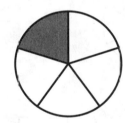

5 equal parts or fifths

One-fifth of the circle is shaded.　$\frac{1}{5}$

6 equal parts or sixths

One-sixth of the circle is shaded.　$\frac{1}{6}$

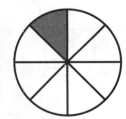

8 equal parts or eighths

One-eighth of the circle is shaded.　$\frac{1}{8}$

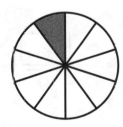

10 equal parts or tenths

One-tenth of the circle is shaded.　$\frac{1}{10}$

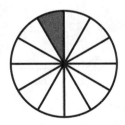

12 equal parts or twelfths

One-twelfth of the circle is shaded.　$\frac{1}{12}$

Fractions: Equivalent

Fractions that name the same part of a whole are equivalent fractions.

Example:

$$\frac{1}{2} = \frac{2}{4}$$

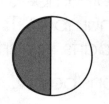

Directions: Fill in the numbers to complete the equivalent fractions.

$$\frac{1}{4} = \frac{\boxed{}}{8}$$

$$\frac{2}{3} = \frac{\boxed{}}{6}$$

$$\frac{1}{6} = \frac{\boxed{}}{12}$$

$$\frac{2}{3} = \frac{\boxed{}}{6}$$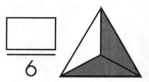

$$\frac{1}{3} = \frac{\boxed{}}{12}$$

$$\frac{1}{5} = \frac{\boxed{}}{15}$$

$$\frac{1}{4} = \frac{\boxed{}}{8}$$

$$\frac{1}{2} = \frac{\boxed{}}{6}$$

$$\frac{2}{3} = \frac{\boxed{}}{9}$$

$$\frac{2}{6} = \frac{\boxed{}}{18}$$

Fractions: Division

A fraction is a number that names part of an object. It can also name part of a group.

Directions: Study the example. Divide by the bottom number of the fraction to find the answers.

Example:

There are 6 cheerleaders.
$\frac{1}{2}$ of the cheerleaders are boys.
How many cheerleaders are boys?

6 cheerleaders $\prod$ 2 groups = 3 boys

$\frac{1}{2}$ of 6 = 3

$\frac{1}{2}$ of 8 = ___4___

$\frac{1}{2}$ of 10 = ____

$\frac{1}{3}$ of 9 = ____

$\frac{1}{5}$ of 10 = ____

$\frac{1}{4}$ of 12 = ____

$\frac{1}{8}$ of 32 = ____

$\frac{1}{3}$ of 27 = ____

$\frac{1}{5}$ of 30 = ____

$\frac{1}{2}$ of 14 = ____

$\frac{1}{9}$ of 18 = ____

$\frac{1}{6}$ of 24 = ____

$\frac{1}{3}$ of 18 = ____

$\frac{1}{10}$ of 50 = ____

Decimals: Addition and Subtraction

Decimals are added and subtracted in the same way as other numbers. Simply carry down the decimal point to your answer.

Directions: Add or subtract.

Examples:

```
   1
  1.3            4.5
+2.8           -2.2
 ----           ----
  4.1           2.3
```

```
  1.3            4.6            5.1            6.7
+2.2           -3.4          +8.8           -4.3
----            ----          ----           ----
```

```
  7.9            6.4           11.4           0.5
-3.7           +8.7          - 9.5          +3.6
----            ----          -----          ----
```

9.3 + 1.2 = _____   2.5 - 0.7 = _____   1.2 + 5.0 = _____

Bob jogs around the school every day. The distance for one time around is 0.7 of a mile. If he jogs around the school two times, how many miles does he jog each day? _____

Problem-Solving: Fractions, Decimals

A fraction is a number that names part of a whole, such as $\frac{1}{2}$ or $\frac{1}{3}$.

Directions: Read and solve each problem.

There are 20 large animals on the Browns' farm. Two-fifths are horses, two-fifths are cows and the rest are pigs. Are there more pigs or cows on the farm? _____

Farmer Brown had 40 eggs to sell. He sold half of them in the morning. In the afternoon, he sold half of what was left. How many eggs did Farmer Brown have at the end of the day? _____

There is a fence running around seven-tenths of the farm. How much of the farm does not have a fence around it? Write the amount as a decimal. _____

The Browns have 10 chickens. Two are roosters and the rest are hens. Write a decimal for the number that are roosters and for the number that are hens. _____ roosters _____ hens

Mrs. Brown spends three-fourths of her day working outside and the rest working inside. Does she spend more time inside or outside? _____

Percentages

A percentage is the amount of a number out of 100. This is the percent sign: %

Directions: Fill in the blanks.

Example: $70\% = \dfrac{70}{100}$ $\qquad$ $\underline{40}\% = \dfrac{40}{100}$

$30\% = \dfrac{}{100}$ $\qquad$ $10\% = \dfrac{}{100}$

$90\% = \dfrac{}{100}$ $\qquad$ $40\% = \dfrac{}{100}$

$70\% = \dfrac{}{100}$ $\qquad$ $80\% = \dfrac{}{100}$

$\underline{}\% = \dfrac{20}{100}$ $\qquad$ $\underline{}\% = \dfrac{60}{100}$

$\underline{}\% = \dfrac{30}{100}$ $\qquad$ $\underline{}\% = \dfrac{10}{100}$

$\underline{}\% = \dfrac{50}{100}$ $\qquad$ $\underline{}\% = \dfrac{90}{100}$

MATH

Level 2

Place Value: Standard Form

For this activity, you will need a number spinner or number cube.

Directions: Roll the cube or spin the spinner the same number of times as there are spaces in each place value box. The first number rolled or spun goes in the ones place, the second number in the tens place, and so on.

Example:

Standard Form

thousands	hundreds	tens	ones
4	5	6	7

4,567

hundreds	tens	ones

_____

thousands	hundreds	tens	ones

_____

ten thousands	thousands	hundreds	tens	ones

_____

hundred thousands	ten thousands	thousands	hundreds	tens	ones

_____

millions	hundred thousands	ten thousands	thousands	hundreds	tens	ones

_____

Directions: Write the number words for the numerals above.

_____

_____

_____

_____

Estimating

Estimating is used for certain mathematical calculations. For example, to figure the cost of several items, round their prices to the nearest dollar, then add up the approximate cost. A store clerk, on the other hand, needs to know the exact prices in order to charge the correct amount. To estimate to the nearest hundred, round up numbers over 50. **Example:** 251 is rounded up to 300. Round down numbers less than 50. **Example:** 128 is rounded down to 100.

Directions: In the following situations, write whether an exact or estimated answer should be used.

Example:

You make a deposit in your bank account. Do you want an estimated total or an exact total?   Exact

1. Your family just ate dinner at a restaurant. Your parents are trying to calculate the tip for your server. Should they estimate by rounding or use exact numbers?

2. You are at the store buying candy, and you want to know if you have enough money to pay for it. Should you estimate or use exact numbers?

3. Some friends are planning a trip from New York City to Washington, D.C. They need to know about how far they will travel in miles. Should they estimate or use exact numbers?

4. You plan a trip to the zoo. Beforehand, you call the zoo for the price of admission. Should the person at the zoo tell you an estimated or exact price?

5. The teacher is grading your papers. Should your scores be exact or estimated?

Addition Games

Directions: Play the following addition games to practice your math facts.

1. ROLL 'EM!

For one or more players.

Materials: 2 number cubes or dice or 2 number spinners per player

How to play: Each player rolls his/her number cubes (dice) or spins his/her spinners simultaneously. As quickly as possible, he/she adds the two numbers rolled or spun. Whoever is first to add the numbers correctly wins the round.

Variation: Subtract the numbers.

2. FLASH 'EM!

For one or more players.

Materials: addition/subtraction flash cards

How to play: An adult shows the flash cards one at a time to each player, who solves the addition problem. Place correctly answered cards in one stack and incorrectly answered cards in another. Which stack is larger? Try again. This time try to answer all the cards correctly.

Variations: Set a time limit for play. How many flash cards can be correctly answered in 5, 4 or 3 minutes?

Adding Larger Numbers

When adding two-, three- and four-digit numbers, add the ones first, then tens, hundreds, thousands, and so on.

Examples:

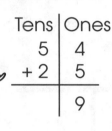

Tens	Ones
5	4
+ 2	5
	9

Tens	Ones
5	4
+ 2	5
7	9

Directions: Add the following numbers.

$$81 + 23$$ $$67 + 22$$ $$34 + 82$$ $$730 + 265$$

$$76 + 73$$ $$1{,}803 + 1{,}104$$ $$523 + 476$$ $$267 + 12$$

$$4{,}254 + 545$$ $$111 + 82$$

$$164 + 425$$ $$727 + 51$$

Addition: Regrouping

Regrouping uses 10 ones to form one 10, 10 tens to form one hundred, one 10 and 5 ones to form 15, and so on.

Directions: Add using regrouping. Color in all the boxes with a 5 in the answer to help the dog find its way home.

	63 + 22	5,268 4,910 + 1,683	248 + 463	291 + 543	2,934 + 112
1,736 + 5,367	2,946 + 7,384	3,245 1,239 + 981	738 + 692	896 + 728	594 + 738
2,603 + 5,004	4,507 + 289	1,483 + 6,753	1,258 + 6,301	27 469 + 6,002	4,637 + 7,531
782 + 65	485 + 276	3,421 + 8,064			
48 93 + 26	90 263 + 864	362 453 + 800			

Going in Circles

Directions: Where the circles meet, write the sum of the numbers from the circles on the right and left and above and below. The first one is done for you.

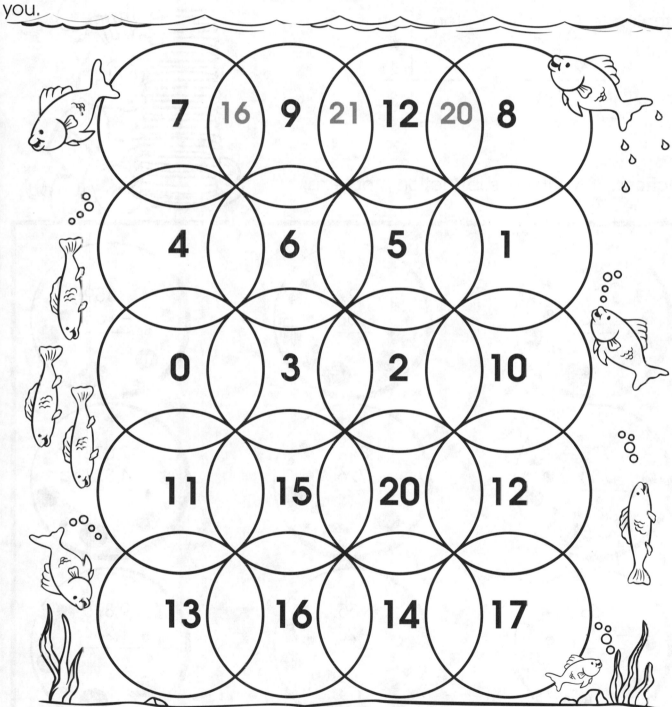

7 16 9 21 12 20 8

4 6 5 1

0 3 2 10

11 15 20 12

13 16 14 17

Subtracting Larger Numbers

When you subtract larger numbers, subtract the ones first, then the tens, hundreds, thousands, and so on.

Example:

Tens	Ones
9	4
− 2	1
	3

Tens	Ones
9	4
− 2	1
7	3

Directions: Solve these subtraction problems.

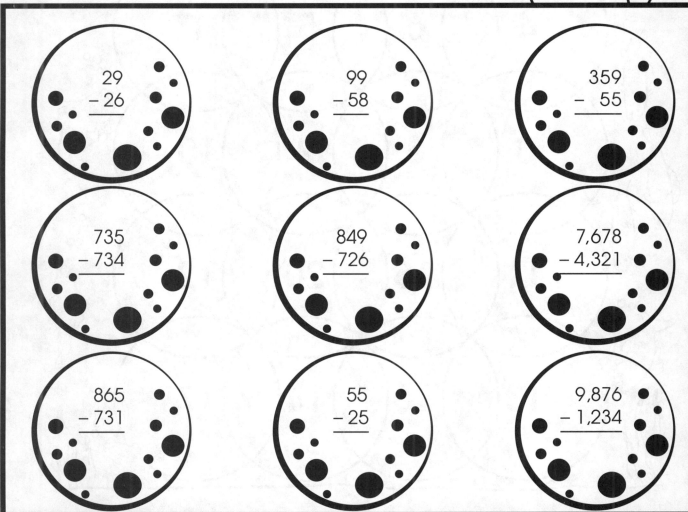

```
   29          99          359
 − 26        − 58         −  55
```

```
  735         849        7,678
− 734       − 726       − 4,321
```

```
  865          55        9,876
− 731        − 25       − 1,234
```

Subtraction: Regrouping

Directions: Subtract using regrouping.

Examples:

23 − 18	$\overset{1}{\cancel{2}}\overset{1}{3}$ − 1 8 —— 5	243 − 96	$\overset{1}{\cancel{2}}\overset{13}{\cancel{4}}\overset{1}{3}$ − 9 6 —— 1 4 7

81 − 53	76 − 49	94 − 38	156 − 77	341 − 83	726 − 29

568 − 173	806 − 738	743 − 550	903 − 336	647 − 289	254 − 69

730 − 518	961 − 846	573 − 76	604 − 55	265 − 19	372 − 59

111 − 82	358 − 99	147 − 49

180 − 106	325 − 68	873 − 35

Addition and Subtraction

Directions: Add or subtract, using regrouping when needed.

```
   32        183        456
   68        246        398        643
 + 43       + 89       + 597      − 377
 ----       ----       -----      -----
```

```
 1,563      3,586      8,711      9,361
 − 941     + 4,218    − 4,937    − 7,452
 ------    -------    -------    -------
```

```
             293                   849
 5,734       431        743        250
+ 6,298     + 93      − 529       + 82
-------     ----      -----       -----
```

```
 1,227
 2,431      9,117
+ 5,792    − 3,828
-------    -------
```

68 + 93 + 146 = _____   73 + 246 + 1,579 = _____

43 + 745 − 29 = _____   128 + 403 + 2,571 = _____

156 + 627 + 541 = _____   97 + 51 + 37 + 79 = _____

Tom walks 389 steps from his house to the video store. It is 149 steps to Elm Street. It is 52 steps from Maple Street to the video store. How many steps is it from Elm Street to Maple Street? _____

Addition and Subtraction

Directions: Add or subtract, using regrouping when needed.

```
   38          1,269                           629
   43          2,453        5,792              491          4,697
 + 21        + 8,219      - 4,814            + 308        - 2,988
 ----        -------      -------            -----        -------


                 68          197
 5,280           27          436            7,321          456
-3,147         + 42        + 213           -2,789        + 974
 -----         ----        -----           ------        -----


                492
 3,932          863        9,873            4,978        6,235
+4,681        +  57       +5,483           +2,131       +2,986
 -----        -----       ------           ------       ------
```

Sue stocked her pond with 263 bass and 187 trout. The turtles ate 97 fish. How many fish are left?

_____

Multiples

A **multiple** is the product of a specific number and any other number. For example, the multiples of 2 are 2 (2 x 1), 4 (2 x 2), 6, 8, 10, 12, and so on.

Directions: Write the missing multiples.

Example: Count by 5's.

5, 10, 15, 20, 25, 30, 35. These are multiples of 5.

Multiplication

Multiplication is a short way to find the sum of adding the same number a certain amount of times, such as 7 x 4 = 28 instead of 7 + 7 + 7 + 7 = 28.

Directions: Multiply.

4 x 7	7 x 6	0 x 8	7 x 2	9 x 5	1 x 5	6 x 4
8 x 3	7 x 1	4 x 2	9 x 6	8 x 5	6 x 7	9 x 8
3 x 5	7 x 8	3 x 9	5 x 6	9 x 9	7 x 5	9 x 4

3 x 6	2 x 8	8 x 6	7 x 7
0 x 7	3 x 3	5 x 9	

How quickly did you complete this page? _____

Fact Factory

Factors are the numbers multiplied together in a multiplication problem. The **product** is the answer.

Directions: Write the missing factors or products.

X	5
1	5
5	
4	20
6	
3	
2	10
7	
9	45

X	9
8	72
3	
4	
9	
6	54
7	
2	
1	9

X	7
2	14
5	
	42
8	
7	
4	
	21
0	

X	3
7	
4	
6	
1	
3	
2	
5	
8	

X	1
1	
12	
10	
3	3
5	
7	
6	
4	

X	8
9	
8	
4	
5	
6	
7	
3	
2	

X	2
	24
2	
	22
4	
	20
6	
	18
8	

X	4
2	
4	
6	
8	
	4
	12
	20
	28

X	6
7	
6	
5	
4	
3	
2	
1	
0	

X	10
	20
3	
	40
5	
	60
7	
	80
9	

X	11
4	
7	
9	
10	
3	
5	
6	
8	

X	12
1	
2	24
3	
4	48
5	
6	
7	
8	

Multiplication:
One-Digit Numbers Times Two-Digit Numbers

Follow the steps for multiplying a one-digit number by a two-digit number using regrouping.

Example: **Step 1:** Multiply the ones.
Regroup.

$$\begin{array}{r} \overset{2}{5}4 \\ \times\ 7 \\ \hline 8 \end{array}$$

Step 2: Multiply the tens.
Add two tens.

$$\begin{array}{r} \overset{2}{5}4 \\ \times\ 7 \\ \hline 3\,7\,8 \end{array}$$

Directions: Multiply.

$$\begin{array}{r} 27 \\ \times\ 3 \\ \hline \end{array} \qquad \begin{array}{r} 63 \\ \times\ 4 \\ \hline \end{array} \qquad \begin{array}{r} 52 \\ \times\ 5 \\ \hline \end{array} \qquad \begin{array}{r} 91 \\ \times\ 9 \\ \hline \end{array} \qquad \begin{array}{r} 45 \\ \times\ 7 \\ \hline \end{array} \qquad \begin{array}{r} 75 \\ \times\ 2 \\ \hline \end{array}$$

$$\begin{array}{r} 64 \\ \times\ 5 \\ \hline \end{array} \qquad \begin{array}{r} 76 \\ \times\ 3 \\ \hline \end{array} \qquad \begin{array}{r} 93 \\ \times\ 6 \\ \hline \end{array} \qquad \begin{array}{r} 87 \\ \times\ 4 \\ \hline \end{array} \qquad \begin{array}{r} 66 \\ \times\ 7 \\ \hline \end{array} \qquad \begin{array}{r} 38 \\ \times\ 2 \\ \hline \end{array}$$

$$\begin{array}{r} 47 \\ \times\ 8 \\ \hline \end{array} \qquad \begin{array}{r} 64 \\ \times\ 9 \\ \hline \end{array} \qquad \begin{array}{r} 51 \\ \times\ 8 \\ \hline \end{array} \qquad \begin{array}{r} 99 \\ \times\ 3 \\ \hline \end{array}$$

$$\begin{array}{r} 13 \\ \times\ 7 \\ \hline \end{array} \qquad \begin{array}{r} 32 \\ \times\ 4 \\ \hline \end{array} \qquad \begin{array}{r} 25 \\ \times\ 8 \\ \hline \end{array} \qquad \begin{array}{r} 15 \\ \times\ 7 \\ \hline \end{array}$$

The chickens on the Smith farm produce 48 dozen eggs each day. How many dozen eggs do they produce in 7 days?

_____

Multiplication: Tens, Hundreds, Thousands

When multiplying a number by 10, the answer is the number with a 0 behind it. It is like counting by tens.

Examples:

10	10	10	10	10	10
x 1	x 2	x 3	x 4	x 5	x 6
10	20	30	40	50	60

When multiplying a number by 100, the answer is the number with two 0's. When multiplying by 1,000, the answer is the number with three 0's.

Examples:

100	100	100	1,000	1,000	1,000
x 1	x 2	x 3	x 1	x 2	x 3
100	200	300	1,000	2,000	3,000

4	400	8	800	7	700
x 2	x 2	x 3	x 3	x 5	x 5
8	800	24	2,400	35	3,500

Directions: Multiply.

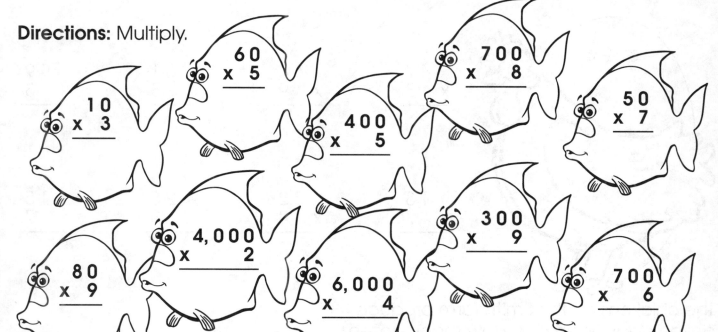

10 x 3

60 x 5

400 x 5

700 x 8

50 x 7

80 x 9

4,000 x 2

6,000 x 4

300 x 9

700 x 6

Multiplication:
Two-Digit Numbers Times Two-Digit Numbers

Follow the steps for multiplying a two-digit number by a two-digit number using regrouping.

Example:

Step 1: Multiply the ones. Regroup.

```
          2
  6 3     6 3
x 6 8   x 6 8
        -----
          5 0 4
```

Step 2: Multiply the tens. Regroup. Add.

```
    1
  6 3       6 3
x 6 8     x 6 8
-----     -----
3,7 8 0     5 0 4
          +3,7 8 0
          -------
          4,2 8 4
```

Directions: Multiply.

```
  1 2      2 7      6 5      1 9      9 9      3 5
x 5 5    x 1 5    x 2 7    x 3 9    x 1 3    x 1 4
```

```
  4 3      3 8      5 3      4 7      5 7      4 8
x 2 6    x 1 7    x 8 6    x 7 2    x 6 2    x 3 3
```

```
  2 7      9 3      6 4      5 3
x 5 4    x 4 5    x 1 6    x 2 3
```

The Jones farm has 24 cows that each produce 52 quarts of milk a day. How many quarts are produced each day altogether? _____

Multiplication:
Two-Digit Numbers Times Three-Digit Numbers

Follow the steps for multiplying a two-digit number by a three-digit number using regrouping.

Example: **Step 1:** Multiply the ones. **Step 2:** Multiply the tens.
Regroup.   Regroup. Add.

```
                    2 2
   287             287                287              287
 x  43           x  43              x  43            x  43
                 ─────                              ─────
                   861             11,480             861
                                               +11,480
                                               ───────
                                                12,341
```

Directions: Multiply.

```
  261            434            357
x  36          x  48          x  75
```

```
  231            754            614
x  46          x  65          x  59
```

```
  549            372            458            368
x  89          x  94          x  85          x  98
```

At the Douglas berry farm, workers pick 378 baskets
of peaches each day. Each basket holds 65 peaches.
How many peaches are picked each day? _____

Multiplication Drill

Directions: Multiply. Color each paintbrush—your choice.

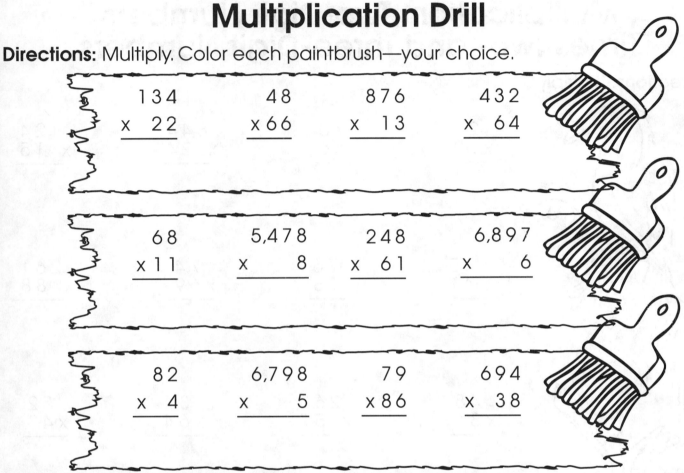

134 x 22	48 x 66	876 x 13	432 x 64
68 x 11	5,478 x 8	248 x 61	6,897 x 6
82 x 4	6,798 x 5	79 x 86	694 x 38

Directions: Color the picture by matching each number with its paintbrush.

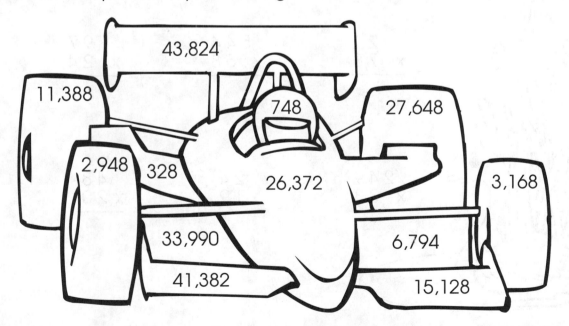

43,824
11,388
748
27,648
2,948 328
26,372
3,168
33,990
6,794
41,382
15,128

Multiplication: Two-Digit Numbers Times Two- and Three-Digit Numbers

Directions: Multiply.

25 x 72	70 x 66	844 x 24	124 x 15
45 x 41	76 x 78	74 x 69	261 x 88
48 x 36	263 x 57	37 x 64	52 x 43
321 x 78	544 x 58	797 x 24	998 x 37
249 x 33	24 x 19	48 x 20	817 x 59

Multiplication:
Three-Digit Numbers Times Three-Digit Numbers

Directions: Multiply. Regroup when needed.

Example:

```
        5 6 3
      x 2 4 8
      ───────
        4,504
       22,520
    +112,600
    ─────────
    1 3 9,6 2 4
```

Hint: When multiplying by the tens, start writing the number in the tens place. When multiplying by the hundreds, start in the hundreds place.

```
    8 4 2          9 3 2          7 5 9          5 3 1
  x 1 6 7        x 2 7 2        x 4 6 8        x 5 5 6
```

```
    3 8 3          5 2 3          2 2 9          7 3 8
  x 4 7 6        x 3 4 9        x 1 8 9        x 5 1 3
```

James grows pumpkins on his farm. He has 362 rows of pumpkins. There are 593 pumpkins in each row. How many pumpkins does James grow? _____

Review

Directions: Multiply. Use the box to solve the problem. Color the ribbons blue if the answer is correct.

$$\begin{array}{r} 5,683 \\ \times\quad 9 \\ \hline 51,147 \end{array}$$

$$\begin{array}{r} 256 \\ \times\quad 38 \\ \hline 8,728 \end{array}$$

$$\begin{array}{r} 356 \\ \times\quad 427 \\ \hline 152,012 \end{array}$$

$$\begin{array}{r} 800 \\ \times\quad 7 \\ \hline 6,300 \end{array}$$

$$\begin{array}{r} 489 \\ \times\quad 56 \\ \hline 27,284 \end{array}$$

$$\begin{array}{r} 60 \\ \times\quad 5 \\ \hline 300 \end{array}$$

Division

Division is a way to find out how many times one number is contained in another number. For example, 28 ∏ 7 = 4 means that there are 4 groups of 7 in 28.

Division problems can be written two ways: 36 ∏ 6 = 6 or $6\overline{)36}$

These are the parts of a division problem: dividend ——→ 36 ∏ 6 = 6 ←— **quotient**
divisor

$$\text{divisor} \longrightarrow 6\overline{)36} \begin{array}{l} \leftarrow\text{— quotient} \\ \leftarrow\text{— dividend} \end{array}$$

Directions: Divide.

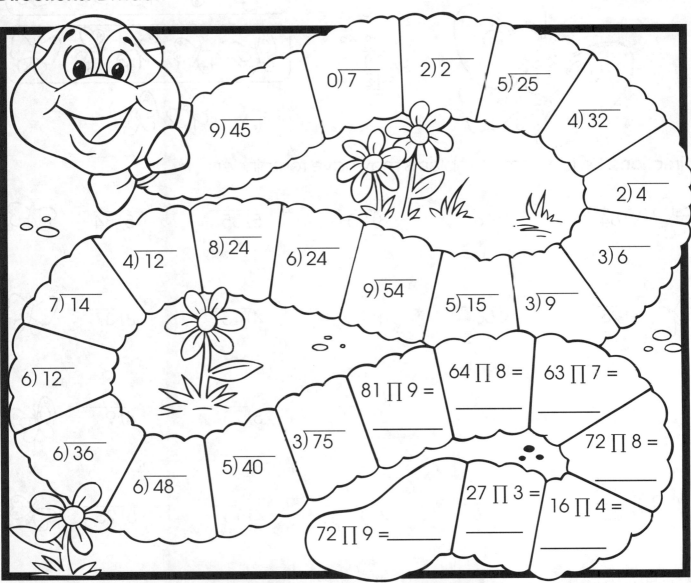

$0\overline{)7}$ $2\overline{)2}$ $5\overline{)25}$

$9\overline{)45}$ $4\overline{)32}$

$2\overline{)4}$

$4\overline{)12}$ $8\overline{)24}$ $6\overline{)24}$ $3\overline{)6}$

$9\overline{)54}$

$7\overline{)14}$ $5\overline{)15}$ $3\overline{)9}$

$6\overline{)12}$ $64 ∏ 8 =$ $63 ∏ 7 =$

$81 ∏ 9 =$ _____   _____

$6\overline{)36}$ $3\overline{)75}$ $72 ∏ 8 =$ _____

$5\overline{)40}$ $27 ∏ 3 =$ $16 ∏ 4 =$

$6\overline{)48}$ _____   _____

$72 ∏ 9 =$ _____

Division With Remainders

Sometimes groups of objects or numbers cannot be divided into equal groups. The **remainder** is the number left over in the quotient of a division problem. The remainder must be smaller than the divisor.

Example:

Divide 18 butterflies into groups of 5.
You have 3 equal groups,
with 3 butterflies left over.

$18 \div 5 = 3 \text{ R}3$

or

$$\begin{array}{r} 3 \text{ R}3 \\ 5\overline{)18} \\ -15 \\ \hline 3 \end{array}$$

Directions: Divide. Some problems may have remainders.

$9\overline{)84}$ $\quad$ $7\overline{)65}$ $\quad$ $8\overline{)25}$ $\quad$ $5\overline{)35}$ $\quad$ $5\overline{)34}$

$4\overline{)25}$ $\quad$ $6\overline{)56}$ $\quad$ $4\overline{)7}$ $\quad$ $4\overline{)16}$ $\quad$ $8\overline{)37}$

$7\overline{)27}$ $\quad$ $2\overline{)5}$ $\quad$ $2\overline{)4}$ $\quad$ $8\overline{)73}$ $\quad$ $4\overline{)9}$

$9\overline{)46}$ $\quad$ $5\overline{)17}$ $\quad$ $2\overline{)3}$ $\quad$ $4\overline{)13}$ $\quad$ $5\overline{)25}$

Division: Larger Numbers

Follow the steps for dividing larger numbers.

Example: **Step 1:** Divide the tens first.   **Step 2:** Divide the ones next.

$$3\overline{)66}$$

$$\begin{array}{r} 2 \\ 3\overline{)66} \\ -6 \\ \hline 06 \end{array}$$

$$\begin{array}{r} 22 \\ 3\overline{)66} \\ -6 \\ \hline 06 \\ -6 \\ \hline 0 \end{array}$$

Directions: Divide.

$$4\overline{)84} \qquad 2\overline{)90} \qquad 2\overline{)64} \qquad 2\overline{)50} \qquad 3\overline{)45}$$

$$3\overline{)75} \qquad 3\overline{)36} \qquad 4\overline{)92} \qquad 2\overline{)76} \qquad 5\overline{)65}$$

In some larger numbers, the divisor goes into the first two digits of the dividend.

Example:

$$9\overline{)729}$$

$$\begin{array}{r} 8 \\ 9\overline{)729} \\ -72 \\ \hline 09 \end{array}$$

$$\begin{array}{r} 81 \\ 9\overline{)729} \\ -72 \\ \hline 09 \\ -9 \\ \hline 0 \end{array}$$

Directions: Divide.

$$7\overline{)630} \qquad 5\overline{)125} \qquad 6\overline{)486} \qquad 5\overline{)100} \qquad 6\overline{)540}$$

Division

Directions: Divide.

$7\overline{)860}$ $6\overline{)611}$ $8\overline{)279}$ $4\overline{)338}$ $6\overline{)979}$

$3\overline{)792}$ $5\overline{)463}$ $6\overline{)940}$ $4\overline{)647}$ $3\overline{)814}$

$7\overline{)758}$ $5\overline{)356}$ $4\overline{)276}$ $8\overline{)328}$ $9\overline{)306}$

$4\overline{)579}$ $8\overline{)932}$ $3\overline{)102}$ $2\overline{)821}$ $6\overline{)489}$

The music store has 491 CD's. The store sells 8 CD's a day. How many days will it take to sell all of the CD's?

_____

Division: Checking the Answers

To check a division problem, multiply the quotient by the divisor. Add the remainder. The answer will be the dividend.

Example:

quotient ⟶
divisor ⟶ 3)175
dividend
remainder ⟶

```
      5 8 R1
3) 1 7 5
    1 5
      2 5
      2 4
        1
```

```
    5 8  ⟵ quotient
  x  3   ⟵ divisor
  ─────
  1 7 4
+     1  ⟵ remainder
  ─────
  1 7 5  ⟵ dividend
```

Directions: Divide each problem, then draw a line from the division problem to the correct checking problem.

33	53	97	135	113	119
x 7	x 7	x 7	x 7	x 7	x 7
	+ 2	+ 3	+ 1	+ 1	+ 1

7)682   7)231   7)373   7)792   7)834   7)946

The toy factory puts 7 robot dogs in each box. The factory has 256 robot dogs. How many boxes will they need?

_____

Division: Checking the Answers

Directions: Divide, then check your answers.

Example:

```
        1 8 2 R1
    4) 7 2 9
      - 4
        3 2
       -3 2
          9
         -8
          1
```

Check:

```
        1 8 2
    x       4
        7 2 8
    +       1
        7 2 9
```

Divide	Check	Divide	Check
35)4 6 8	☐ x 3 5	77)8 1 9	☐ x 7 7
29)5 6 8	☐ x 2 9	53)2,7 9 5	☐ x 5 3

The bookstore puts 53 books on a shelf. How many shelves will it need for 1,590 books? _____

Division: Two-Digit Divisors

Directions: Divide. Then check each answer on another sheet of paper by multiplying it by the divisor and adding the remainder.

Example:

```
      2                21 R4
12)256            12)256
   -24               -24
     1                 16
                      -12
                        4
```

Check:

```
    21
 x  12
    42
   210
   252
 +   4
   256
```

$27)\overline{880}$ $81)\overline{913}$ $65)\overline{790}$ $42)\overline{674}$ $67)\overline{823}$

$72)\overline{977}$ $54)\overline{743}$ $45)\overline{863}$ $24)\overline{432}$ $18)\overline{372}$

$28)\overline{175}$ $49)\overline{538}$ $77)\overline{936}$ $37)\overline{603}$ $63)\overline{835}$

The Allen farm has 882 chickens. The chickens are kept in 21 coops. How many chickens are there in each coop? _____

Averaging

An **average** is found by adding two or more quantities and dividing by the number of quantities.

Example:

Step 1: Find the sum of the numbers.
24 + 36 + 30 = 90

Step 2: Divide by the number of quantities.
90 $\overline{)}$ 3 = 30
The average is 30.

Directions: Find the average of each group of numbers. Draw a line from each problem to the correct average.

12 + 14 + 29 + 1 =   410

4 + 10 + 25 =   83

33 + 17 + 14 + 20 + 16 =   40

782 + 276 + 172 =   15

81 + 82 + 91 + 78 =   13

21 + 34 + 44 =   33

14 + 24 + 10 + 31 + 5 + 6 =   14

278 + 246 =   20

48 + 32 + 18 + 62 =   262

A baseball player had 3 hits in game one, 2 hits in game two and 4 hits in game three. How many hits did she average over the three games? _____

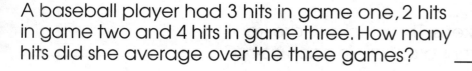

Averaging

Directions: Find the averages.

Ted went bowling. He had scores of 112, 124 and 100. What was his average?

_____

Sue ran 3 races. Her times were 9 seconds, 10 seconds and 8 seconds. What was her average?

_____

The baseball team played 6 games. They had 12 hits, 6 hits, 18 hits, 36 hits, 11 hits and 7 hits. What is the average number of hits in a game?

_____

In 3 games of football, Chris gained 156, 268 and 176 yards running. How many yards did he average in a game?

_____

Jane scored 18, 15, 26 and 21 points in 4 basketball games. How many points did she average?

_____

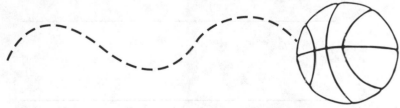

Averaging

Averaging can be used to keep track of your grades.

Example: Average the grades for each subject.

Sally has the following grades:
English — 75, 84, 95; Spelling — 98, 92, 80;
Math — 80, 88, 95.

Her averages are:
English — 75 + 84 + 95 = 254 $\prod$ 3 = 84.7
Spelling — 98 + 92 + 80 = 270 $\prod$ 3 = 90.0
Math — 80 + 88 + 95 = 263 $\prod$ 3 = 87.7

Directions: Find the averages.

1. Write the number of minutes you do homework each night for a week. What is the average of those times?

_____

2. Keep track of the following for 1 week and find the average:

a. Time spent watching TV

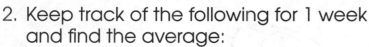

b. Time spent playing video games

c. Time spent on the computer

d. Time spent doing chores

e. Time spent practicing sports or a musical instrument

Graphing

A **graph** is a drawing that shows information about changes in numbers.

Directions: Answer the questions by reading the graphs.

Bar Graph

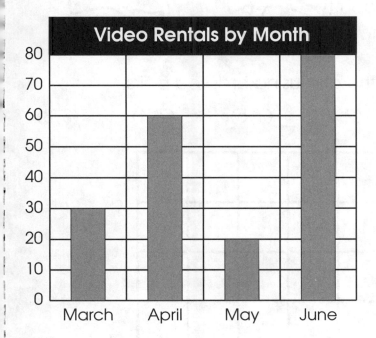

How many videos did the store rent in June?

_____

In which month did the store rent the fewest videos?

_____

How many videos did the store rent for all 4 months?

_____

Line Graph

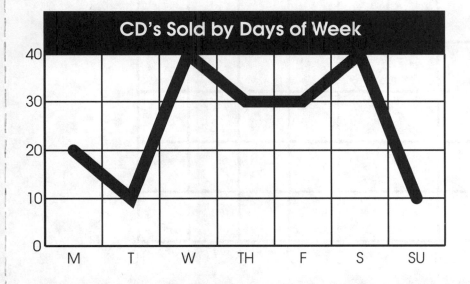

On which days did the store sell the fewest CD's?

_____

How many CD's did the store sell in 1 week?

_____

Ordered Pairs

An **ordered pair** is a pair of numbers
used to locate a point.

Example: (8, 3)

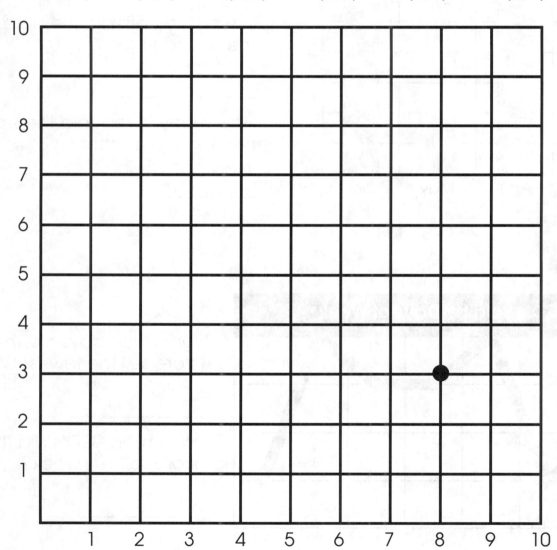

Step 1: Count across to line 8 on the graph.
Step 2: Count up to line 3 on the graph.
Step 3: Draw a dot to mark the spot.

Directions: Map the following spots on the grid using ordered pairs.

(4, 7)   (9, 10)   (2, 1)   (5, 6)   (2, 2)   (1, 5)   (7, 4)   (3, 8)

Graphing: Finding Ordered Pairs

Graphs or grids are sometimes used to find the location of objects.

Example: The ice-cream cone is located at point (5, 6) on the graph. To find the ice cream's location, follow the line to the bottom of the grid to get the first number — 5. Then go back to the ice cream and follow the grid line to the left for the second number — 6.

Directions: Write the ordered pair for the following objects. The first one is done for you.

book __(4, 8)__   bike _____   suitcase _____   house _____

globe _____   cup _____   triangle _____   airplane _____

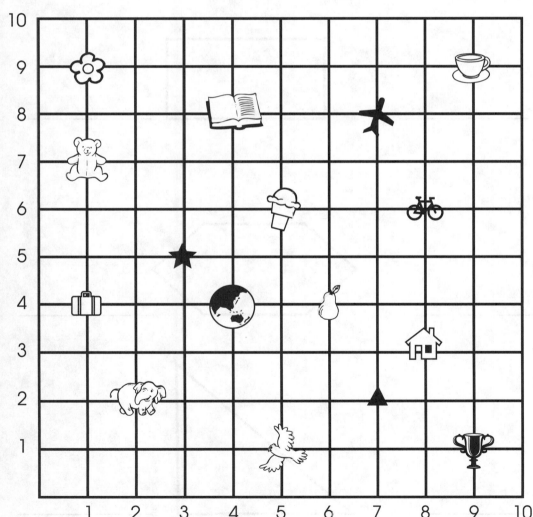

Directions: Identify the objects located at the following points. The first one is done for you.

(9, 1) __trophy__

(3, 5) _____

(2, 2) _____

(6, 4) _____

(1, 9) _____

(5, 1) _____

(1, 7) _____

Geometry: Polygons

A **polygon** is a closed figure with three or more sides.

Examples:

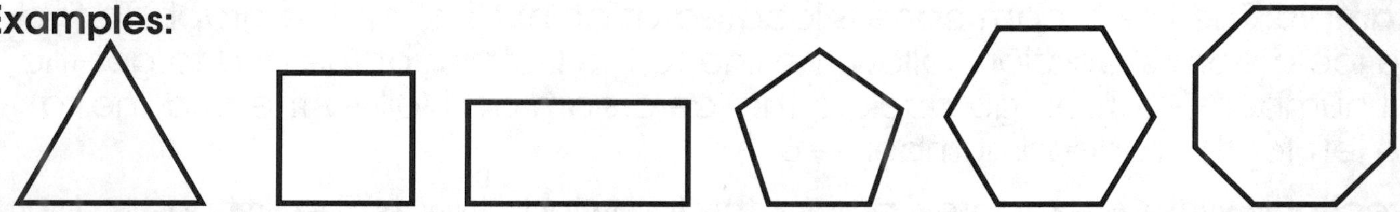

triangle
3 sides

square
4 equal
sides

rectangle
4 sides

pentagon
5 sides

hexagon
6 sides

octagon
8 sides

Directions: Identify the polygons.

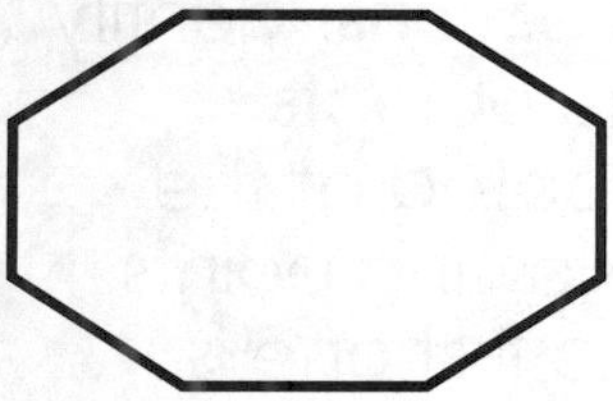

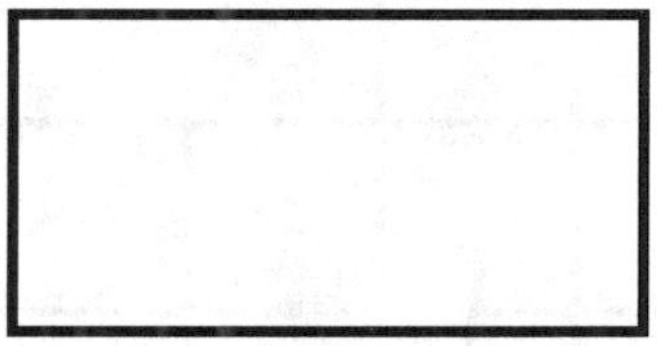

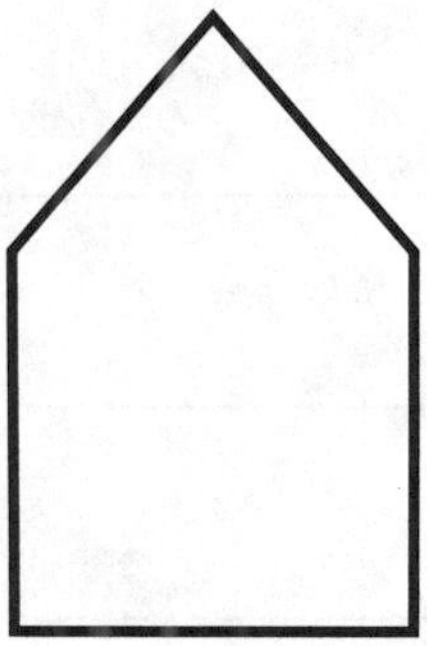

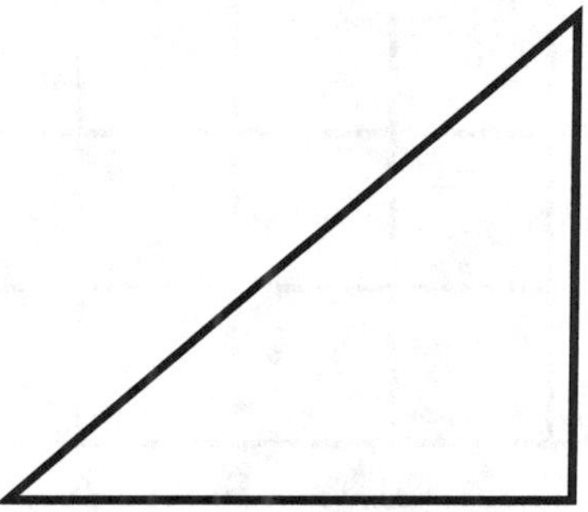

Measurement: Inches

An **inch** is a unit of length in the standard system equal to $\frac{1}{12}$ of a foot. A ruler is used to measure inches.

This illustration shows a ruler measuring a 4-inch pencil, which can be written as 4" or 4 in.

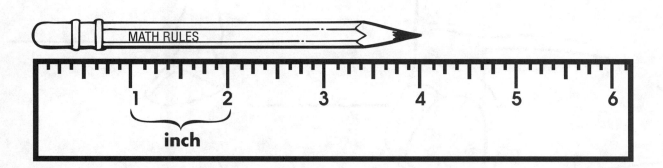

Directions: Use a ruler to measure each object to the nearest inch.

1. The length of your foot   _____

2. The width of your hand   _____

3. The length of this page   _____

4. The width of this page   _____

5. The length of a large paper clip _____

6. The length of your toothbrush   _____

7. The length of a comb   _____

8. The height of a juice glass   _____

9. The length of your shoe   _____

10. The length of a fork   _____

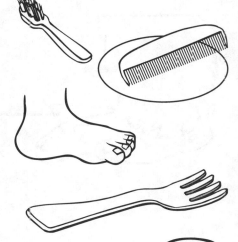

Measurement: Inches

Directions: Use a ruler to measure the width of each foot to the nearest inch.

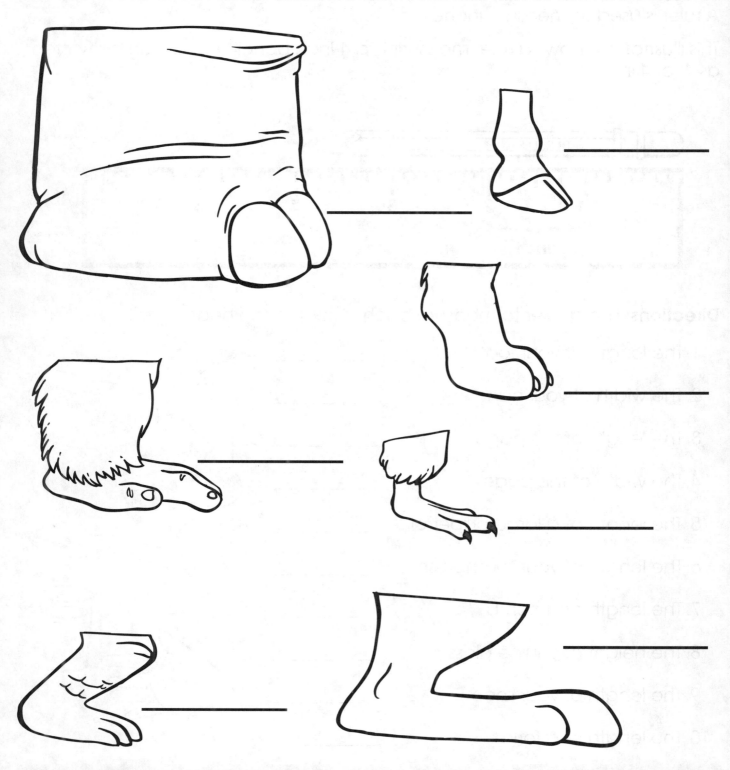

Measurement: Fractions of an Inch

An inch is divided into smaller units, or fractions of an inch.

Example: This stick of gum is $2\frac{3}{4}$ inches long.

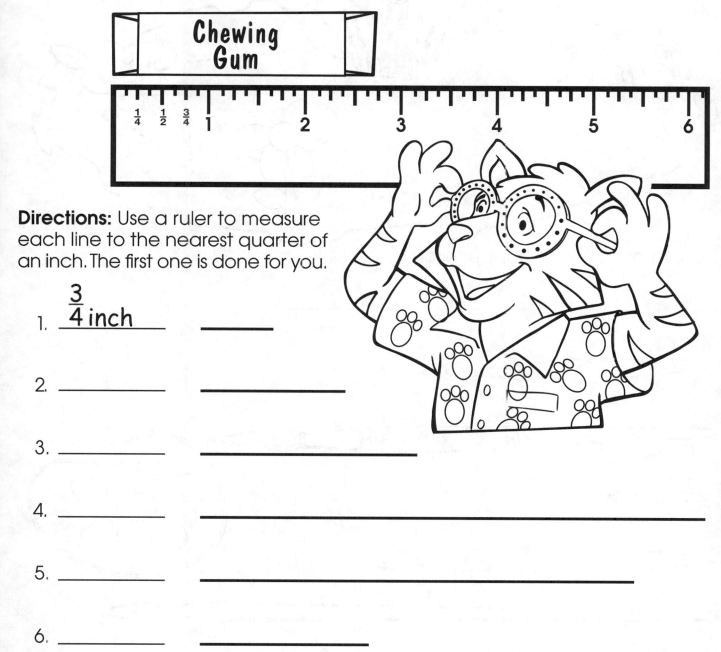

Directions: Use a ruler to measure each line to the nearest quarter of an inch. The first one is done for you.

1. $\dfrac{3}{4}$ inch _____

2. _____ _____

3. _____ _____

4. _____ _____

5. _____ _____

6. _____ _____

7. _____ _____

Measurement: Fractions of an Inch

Directions: Use a ruler to measure to the nearest quarter of an inch.

How far did the grasshopper jump?

_____ + _____ + _____ + _____ = _____

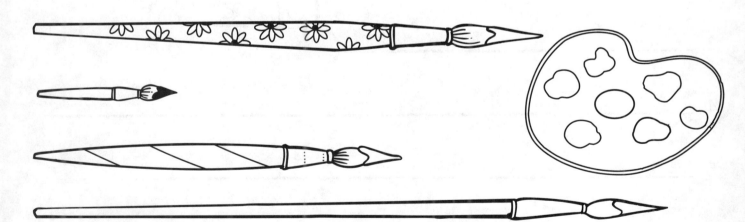

What is the total length of the paintbrushes?

_____ + _____ + _____ + _____ + _____ = _____

Measurement: Foot, Yard, Mile

Directions: Choose the measure of distance you would use for each object.

1 foot = 12 inches
1 yard = 3 feet
1 mile = 1,760 yards or 5,280 feet

inches _____

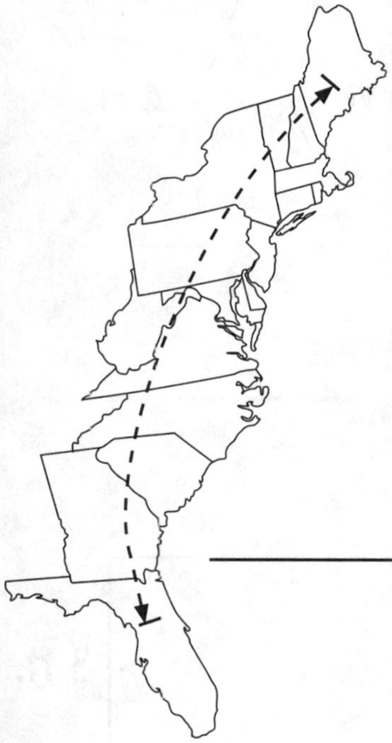

_____

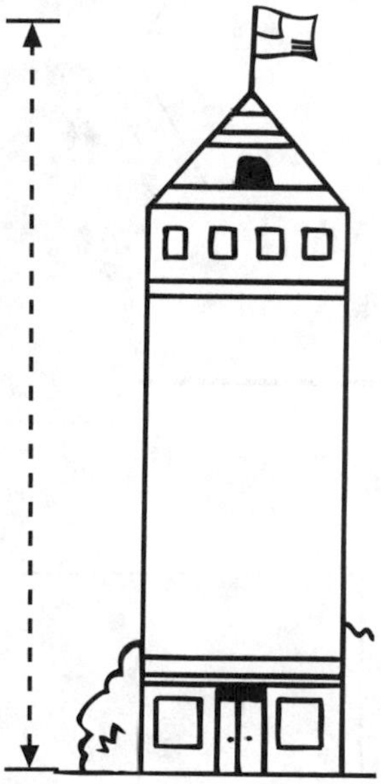

_____

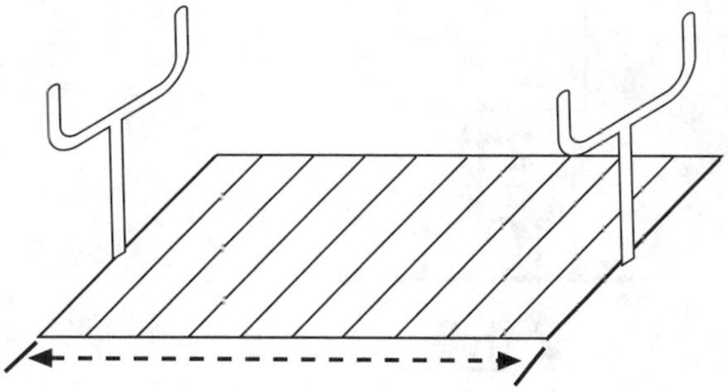

_____

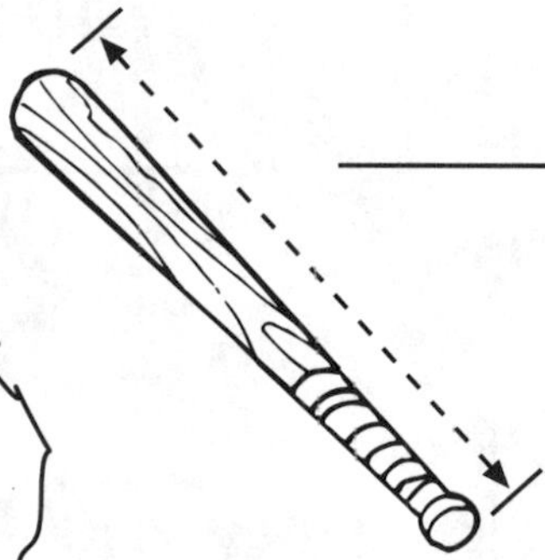

_____

_____

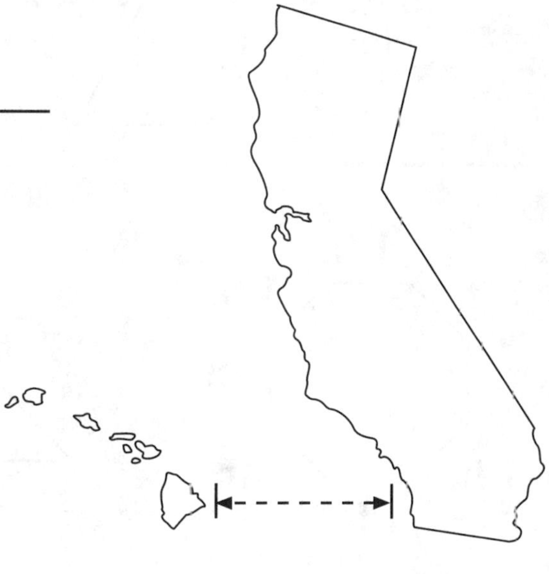

_____

_____

Geometry: Perimeter

The **perimeter** is the distance around an object. Find the perimeter by adding the lengths of all the sides.

Directions: Find the perimeter for each object (ft. = feet).

2 ft.

3 ft.　　3 ft.

2 ft.

__10 ft.__

6 ft.

6 ft.　　6 ft.

6 ft.　　6 ft.

6 ft.

_____

4 ft.　　4 ft.

3 ft.

_____

2 ft.

5 ft.

5 ft.

2 ft.

_____

10 ft.

3 ft.　　　　　3 ft.

10 ft.

_____

1 ft.

1 ft.　　1 ft.

1 ft.　　1 ft.

1 ft.　　1 ft.

1 ft.

_____

7 ft.　　5 ft.

5 ft.

_____

1 ft.　　3 ft.　　1 ft.

5 ft.

_____

Measurement: Perimeter

Directions: Find the perimeter of the following figures.

Examples:

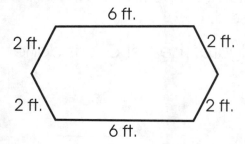

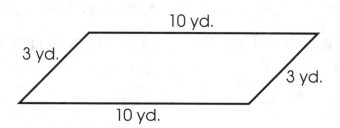

2 + 2 + 2 + 2 + 6 + 6 = 20
The perimeter of this
hexagon is 20 ft.

10 + 10 + 3 + 3 = 26
The perimeter of this
parallelogram is 26 yd.

Perimeter

Perimeter

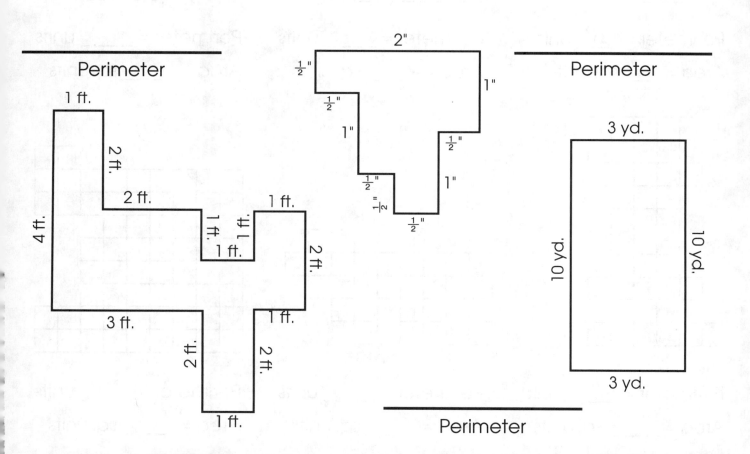

Perimeter

Measurement: Perimeter and Area

Perimeter is the distance around a figure. It is found by adding the lengths of the sides. **Area** is the number of square units needed to cover a region. The area is found by adding the number of square units. A unit can be any unit of measure. Most often, inches, feet or yards are used.

Directions: Find the perimeter and area for each figure. The first one is done for you. ☐ = 1 square unit

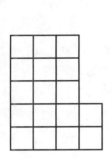

Perimeter = __18__ units

Area = __17__ sq. units

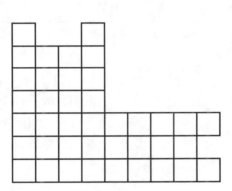

Perimeter = _____ units

Area = _____ sq. units

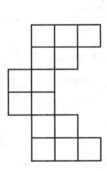

Perimeter = _____ units

Area = _____ sq. units

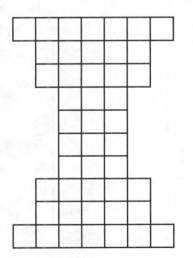

Perimeter = _____ units

Area = _____ sq. units

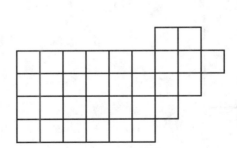

Perimeter = _____ units

Area = _____ sq. units

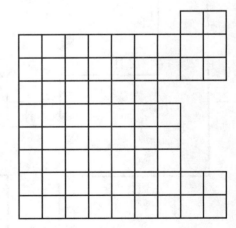

Perimeter = _____ units

Area = _____ sq. units

Measurement: Perimeter and Area

Area is also calculated by multiplying the length times the width of a square or rectangular figure. Use the formula: A = l x w.

Directions: Calculate the perimeter of each figure.

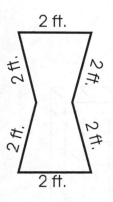

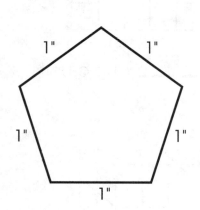

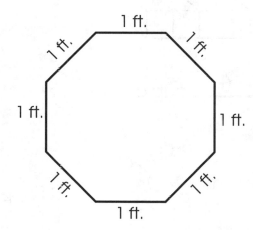

_____

_____

_____

Directions: Calculate the area of each figure.

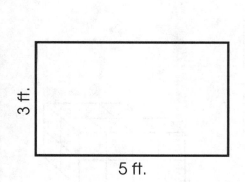

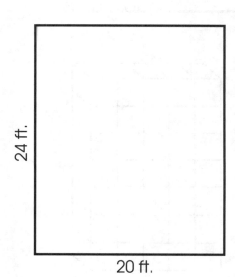

_____

_____

_____

Measurement: Volume

Volume is the number of cubic units that fit inside a figure.

Directions: Find the volume of each figure. The first one is done for you.

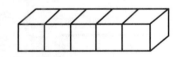

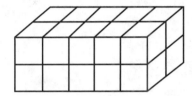

__4__ cubic units

_____ cubic units

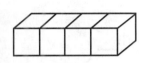

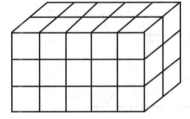

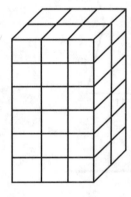

_____ cubic units

_____ cubic units

_____ cubic units

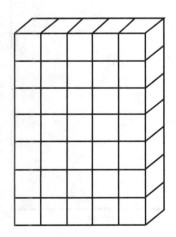

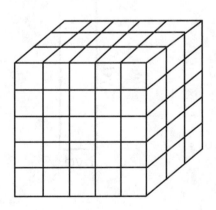

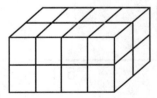

_____ cubic units

_____ cubic units

_____ cubic units

Measurement: Volume

The volume of a figure can also be calculated by multiplying the length times the width times the height.
Use the formula: l x w x h.

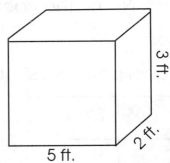

Example:

3 x 5 x 2 = 30 cubic feet

Directions: Find the volume of the following figures. Label your answers in feet, inches or yards. The first one is done for you.

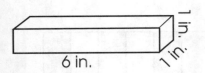

6 in.   1 in.   1 in.

6 cubic inches

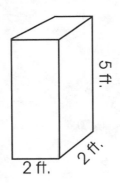

5 ft.   2 ft.   2 ft.

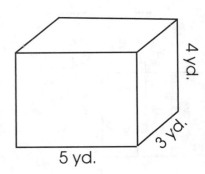

4 yd.   3 yd.   5 yd.

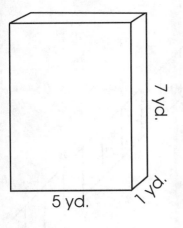

7 yd.   5 yd.   1 yd.

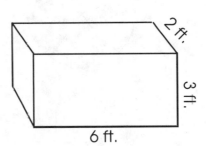

2 ft.   3 ft.   6 ft.

Fractions

Directions: Name the fraction that is shaded.

Examples:

3 of 4 equal parts are shaded.

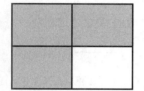

$$\frac{3}{4}$$

12 of 16 equal parts are shaded.

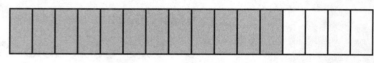

$$\frac{12}{16}$$

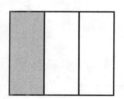

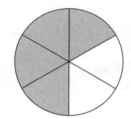

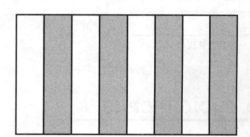

_____

_____

_____

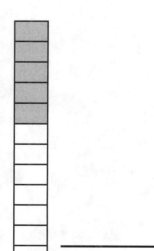

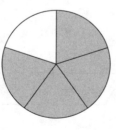

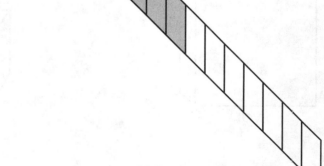

_____

_____

_____

Fractions: Addition

When adding fractions with the same denominator, the denominator stays the same. Add only the numerators.

Example: **numerator**
denominator $\dfrac{1}{8}$ + $\dfrac{2}{8}$ = $\dfrac{3}{8}$

Directions: Begin in the center of each flower and add each petal.

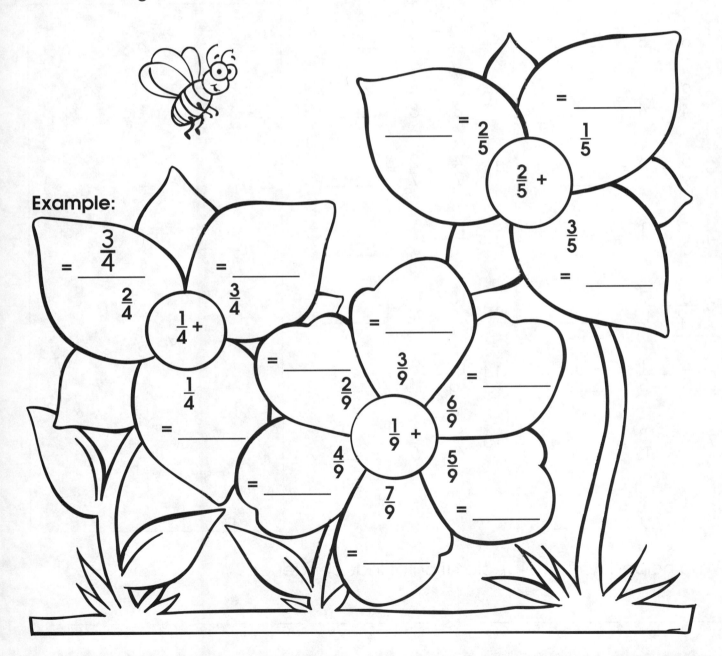

Fractions

Fractions: Subtraction

When subtracting fractions with the same denominator, the denominator stays the same. Subtract only the numerators.

Directions: Solve the problems. Match the answer to a letter from the key. The answer is the name of a famous American.

1. $\frac{3}{8} - \frac{2}{8} = \underline{\frac{1}{8}}$

2. $\frac{2}{4} - \frac{1}{4} = \underline{\hspace{1cm}}$

3. $\frac{5}{9} - \frac{3}{9} = \underline{\hspace{1cm}}$

4. $\frac{2}{3} - \frac{1}{3} = \underline{\hspace{1cm}}$

5. $\frac{8}{12} - \frac{7}{12} = \underline{\hspace{1cm}}$

6. $\frac{4}{5} - \frac{1}{5} = \underline{\hspace{1cm}}$

7. $\frac{6}{12} - \frac{3}{12} = \underline{\hspace{1cm}}$

8. $\frac{4}{9} - \frac{1}{9} = \underline{\hspace{1cm}}$

9. $\frac{11}{12} - \frac{7}{12} = \underline{\hspace{1cm}}$

10. $\frac{7}{8} - \frac{3}{8} = \underline{\hspace{1cm}}$

11. $\frac{4}{7} - \frac{2}{7} = \underline{\hspace{1cm}}$

12. $\frac{14}{16} - \frac{7}{16} = \underline{\hspace{1cm}}$

13. $\frac{18}{20} - \frac{13}{20} = \underline{\hspace{1cm}}$

14. $\frac{13}{15} - \frac{2}{15} = \underline{\hspace{1cm}}$

15. $\frac{5}{6} - \frac{3}{6} = \underline{\hspace{1cm}}$

T $\frac{1}{8}$		P $\frac{5}{24}$		H $\frac{1}{4}$
F $\frac{4}{12}$		E $\frac{2}{7}$		J $\frac{3}{12}$
E $\frac{3}{9}$		O $\frac{2}{9}$		F $\frac{4}{8}$
R $\frac{7}{16}$		O $\frac{2}{8}$		Y $\frac{8}{20}$
Q $\frac{1}{32}$		M $\frac{1}{3}$		S $\frac{5}{20}$
A $\frac{1}{12}$		R $\frac{12}{15}$		S $\frac{3}{5}$
N $\frac{2}{6}$		O $\frac{11}{15}$		

Who helped write the Declaration of Independence?

$\overline{1}$ $\overline{2}$ $\overline{3}$ $\overline{4}$ $\overline{5}$ $\overline{6}$ $\overline{7}$ $\overline{8}$ $\overline{9}$ $\overline{10}$ $\overline{11}$ $\overline{12}$ $\overline{13}$ $\overline{14}$ $\overline{15}$

Equivalent Fractions

Equivalent fractions are two different fractions that represent the same number. **Example:**

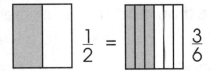

Directions: Complete these equivalent fractions.

$$\frac{1}{3} = \frac{}{6} \qquad \frac{1}{2} = \frac{}{4} \qquad \frac{3}{4} = \frac{}{8} \qquad \frac{1}{3} = \frac{}{9}$$

Directions: Circle the figures that show a fraction equivalent to figure a. Write the fraction for the shaded area under each figure.

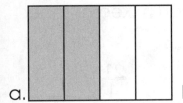

a.

b.

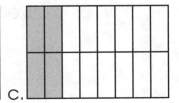

c.

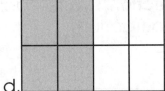

d.

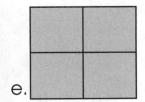

e.

f.

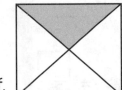

g.

h.

Directions: Find the equivalent fraction by multiplying both parts of the fraction by the same number.

Example: $\frac{2}{3} \times \frac{3}{3} = \frac{6}{9}$

$$\frac{1}{4} = \frac{}{8} \qquad \frac{3}{4} = \frac{}{16} \qquad \frac{4}{5} = \frac{8}{} \qquad \frac{3}{8} = \frac{}{24}$$

Fractions: Mixed Numbers

A **mixed number** is a number written as a whole number and a fraction, such as $6\frac{5}{8}$.

To change a fraction into a mixed number, divide the denominator (bottom number) into the numerator (top number). Write the remainder over the denominator.

Example:

$$\frac{14}{6} = 2\frac{2}{6} \qquad 6)\overline{14} \begin{array}{c} 2 \text{ R2} \\ 12 \\ \hline 2 \end{array}$$

To change a mixed number into a fraction, multiply the denominator by the whole number, add the numerator and write it on top of the denominator.

Example:

$$3\frac{1}{7} = \frac{22}{7} \qquad (7 \times 3) + 1 = \frac{22}{7}$$

Directions: Write each fraction as a mixed number. Write each mixed number as a fraction.

$\frac{21}{6} = \underline{\hspace{2cm}}$ $\qquad$ $\frac{24}{5} = \underline{\hspace{2cm}}$ $\qquad$ $\frac{10}{3} = \underline{\hspace{2cm}}$ $\qquad$ $\frac{21}{4} = \underline{\hspace{2cm}}$

$\frac{11}{6} = \underline{\hspace{2cm}}$ $\qquad$ $\frac{13}{4} = \underline{\hspace{2cm}}$ $\qquad$ $\frac{12}{5} = \underline{\hspace{2cm}}$ $\qquad$ $\frac{10}{9} = \underline{\hspace{2cm}}$

$4\frac{3}{8} = \frac{\Box}{8}$ $\qquad$ $2\frac{1}{3} = \frac{\Box}{3}$ $\qquad$ $4\frac{3}{5} = \frac{\Box}{5}$ $\qquad$ $3\frac{4}{6} = \frac{\Box}{6}$

$7\frac{1}{4} = \frac{\Box}{4}$ $\qquad$ $2\frac{3}{5} = \frac{\Box}{5}$ $\qquad$ $7\frac{1}{2} = \frac{\Box}{2}$ $\qquad$ $6\frac{5}{7} = \frac{\Box}{7}$

$\frac{11}{8} = \underline{\hspace{2cm}}$ $\qquad$ $\frac{21}{4} = \underline{\hspace{2cm}}$ $\qquad$ $\frac{33}{5} = \underline{\hspace{2cm}}$ $\qquad$ $\frac{13}{6} = \underline{\hspace{2cm}}$

$\frac{23}{7} = \underline{\hspace{2cm}}$ $\qquad$ $8\frac{1}{3} = \underline{\hspace{2cm}}$ $\qquad$ $9\frac{3}{7} = \underline{\hspace{2cm}}$ $\qquad$ $\frac{32}{24} = \underline{\hspace{2cm}}$

Fractions: Adding Mixed Numbers

When adding mixed numbers, add the whole numbers first, then the fractions.

Examples:

$$9\frac{1}{3}$$
$$+3\frac{1}{3}$$
$$\overline{12\frac{2}{3}}$$

$$2\frac{3}{6}$$
$$+1\frac{1}{6}$$
$$\overline{3\frac{4}{6}}$$

Directions: Add the number in the center to the number in each surrounding section.

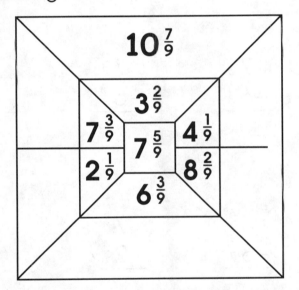

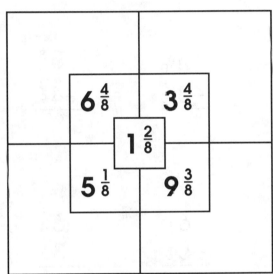

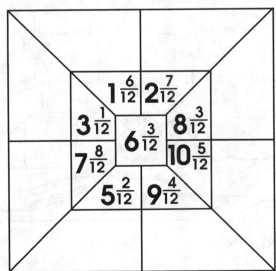

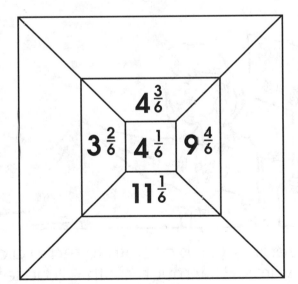

Fractions: Subtracting Mixed Numbers

When subtracting mixed numbers, subtract the fractions first, then the whole numbers.

Directions: Subtract the mixed numbers. The first one is done for you.

$$7\frac{3}{8}$$
$$-4\frac{2}{8}$$
$$\overline{3\frac{1}{8}}$$

$$4\frac{5}{6}$$
$$-3\frac{1}{6}$$

$$4\frac{1}{2}$$
$$-3$$

$$7\frac{5}{8}$$
$$-6\frac{3}{8}$$

$$6\frac{6}{8}$$
$$-1\frac{1}{8}$$

$$5\frac{3}{4}$$
$$-1\frac{1}{4}$$

$$5\frac{2}{3}$$
$$-3\frac{1}{3}$$

$$4\frac{8}{10}$$
$$-3\frac{3}{10}$$

$$9\frac{8}{9}$$
$$-4\frac{3}{9}$$

$$7\frac{2}{3}$$
$$-6\frac{1}{3}$$

$$7\frac{2}{3}$$
$$-5$$

$$9\frac{8}{10}$$
$$-6\frac{3}{10}$$

$$4\frac{7}{9}$$
$$-2$$

$$6\frac{7}{8}$$
$$-5\frac{3}{8}$$

$$6\frac{3}{4}$$
$$-3\frac{1}{4}$$

$$5\frac{6}{7}$$
$$-3\frac{1}{7}$$

$$7\frac{6}{7}$$
$$-2\frac{4}{7}$$

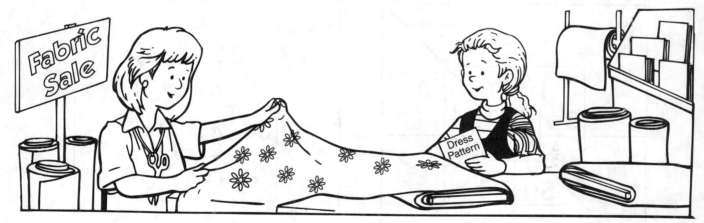

Sally needs $1\frac{3}{8}$ yards of cloth to make a dress. She has $4\frac{5}{8}$ yards. How much cloth will be left over? _____

Reducing Fractions

Reducing a fraction means to find the greatest common factor and divide.

Example: $\dfrac{5}{15}$ factors of 5: 1, 5
factors of 15: 1, 3, 5, 15

5 is the greatest common factor. Divide both the numerator and denominator by 5.

$$5 \sqcap 5 = 1$$
$$15 \sqcap 5 = 3$$

Directions: Reduce each fraction. Circle the correct answer.

$\dfrac{2}{4} = \dfrac{1}{2}, \dfrac{1}{6}, \dfrac{1}{8}$ $\dfrac{3}{9} = \dfrac{1}{6}, \dfrac{1}{3}, \dfrac{3}{6}$ $\dfrac{5}{10} = \dfrac{1}{5}, \dfrac{1}{2}, \dfrac{5}{6}$ $\dfrac{4}{12} = \dfrac{1}{4}, \dfrac{1}{3}, \dfrac{2}{3}$ $\dfrac{10}{15} = \dfrac{2}{3}, \dfrac{2}{5}, \dfrac{2}{7}$

$\dfrac{12}{14} = \dfrac{1}{8}, \dfrac{6}{7}, \dfrac{3}{5}$ $\dfrac{3}{24} = \dfrac{2}{12}, \dfrac{3}{6}, \dfrac{1}{8}$ $\dfrac{1}{11} = \dfrac{1}{11}, \dfrac{2}{5}, \dfrac{3}{4}$ $\dfrac{11}{22} = \dfrac{1}{12}, \dfrac{1}{2}, \dfrac{2}{5}$

Directions: Find the way home. Color the boxes with fractions equivalent to $\frac{1}{8}$ and $\frac{1}{3}$.

Review

Directions: Add or subtract the fractions and mixed numbers.

$$4\tfrac{7}{8}$$
$$-2\tfrac{5}{8}$$

$$8\tfrac{3}{9}$$
$$+2\tfrac{5}{9}$$

$$3\tfrac{1}{8}$$
$$+1\tfrac{3}{8}$$

$$4\tfrac{5}{6}$$
$$-3\tfrac{1}{6}$$

$$7\tfrac{5}{11}$$
$$+3\tfrac{3}{11}$$

$\dfrac{4}{12} + \dfrac{3}{12} =$ _____

$\dfrac{3}{5} + \dfrac{1}{5} =$ _____

$\dfrac{3}{8} - \dfrac{1}{8} =$ _____

$\dfrac{3}{9} + \dfrac{1}{9} =$ _____

$\dfrac{3}{4} - \dfrac{2}{4} =$ _____

Directions: Reduce the fractions.

$\dfrac{4}{6} =$ _____

$\dfrac{7}{21} =$ _____

$\dfrac{9}{12} =$ _____

$\dfrac{2}{4} =$ _____

$\dfrac{6}{24} =$ _____

$\dfrac{8}{32} =$ _____

Directions: Change the mixed numbers to fractions and the fractions to mixed numbers.

$3\tfrac{1}{3} = \dfrac{\boxed{}}{3}$ 　　 $\dfrac{14}{4} =$ _____ 　　 $\dfrac{26}{6} =$ _____ 　　 $3\tfrac{7}{12} = \dfrac{\boxed{}}{12}$ 　　 $\dfrac{22}{7} =$ _____

Fractions to Decimals

When a figure is divided into 10 equal parts, the parts are called tenths. Tenths can be written two ways—as a fraction or a decimal. A **decimal** is a number with one or more places to the right of a decimal point, such as 6.5 or 2.25. A **decimal point** is the dot between the ones place and the tenths place.

Examples:

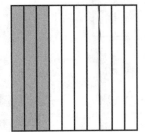

ones	tenths
0	3

$\frac{3}{10}$ or 0.3 of the square is shaded.

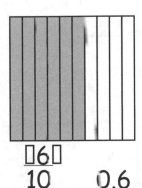

$\frac{6}{10}$ 0.6

Directions: Write the decimal and fraction for the shaded parts of the following figures. The first one is done for you.

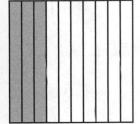

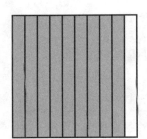

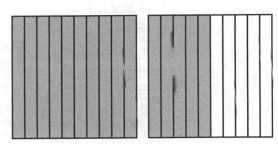

_____   _____

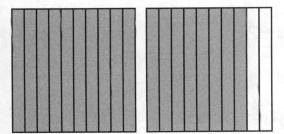

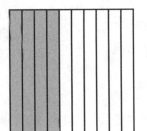

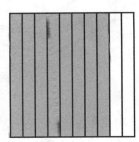

_____   _____

Decimals

Directions: Add or subtract. Remember to include the decimal point in your answers.

Example:

$1\frac{3}{10} = 1.3$

$1\frac{6}{10} = 1.6$

$$\begin{array}{r} 1.3 \\ + 1.6 \\ \hline 2.9 \end{array}$$

8.1	4.1	0.5	7.6	7.2	1.2	8.7	6.8
+ 1.7	+ 6.2	+ 1.6	− 6.5	− 2.6	+ 5.0	− 3.9	− 3.7

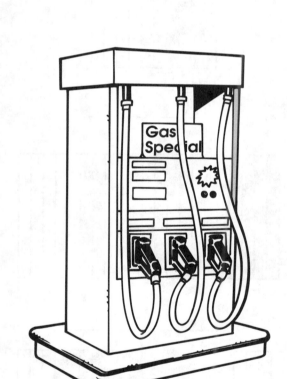

$$\begin{array}{r} 7.8 \\ - 6.8 \\ \hline \end{array} \qquad \begin{array}{r} 16.5 \\ - 7.3 \\ \hline \end{array} \qquad \begin{array}{r} 6.4 \\ + 5.3 \\ \hline \end{array} \qquad \begin{array}{r} 10.0 \\ + 3.5 \\ \hline \end{array}$$

$$\begin{array}{r} 0.42 \\ + 0.35 \\ \hline \end{array} \qquad \begin{array}{r} 0.98 \\ - 0.87 \\ \hline \end{array} \qquad \begin{array}{r} 0.78 \\ - 0.13 \\ \hline \end{array} \qquad \begin{array}{r} 0.83 \\ + 0.12 \\ \hline \end{array}$$

$$\begin{array}{r} 0.95 \\ - 0.14 \\ \hline \end{array} \qquad \begin{array}{r} 3.23 \\ + 2.48 \\ \hline \end{array} \qquad \begin{array}{r} 4.68 \\ - 2.65 \\ \hline \end{array} \qquad \begin{array}{r} 5.86 \\ - 2.73 \\ \hline \end{array}$$

$$\begin{array}{r} 6.98 \\ + 1.40 \\ \hline \end{array} \qquad \begin{array}{r} 3.27 \\ + 1.82 \\ \hline \end{array} \qquad \begin{array}{r} 4.65 \\ - 1.32 \\ \hline \end{array} \qquad \begin{array}{r} 5.97 \\ + 2.77 \\ \hline \end{array}$$

Mr. Martin went on a car trip with his family. Mr. Martin purchased gas 3 times. He bought 6.7 gallons, 7.3 gallons, then 5.8 gallons of gas. How much gas did he purchase in all? _____

Decimals: Hundredths

The next smallest decimal unit after a tenth is called a hundredth. One hundredth is one unit of a figure divided into 100 units. Written as a decimal, it is one digit to the right of the tenths place.

Examples:

One square divided into hundredths, 34 hundredths are shaded. Write: 0.34.

ones	tenths	hundredths
0	3	4

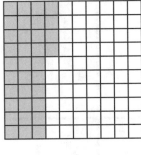

0.34

Directions: Write the decimal for the shaded parts of the following figures.

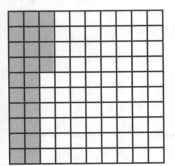 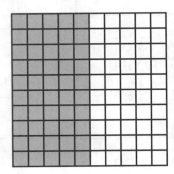  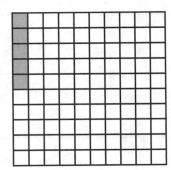

_____   _____   _____   _____

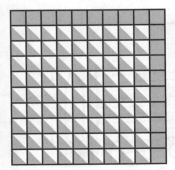 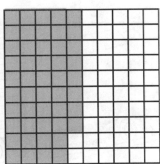 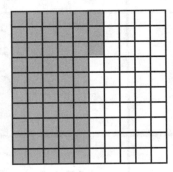 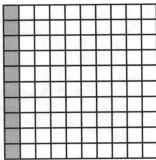

_____   _____

Adding and Subtracting Decimals

Directions: Add or subtract. Then fill in the circle next to the correct answer.

Example:

$$\begin{array}{r} 2.4 \\ + 1.7 \\ \hline \end{array}$$
○ 2.5
○ 3.1
● 4.1

$\begin{array}{r} 2.8 \\ + 3.4 \\ \hline \end{array}$ ○ 5.2 ○ 7.4 ○ 6.2	$\begin{array}{r} 5.7 \\ - 3.8 \\ \hline \end{array}$ ○ 1.9 ○ 2.5 ○ 2.9	$\begin{array}{r} 7.6 \\ + 8.9 \\ \hline \end{array}$ ○ 15.9 ○ 16.5 ○ 17.3
$\begin{array}{r} 16.3 \\ + 9.8 \\ \hline \end{array}$ ○ 25.11 ○ 26.1 ○ 26.01	$\begin{array}{r} 28.6 \\ + 43.9 \\ \hline \end{array}$ ○ 73.6 ○ 72.5 ○ 71.9	$\begin{array}{r} 43.9 \\ + 56.5 \\ \hline \end{array}$ ○ 100.4 ○ 107.4 ○ 101.4
$\begin{array}{r} 12.87 \\ - 3.45 \\ \hline \end{array}$ ○ 16.32 ○ 10.31 ○ 9.42	$\begin{array}{r} 47.56 \\ - 33.95 \\ \hline \end{array}$ ○ 13.61 ○ 80.41 ○ 14.61	$\begin{array}{r} 93.6 \\ - 79.8 \\ \hline \end{array}$ ○ 14.8 ○ 15.3 ○ 13.8
$\begin{array}{r} 11.57 \\ + 10.64 \\ \hline \end{array}$ ○ 22.21 ○ 1.93 ○ 21.12	$\begin{array}{r} 27.83 \\ - 14.94 \\ \hline \end{array}$ ○ 14.09 ○ 12.89 ○ 11.97	$\begin{array}{r} 106.935 \\ - 95.824 \\ \hline \end{array}$ ○ 111.1 ○ 111.11 ○ 11.111

The high-speed train traveled 87.90 miles on day one, 127.86 miles on day two and 113.41 miles on day three. How many miles did it travel in all? _____

Fractions and Decimals

Directions: Compare the fraction to the decimal in each box. Circle the larger number.

Example:

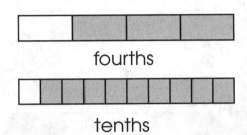

fourths

tenths

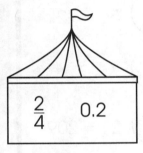 $\frac{2}{4}$ 0.2

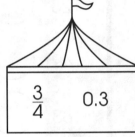 $\frac{3}{4}$ 0.3

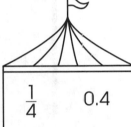 $\frac{1}{2}$ 0.6

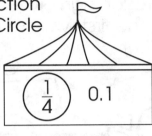 $\frac{1}{4}$ 0.4

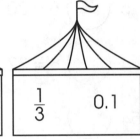 $\frac{1}{3}$ 0.1

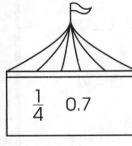 $\frac{1}{4}$ 0.7

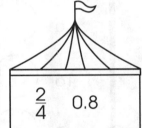 $\frac{2}{4}$ 0.8

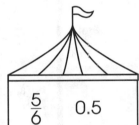 $\frac{3}{4}$ 0.9

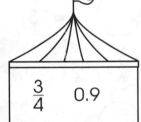 $\frac{5}{6}$ 0.5

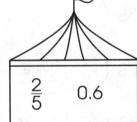 $\frac{2}{5}$ 0.6

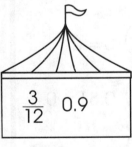 $\frac{3}{12}$ 0.9

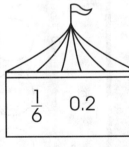 $\frac{1}{6}$ 0.2

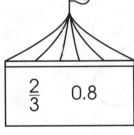 $\frac{2}{3}$ 0.8

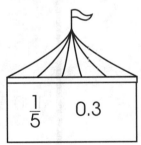 $\frac{1}{5}$ 0.3

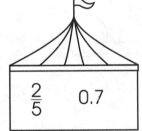 $\frac{2}{5}$ 0.7

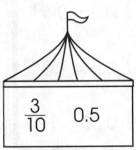 $\frac{3}{10}$ 0.5

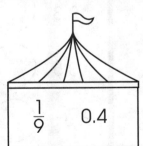 $\frac{1}{9}$ 0.4

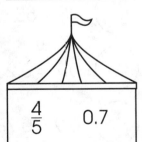 $\frac{4}{5}$ 0.7

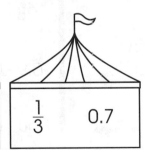 $\frac{1}{3}$ 0.7

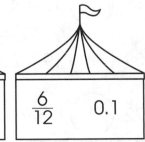 $\frac{6}{12}$ 0.1

Identifying Operations

Directions: Write the correct operation sign (**+**, **−**, **x**, ∏) in each circle to correctly complete the problem. The first two are done for you.

5 (**X**) 6 = 30	0.3 (**−**) 0.2 = 0.1	128 ( ) 56 = 72
4 ( ) 8 = 32	$1\frac{3}{6}$ ( ) $2\frac{2}{6}$ = $3\frac{5}{6}$	49 ( ) 7 = 7
54 ( ) 6 = 9	$\frac{1}{10}$ ( ) $\frac{4}{10}$ = $\frac{5}{10}$	188 ( ) 21 = 209
38 ( ) 7 = 31	5 ( ) 7 = 35	5 ( ) 3 = 15
28 ( ) 16 = 44	$3\frac{3}{8}$ ( ) $2\frac{2}{8}$ = $1\frac{1}{8}$	16 ( ) 4 = 4
32 ( ) 8 = 4	9 ( ) 3 = 6	47 ( ) 38 = 9
63 ( ) 7 = 9	12 ( ) 12 = 144	10 ( ) 0 = 0
49 ( ) 9 = 40	100 ( ) 5 = 20	0.91 ( ) 0.81 = 0.1
48 ( ) 12 = 4	98 ( ) 43 = 55	0.3 ( ) 0.3 = 0.6
39 ( ) 19 = 20	0.9 ( ) 0.7 = 0.2	0.5 ( ) 0.5 = 1.0
72 ( ) 8 = 9	1.68 ( ) 0.9 = 0.78	0.97 ( ) 0.50 = 1.47

Identifying Operations

Directions: Solve the problems. Circle the letter with the correct answer. Write the letters in order to read the message.

1. 348 − 227 =	121	M	425	S
2. 542 x 6 =	5,683	W	3,252	A
3. 328 + 593 =	921	T	149	N
4. 1,280 ∏ 40 =	92	L	32	H
5. 24 x 52 =	2,386	W	1,248	I
6. 863 − 438 =	425	S	234	U
7. 4,586 + 1,097 =	3,489	Q	5,683	W
8. 480 ∏ 4 =	32	H	120	O
9. 0.5 + 0.9 =	1.4	N	0.14	E
10. 1.6 − 0.9 =	0.7	D	0.9	T
11. $3\frac{1}{4} + 2\frac{1}{5}$ =	$5\frac{9}{20}$	E	$4\frac{7}{20}$	L
12. $\frac{4}{8} - \frac{1}{4}$ =	$\frac{3}{8}$	Y	$\frac{1}{4}$	R
13. 2,193 − 1,864 =	329	F	591	Y
14. 26 x 9 =	234	U	744	L
15. 42 ∏ 6 =	8	M	7	L

$\underline{M}$ $\underline{\hphantom{M}}$ $\underline{\hphantom{M}}$ $\underline{\hphantom{M}}$ $\underline{\hphantom{M}}$ $\underline{\hphantom{M}}$
1   2   3   4   5   6

$\underline{\hphantom{M}}$ $\underline{\hphantom{M}}$ $\underline{\hphantom{M}}$ $\underline{\hphantom{M}}$ $\underline{\hphantom{M}}$ $\underline{\hphantom{M}}$ $\underline{\hphantom{M}}$ $\underline{\hphantom{M}}$ $\underline{\hphantom{M}}$!
7   8   9   10   11   12   13   14   15

Review

Directions: Add or subtract to find the answers.

Bill jumped 28.5 feet. Jim jumped 27.3 feet. How much farther did Bill jump than Jim?

_____

Sue threw the discus 86.4 feet. Julie threw the discus 93.8 feet. How much farther did Julie throw the discus than Sue?

_____

Kim, Monica and Kelly swam on the same team in the butterfly relay race. Their individual times were 32.8 seconds, 29.9 seconds and 31.7 seconds. The winning team's time was 93.5 seconds. Did Kim, Monica and Kelly swim the fastest race?

_____

Jake's times for the 100-meter dash were 10.1 seconds, 12.5 seconds and 11.8 seconds. What was his total time?

_____

Directions: Write the correct sign in the circle.

5 $\bigcirc$ 5 = 25   100 $\bigcirc$ 25 = 4   42 $\bigcirc$ 38 = 80

152 $\bigcirc$ 38 = 114   72 $\bigcirc$ 12 = 6   9 $\bigcirc$ 5 = 45

Directions: Round the numbers, then estimate each answer.

592 →   802 →   499 →   612 →
+ 312 →   − 695 →   − 299 →   + 499 →

Magic Squares

Directions: Some of the number squares below are "magic" and some are not. Squares that add up to the same number horizontally, vertically and diagonally are "magic." Add the numbers in each square to discover which ones are "magic."

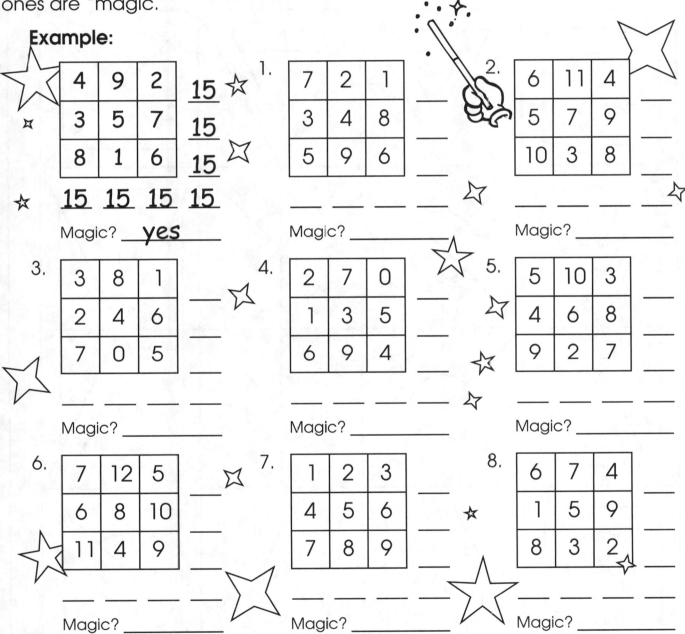

Example:

4	9	2	15
3	5	7	15
8	1	6	15
15	15	15	15

Magic? **yes**

1.

7	2	1
3	4	8
5	9	6

Magic? _____

2.

6	11	4
5	7	9
10	3	8

Magic? _____

3.

3	8	1
2	4	6
7	0	5

Magic? _____

4.

2	7	0
1	3	5
6	9	4

Magic? _____

5.

5	10	3
4	6	8
9	2	7

Magic? _____

6.

7	12	5
6	8	10
11	4	9

Magic? _____

7.

1	2	3
4	5	6
7	8	9

Magic? _____

8.

6	7	4
1	5	9
8	3	2

Magic? _____

Challenge: Can you discover a pattern for number placement in the magic squares? Try to make a magic square of your own.

Geometric Coloring

Directions: Color the geometric shapes in the box below.

Answer Key

Vocabulary: Synonyms

A **synonym** is a word that means the same, or nearly the same, as another word.
Example: quick and **fast**

Directions: Draw lines to match the words in Column A with their synonyms in Column B.

Column A	Column B
plain	unusual
career	vocation
rare	disappear
vanish	greedy
beautiful	finish
selfish	simple
complete	lovely

Directions: Choose a word from Column A or Column B to complete each sentence below. **Sample answers:**

1. Dad was very excited when he discovered the _rare/unusual_ coin for sale on the display counter.

2. My dog is a real magician; he can _vanish/disappear_ into thin air when he sees me getting his bath ready!

3. Many of my classmates joined the discussion about _career/vocation_ choices we had considered.

4. "You will need to _finish/complete_ your report on ancient Greece before you sign up for computer time," said Mr. Rastetter.

5. Your _beautiful/lovely_ painting will be on display in the art show.

4

Synonym Search

Directions: Complete the puzzle using a synonym for each clue from the box.

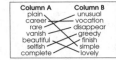

Down:
1. shirt
2. kind
3. coat
4. forest
5. sleepy

Across:
1. skinny
2. hop
4. us
5. jacket
7. top

tired, jacket, top, woods, thin, we, shirt, coat, jump, nice

Across: thin, jump, we, coat, shirt
Down: nice, nod, woods, tired

5

Vocabulary: Synonyms

tired greedy easy rough minute melted friend smart

Directions: For each sentence, choose a word from the box that is a synonym for the bold word. Write the synonym above the word.

1. Boy, this road is really **bumpy**! _rough_

2. The operator said politely, "One **moment**, please." _minute_

3. My parents are usually **exhausted** when they get home from work. _tired_

4. "Don't be so **selfish**! Can't you share with us?" asked Rob. _greedy_

5. That puzzle was actually quite **simple**. _easy_

6. "Who's your **buddy**?" Dad asked, as we walked onto the porch. _friend_

7. When it comes to animals, my Uncle Steve is quite **intelligent**. _smart_

8. The frozen treat **thawed** while I stood in line for the bus. _melted_

6

Vocabulary: Antonyms

An **antonym** is a word that means the opposite of another word.
Example: difficult and **easy**

Directions: Choose words from the box to complete the crossword puzzle.

friend vanish quit safety liquids scatter help noisy

Across:
2. Opposite of **gather** SCATTER
3. Opposite of **enemy** FRIEND
4. Opposite of **prevent** HELP
6. Opposite of **begin** QUIT
7. Opposite of **silent** NOISY

Down:
1. Opposite of **appear** VANISH
2. Opposite of **danger** SAFETY
5. Opposite of **solids** LIQUIDS

7

Antonyms

Directions: Complete the word pyramids using the antonym of the bold word in each sentence.

1. When I passed the test, it was the **saddest** day of my life.
2. I **dropped** the dishes on the way to the kitchen.
3. You may play after you **start** the dishes.
4. My sister is **little** compared to me.
5. He was **sad** because he won the prize.
6. How **short** was the snake we saw?

4. big
5. happy
2. carried
6. long
3. finish
1. happiest

8

Homophones

Homophones are words that sound the same but have different spellings and meanings.

Directions: Complete each sentence using a word from the box.

blew night blue knight hour in ant inn
our aunt meet too two to meat

1. A red _ant_ crawled up the wall.
2. It will be one _hour_ before we can go back home.
3. Will you _meet_ us later?
4. We plan to stay at an _inn_ during our trip.
5. The king had a _knight_ who fought bravely.
6. The wind _blew_ so hard that I almost lost my hat.
7. His jacket was _blue_.
8. My _aunt_ plans to visit us this week.
9. I will come _in_ when it gets too cold outside.
10. It was late at _night_ when we finally got there.
11. _Two_ of us will go with you.
12. I will mail a note _to_ someone at the bank.

9

Answer Key

Multiple-Meaning Words

Directions: Complete each sentence on pages 10 and 11 using one of the words below. Each word will be used only twice.

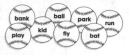

1. The kitten watched the ___fly___ crawl slowly up the wall.
2. "You wouldn't ___kid___ me, would you?" asked Dad.
3. Do you think Aunt Donna and Uncle Mike will come to my school ___play___?
4. He hit the ball so hard it broke the ___bat___.
5. "My favorite part of the story is when the princess goes to the ___ball___," sighed Veronica.
6. My brother scored the first ___run___ in the game.

10

Multiple-Meaning Words

7. We will have to ___play___ quietly while the baby is sleeping.
8. Before we go to the store, I want to get some coins out of my ___bank___.
9. The nature center will bring a live ___bat___ for our class to see.
10. We sat on the ___bank___ as we fished in the river.
11. The umpire decided the pitcher needed a new ___ball___.
12. We will ___run___ in a race tomorrow.
13. "Can we please go to the ___park___ after I clean my room?" asked Jordan.
14. That boomerang can really ___fly___!
15. Is it okay to ___park___ my bike here?
16. The baby goat, or ___kid___, follows its mother everywhere.

11

Nouns

A noun names a person, place or thing.
Examples:
   person — sister, uncle, boy, woman
   place — building, city, park, street
   thing — workbook, cat, candle, bed

Directions: Circle the nouns in each sentence. The first one has been done for you.

1. The (dog) ran into the (street.)
2. Please take this (book) to the (librarian.)
3. The red (apples) are in the (kitchen.)
4. That (scarf) belongs to the bus (driver.)
5. Get some blue (paper) from the (office) to make a (card.)
6. Look at the (parachute!)
7. Autumn (leaves) are beautiful.
8. The (lion) roared loudly at the (visitors.)

Directions: Write the nouns you circled in the correct group.

Persons	Places	Things	
librarian	street	dog	paper
driver	kitchen	book	card
visitors	office	apples	parachute
		scarf	leaves
			lion

12

Verbs

When a verb tells what one person or thing is doing now, it usually ends in **s**. Example: She **sings**.

When a verb is used with **you, I** or **we**, we do not add an **s**.

Example: I **sing**.

Directions: Write the correct verb in each sentence.

Example:
I ___write___ a newspaper about our street.   **writes, write**
1. My sister ___helps___ me sometimes.   **helps, help**
2. She ___draws___ the pictures.   **draw, draws**
3. We ___deliver___ them together.   **delivers, deliver**
4. I ___tell___ the news about all the people.   **tell, tells**
5. Mr. Macon ___grows___ the most beautiful flowers.   **grow, grows**
6. Mrs. Jones ___talks___ to her plants.   **talks, talk**
7. Kevin Turner ___lets___ his dog loose everyday.   **lets, let**
8. Little Mikey Smith ___gets___ lost once a week.   **get, gets**
9. You may ___think___ I live on an interesting street.   **thinks, think**
10. We ___say___ it's the best street in town.   **say, says**

13

Irregular Verbs

Directions: Circle the verb that completes each sentence.

1. Scientists will try to (find) found) the cure.
2. Eric (brings (brought) his lunch to school yesterday.
3. Everyday, Betsy (sings) sang) all the way home.
4. Jason (breaks (broke) the vase last night.
5. The ice had (freezes (frozen) in the tray.
6. Mitzi has (swims (swum) in that pool before.
7. Now I (choose) chose) to exercise daily.
8. The teacher has (rings (rung) the bell.
9. The boss (speaks (spoke) to us yesterday.
10. She (says (said) it twice already.

14

Irregular Verbs

Irregular verbs are verbs that do not change from the present tense to the past tense in the regular way with **d** or **ed**.
Example: sing, sang

Directions: Read the sentence and underline the verbs. Choose the past-tense form from the box and write it next to the sentence.

blow — blew	fly — flew
come — came	give — gave
take — took	wear — wore
make — made	sing — sang
grow — grew	

Example:
Dad will make a cake tonight.   ___made___
1. I will probably grow another inch this year.   ___grew___
2. I will blow out the candles.   ___blew___
3. Everyone will give me presents.   ___gave___
4. I will wear my favorite red shirt.   ___wore___
5. My cousins will come from out of town.   ___came___
6. It will take them four hours.   ___took___
7. My Aunt Betty will fly in from Cleveland.   ___flew___
8. She will sing me a song when she gets here.   ___sang___

15

Answer Key

Adjectives

Adjectives are words that tell more about nouns, such as a **happy** child, a **cold** day or a **hard** problem. Adjectives can tell how many (**one** airplane) or which one (**those** shoes).

Directions: The nouns are in bold letters. Circle the adjectives that describe the nouns.

Example: Some people have (unusual) **pets**.

1. Some people keep (wild) **animals**, like lions and bears.
2. (These) **pets** need special care.
3. (These) **animals** want to be free when they get older.
4. Even (small) **animals** can be difficult if they are wild.
5. Raccoons and squirrels are not (tame) **pets**.
6. Never touch a (wild) **animal** that may be sick.

Complete the story below by writing in your own adjectives. Use your imagination.

My Cat

My cat is a very _____ animal. She has _____
and _____ fur. Her _____ _____ ball.
She has _____ _____ has a _____ tail.
She has a _____ face and _____ whiskers.
I think she is the _____ cat in the world!

Answers will vary.

16

And and But

We can use **and** or **but** to make one longer sentence from two short ones.

Directions: Use **and** or **but** to make two short sentences into a longer, more interesting one. Write the new sentence on the line below the two short sentences.

Example:
The skunk has black fur. The skunk has a white stripe.
The skunk has black fur and a white stripe.

1. The skunk has a small head. The skunk has small ears.
The skunk has a small head and small ears.
2. The skunk has short legs. The skunk can move quickly.
The skunk has short legs but can move easily.
3. Skunks sleep in hollow trees. Skunks sleep underground.
Skunks sleep in hollow trees and underground.
4. Skunks are chased by animals. Skunks do not run away.
Skunks are chased by animals but do not run away.
5. Skunks sleep during the day. Skunks hunt at night.
Skunks sleep during the day and hunt at night.

17

Prepositions

Prepositions show relationships between the noun or pronoun and another noun in the sentence. The preposition comes before that noun.

Example: The <u>book</u> is (on) the table.

Common Prepositions

above	behind	by	near	over
across	below	in	off	through
around	beside	inside	on	under

Directions: Circle the prepositions in each sentence.

1. The dog ran fast (around) the house.
2. The plates (in) the cupboard were clean.
3. Put the card (inside) the envelope.
4. The towel (on) the sink was wet.
5. I planted flowers (in) my garden.
6. My kite flew high (above) the trees.
7. The chair (near) the counter was sticky.
8. (Under) the ground, worms live (in) their homes.
9. I put the bow (around) the box.
10. (Beside) the pond, there was a playground.

18

Parts of Speech

Nouns, pronouns, verbs, adjectives, adverbs and prepositions are all **parts of speech**.

Directions: Label the words in each sentence with the correct part of speech.

Example: The (article) cat (noun) is (verb) fat (adjective).

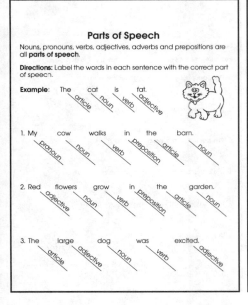

1. My (pronoun) cow (noun) walks (verb) in (preposition) the (article) barn (noun).

2. Red (adjective) flowers (noun) grow (verb) in (preposition) the (article) garden (noun).

3. The (article) large (adjective) dog (noun) was (verb) excited (adjective).

19

Subjects and Predicates

Directions: Write the words for the subject to answer the **who** or **what** questions. Write the words for the predicate to answer the **does**, **did**, **is** or **has** questions.

Example:
My friend has two pairs of sunglasses.   who? My friend
has? has two pairs of sunglasses.

1. John's dog went to school with him.   what? John's dog
did? went to school with him.
2. The Eskimo traveled by dog sled.   who? The Eskimo
did? traveled by dog sled.
3. Alex slept in his treehouse last night.   who? Alex
did? slept in his treehouse last night.
4. Cherry pie is my favorite kind of pie.   what? Cherry pie
is? is my favorite kind of pie.
5. The mail carrier brings the mail to the door.   who? The mail carrier
does? brings the mail to the door.
6. We have more than enough bricks to build the wall.   who? We
has? have more than enough bricks to build the wall.
7. The bird has a worm in its beak.   what? The bird
has? has a worm in its beak.

20

Subjects and Predicates

The **subject** tells who or what the sentence is about. The **predicate** tells what the subject does, did, is doing or will do. A complete sentence must have a subject and a predicate.

Examples:

Subject	Predicate
Sharon	writes to her grandmother every week.
The horse	ran around the track quickly.
My mom's car	is bright green.
Denise	will be here after lunch.

Directions: Circle the subject of each sentence. Underline the predicate.

1. (My sister) is a very happy person.
2. (I) wish we had more holidays in the year.
3. (Laura) is one of the nicest girls in our class.
4. (John) is fun to have as a friend.
5. (The rain) nearly ruined our picnic!
6. (My birthday present) was exactly what I wanted.
7. (Your bicycle) is parked beside my skateboard.
8. (The printer) will need to be filled with paper before you use it.
9. (Six dogs) chased my cat home yesterday!
10. (Anthony) likes to read anything he can get his hands on.

21

Answer Key

Subjects and Predicates

A **sentence** is a group of words that expresses a complete thought. It must have at least one subject and one verb.

Examples:
    Sentence: John felt tired and went to bed early.
    Not a sentence: Went to bed early.

Directions: Write **S** if the group of words is a complete sentence. Write **NS** if the group of words is not a sentence.

NS 1. Which one of you?
S 2. We're happy for the family.
S 3. We enjoyed the program very much.
NS 4. Felt left out and lonely afterwards.
S 5. Everyone said it was the best party ever!
S 6. No one knows better than I what the problem is.
NS 7. Seventeen of us!
NS 8. Quickly, before they.
S 9. Squirrels are lively animals.
S 10. Not many people believe it really happened.
S 11. Certainly, we enjoyed ourselves.

22

Simple Subjects

A **simple subject** is the main noun or pronoun in the complete subject.

Directions: Draw a line between the subject and the predicate. Circle the simple subject.

Example: The black (bear) lives in the zoo.

1. (Penguins) look like they wear tuxedos.
2. The (seal) enjoys raw fish.
3. The (monkeys) like to swing on bars.
4. The beautiful (peacock) has colorful feathers.
5. (Bats) like dark places.
6. Some (snakes) eat small rodents.
7. The orange and brown (giraffes) have long necks.
8. The baby (zebra) is close to his mother.

23

Compound Subjects

Compound subjects are two or more nouns that have the same predicate.

Directions: Combine the subjects to create one sentence with a compound subject.

Example: Jill can swing
             Whitney can swing.
             Luke can swing.
             Jill, Whitney and Luke can swing.

1. Roses grow in the garden. Tulips grow in the garden.

Roses and tulips grow in the garden.

2. Apples are fruit. Oranges are fruit. Bananas are fruit.

Apples, oranges and bananas are fruit.

3. Bears live in the zoo. Monkeys live in the zoo.

Bears and monkeys live in the zoo.

4. Jackets keep us warm. Sweaters keep us warm.

Jackets and sweaters keep us warm.

24

Simple Predicates

A **simple predicate** is the main verb or verbs in the complete predicate.

Directions: Draw a line between the complete subject and the complete predicate. Circle the simple predicate.

Example: The ripe apples (fell) to the ground.

1. The farmer (scattered) feed for the chickens.
2. The horses (galloped) wildly around the corral.
3. The baby chicks (were staying) warm by the light.
4. The tractor (was bailing) hay.
5. The silo (was) full of grain.
6. The cows (were being) milked.
7. The milk truck (drove) up to the barn.
8. The rooster (woke) everyone up.

25

Compound Predicates

Compound predicates have two or more verbs that have the same subject.

Directions: Combine the predicates to create one sentence with a compound predicate.

Example: We went to the zoo.
         We watched the monkeys.
         We went to the zoo and watched the monkeys.

1. Students read their books. Students do their work.

Students read their books and do their work.

2. Dogs can bark loudly. Dogs can do tricks.

Dogs can bark loudly and do tricks.

3. The football player caught the ball. The football player ran.

The football player caught the ball and ran.

4. My dad sawed wood. My dad stacked wood.

My dad sawed and stacked wood.

5. My teddy bear is soft. My teddy bear likes to be hugged.

My teddy bear is soft and likes to be hugged.

26

Compound Predicates

Directions: Underline the simple predicates (verbs) in each predicate.

Example: The fans <u>clapped</u> and <u>cheered</u> at the game.

1. The coach <u>talks</u> and <u>encourages</u> the team.
2. The cheerleaders <u>jump</u> and <u>yell</u>.
3. The basketball players <u>dribble</u> and <u>shoot</u> the ball.
4. The basketball <u>bounces</u> and <u>hits</u> the backboard.
5. The ball <u>rolls</u> around the rim and <u>goes</u> into the basket.
6. Everyone <u>leaps</u> up and <u>cheers</u>.
7. The team <u>scores</u> and <u>wins</u>!

27

Answer Key

Abbreviations

An **abbreviation** is the shortened form of a word. Most abbreviations begin with a capital letter and end with a period.

Mr.	Mister	St.	Street
Mrs.	Missus	Ave.	Avenue
Dr.	Doctor	Blvd.	Boulevard
A.M.	before noon	Rd.	Road
P.M.	after noon		

Days of the week: Sun. Mon. Tues. Wed. Thurs. Fri. Sat.
Months of the year: Jan. Feb. Mar. Apr. Aug. Sept. Oct. Nov. Dec.

Directions: Write the abbreviations for each word.

street	St.	doctor	Dr.	Tuesday	Tues.
road	Rd.	mister	Mr.	avenue	Ave.
missus	Mrs.	October	Oct.	Friday	Fri.
before noon	A.M.	March	Mar.	August	Aug.

Directions: Write each sentence using abbreviations.

1. On Monday at 9:00 before noon, Mister Jones had a meeting.

On Mon. at 9:00 A.M., Mr. Jones had a meeting.

2. In December, Doctor Carlson saw Missus Zuckerman.

In Dec., Dr. Carlson saw Mrs. Zuckerman.

3. One Tuesday in August, Mister Wood went to the park.

One Tues. in Aug., Mr. Wood went to the park.

28

Possessive Nouns

Possessive nouns tell who or what is the owner of something. With singular nouns, we use an apostrophe **before** the s. With plural nouns, we use an apostrophe **after** the s.

Example:
singular: one elephant
The **elephant's** dance was wonderful.
plural: more than one elephant
The **elephants'** dance was wonderful.

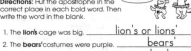

Directions: Put the apostrophe in the correct place in each bold word. Then write the word in the blank.

1. The **lion's** cage was big. _lion's or lions'_
2. The **bears'** costumes were purple. _bears'_
3. One **boy's** laughter was very loud. _boy's_
4. The **trainer's** dogs were dancing about. _trainer's or trainers'_
5. The **man's** popcorn was tasty and good. _man's_
6. **Mark's** cotton candy was delicious. _Mark's_
7. A little **girl's** balloon burst in the air. _girl's_
8. The big **clown's** tricks were very funny. _clown's or clowns'_
9. **Laura's** sister clapped for the clowns. _Laura's_
10. The **woman's** money was lost in the crowd. _woman's_
11. **Kelly's** mother picked her up early. _Kelly's_

29

Punctuation: Quotation Marks

Use quotation marks (" ") before and after the exact words of a speaker.

Examples:
I asked Aunt Martha, "How do you feel?"
"I feel awful," Aunt Martha replied.

Do not put quotation marks around words that report what the speaker said.

Examples:
Aunt Martha said she felt awful.
I asked Aunt Martha how she felt.

Directions: Write **C** if the sentence is punctuated correctly. Draw an **X** if the sentence is not punctuated correctly. The first one has been done for you.

C 1. "I want it right now!" she demanded angrily.
X 2. "Do you want it now? I asked."
X 3. She said "she felt better" now.
C 4. Her exact words were, "I feel much better now!"
C 5. "I am so thrilled to be here!" he shouted.
C 6. "Yes, I will attend," she replied.
X 7. Elizabeth said "she was unhappy."
C 8. "I'm unhappy," Elizabeth reported.
C 9. "Did you know her mother?" I asked.
X 10. I asked "whether you knew her mother."
C 11. I wondered, "What will dessert be?"
C 12. "Which will it be, salt or pepper?" the waiter asked.

30

Review

Directions: Unscramble this sentence and write it on the line below.

1. have tails short bodies wide and pigs

Pigs have wide bodies and short tails.

Directions: Put a question mark, a period or an exclamation point at the end of the following sentences:

1. Tiny pigs, called miniature pigs, weigh only 60 pounds.
2. Pigs can weigh as much as 800 pounds.
3. Wow!
4. Do pigs have spots?

Directions: Put the apostrophes in the sentences to replace a letter or to show ownership.

1. A pig's pen should have water in it.
2. They're really not animals that like mud.
3. It's an animal that needs water to keep cool.
4. Most farmers don't give them their own pools.

Directions: Put quotation marks in the sentences below.

1. "You eat like a pig," said my Uncle Homer.
2. "That is not an insult," I told him.
3. "Pigs are really clean animals," I said.

31

Vocabulary: Prefixes

A **prefix** is a syllable at the beginning of a word that changes its meaning.

Directions: Add a prefix to the beginning of each word in the box to make a word with the meaning given in each sentence below. The first one is done for you.

PREFIX	MEANING
bi	two or twice
en	to make
in	within
mis	wrong
non	not or without
pre	before
re	again
un	not

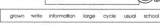
| grown | write | information | large | cycle | usual | school | sense |

1. Jimmy's foot hurt because his toenail was (growing within). ingrown
2. If you want to see what is in the background, you will have to (make bigger) the photograph. enlarge
3. I didn't do a very good job on my homework, so I will have to (write it again) it. rewrite
4. The newspaper article about the event has some (wrong facts). misinformation
5. I hope I get a (vehicle with two wheels) for my birthday. bicycle
6. The story he told was complete (words without meaning)! nonsense
7. Did you go to (school that comes before kindergarten) before you went to kindergarten? preschool
8. The ability to read words upside down is most (not usual). unusual

33

Vocabulary: Prefixes

Directions: Circle the correct word for each sentence.

1. You will need to _____ the directions before you complete this page.
   reset   (reread)   repair

2. Since she is allergic to milk products, she has to use _____ products.
   (nondairy)   nonsense   nonmetallic

3. That certainly was an _____ costume he selected for the Halloween party.
   untied   (unusual)   unable

4. The directions on the box said to _____ the oven before baking the brownies.
   (preheat)   preschool   prevent

5. "I'm sorry if I _____ you as to the cost of the trip," explained the travel agent.
   misdialed   misread   (misinformed)

6. You may use the overhead projector to _____ the picture so the whole class can see it.
   (enlarge)   enable   endanger

34

Answer Key

Vocabulary: Suffixes

A **suffix** is a syllable at the end of a word that changes its meaning. In most cases, when adding a suffix that begins with a vowel, drop the final **e** of the root word. For example, **fame** becomes **famous**. Also, change a final **y** in the root word to **i** before adding any suffix except **ing**. For example, **silly** becomes **silliness**.

Directions: Add a suffix to the end of each word in the box to make a word with the meaning given (in parentheses) in each sentence below. The first one is done for you.

SUFFIX	MEANING
ful	full of
ity	quality or degree
ive	have or tend to be
less	without or lacking
able	able to be
ness	state of
ment	act of
or	person that does something
ward	in the direction of

effect   like   thought   pay   beauty   thank   back   act   happy

1. Mike was (full of thanks) for a hot meal. __thankful__
2. I was (without thinking) for forgetting your birthday. __thoughtless__
3. The mouse trap we put out doesn't seem to have an effect. __effective__
4. In spring, the flower garden is (full of beauty). __beautiful__
5. Sally is such a (able to be liked) girl. __likable__
6. Tim fell over (in the direction of the back) because he wasn't watching where he was going. __backward__
7. Jill's wedding day was one of great (the state of being happy). __happiness__
8. The (person who performs) was very good in the play. __actor__
9. I have to make a (act of paying) for the stereo I bought. __payment__

35

Vocabulary: Suffixes

Directions: Read the story. Choose the correct word from the box to complete the sentences.

beautiful   colorful   payment   careless   director   agreement
breakable   careful   backward   basement   forward   firmness

Colleen and Marj carried the boxes down to the __basement__ apartment. "Be __careful__ with those," cautioned Colleen's mother. "All the things in that box are __breakable__." As soon as the two girls helped carry all the boxes from the moving van down the stairs, they would be able to go to school for the play tryouts. That was the __agreement__ made with Colleen's mother earlier that day.

"It won't do any good to get __careless__ with your work. Just keep at it and the job will be done quickly," she spoke with a __firmness__ in her voice.

"It's hard to see where I'm going when I walk __backward__," groaned Marj.

Colleen agreed to switch places, but they soon discovered that the last two boxes were lightweight. Each girl had her own box to carry, so each of them got to walk looking __forward__. "These are so light," remarked Marj. "What's in them?"

"These have the __beautiful__ __colorful__ hats I was telling you about. We can take them to the play tryouts with us," answered Colleen. "I bet we'll impress the __director__. Even if we don't get parts in the play, I bet our hats will!"

Colleen's mother handed each of the girls a 5-dollar bill. "I really appreciate your help. Will this be enough?"

"Thanks, Mom. You bet!" Colleen shouted as the girls ran down the sidewalk.

36

Vocabulary: Synonyms

Directions: For each paragraph, choose a word from the box that is a synonym for each bold word. Write the synonym above the word.

manual   beautiful   simple   wonderful   greatest   finished

Danielle and Mackenzie worked hard to earn the __greatest__ **best** badge for Girl Scouts. Each knew that her **workbook** __manual__ had to be __finished__ **completed** by the meeting on Saturday. Danielle's mother suggested that they work at the park and change it from a __simple__ **plain** setting to something more __beautiful__ **lovely**. The girls agreed that Danielle's mother had a __wonderful__ **great** idea to help them earn the environmental badge.

beside   tired   evening   important   competition   hopped

The two boys **jumped** __hopped__ on their bikes and headed down the hill toward the park. Corey and Justin knew that they needed to be at ball practice today or they would be unable to play in the **game** __competition__ Friday **night** __evening__. They had worked all day in the fields **alongside** __beside__ their father. They were **exhausted** __tired__, but knew that it was **crucial** __important__ that they not be late.

37

Vocabulary: Antonyms

Directions: Each bold word below has an antonym in the box. Use these words to write new sentences. The first one is done for you.

friend   vanish   quit   safety   liquids   help   scatter   worse

1. I'll **help** you **gather** all the papers on the lawn.
   The strong winds will scatter the leaves.
2. The fourth graders were learning about the many **solids** in their classroom.
   Answer should include "liquids."
3. "It's time to **begin** our lesson on the continents," said Ms. Haynes.
   Answer should include "quit."
4. "That's strange. The stapler decided to **appear** all of a sudden," said Mr. Jonson.
   Answer should include "vanish."
5. The doctor said this new medicine should **prevent** colds.
   Answer should include "help."
6. "She is our **enemy**, boys, we can't let her in our clubhouse!" cried Paul.
   Answer should include "friend."
7. I'm certain that dark cave is full of **danger!**
   Answer should include "safety."
8. Give me a chance to make the situation **better**.
   Answer should include "worse."

38

Vocabulary: Synonyms and Antonyms

Directions: Use the words in the box to write a synonym for each word below. Write it next to the S. Next to the A, write an antonym. The first one is done for you.

appear   proud   merry   straight   repair   plain
under   melted   unnecessary   late   new   smooth
embarrassed   gloomy   bent   break   fancy   above
icy   valuable   immediate   old   bumpy   vanish

1. crooked
   S: bent
   A: straight
2. frozen
   S: icy
   A: melted
3. instant
   S: immediate
   A: late
4. damage
   S: break
   A: repair
5. important
   S: valuable
   A: unnecessary
6. ashamed
   S: embarrassed
   A: proud
7. cheerful
   S: merry
   A: gloomy
8. elegant
   S: fancy
   A: plain
9. rough
   S: bumpy
   A: smooth
10. beneath
    S: under
    A: above
11. disappear
    S: vanish
    A: appear
12. ancient
    S: old
    A: new

39

Vocabulary: Homophones

Homophones are two words that sound the same, have different meanings and are usually spelled differently.
Example: write and **right**

Directions: Write the correct homophone in each sentence below.

weight — how heavy something is
wait — to be patient

threw — tossed
through — passing between

steal — to take something that doesn't belong to you
steel — a heavy metal

1. The bands marched __through__ the streets lined with many cheering people.
2. __Wait__ for me by the flagpole.
3. One of our strict rules at school is: Never __steal__ from another person.
4. Could you estimate the __weight__ of this bowling ball?
5. The bleachers have __steel__ rods on both ends and in the middle.
6. He walked in the door and __threw__ his jacket down.

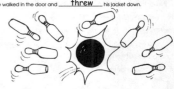

40

Answer Key

Vocabulary: Words That Sound Alike

Directions: Choose the correct word in parentheses to complete each sentence. The first one is done for you.

1. Jimmy was so **bored** that he fell asleep. (board, bored)
2. We'll need a **board** and some nails to repair the fence. (board, bored)
3. Do you want **dessert** after dinner? (desert, dessert)
4. A **desert** is hot and sandy. (desert, dessert)
5. The soldier had a **medal** pinned to his uniform. (medal, metal)
6. Gold is a precious **metal**. (medal, metal)
7. Don't **peek** at your present before Christmas! (peak, peek)
8. They climbed to the **peak** of the mountain. (peak, peek)
9. Jack had to repair the emergency **brake** on his car. (brake, break)
10. Please be careful not to **break** my bicycle. (brake, break)
11. The race **course** was a very difficult one. (coarse, course)
12. We will need some **coarse** sandpaper to finish the job. (coarse, course)

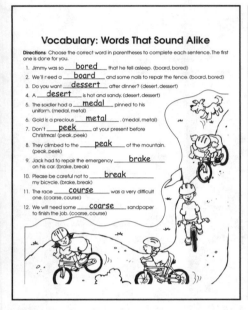

41

Proper Nouns

Proper nouns name specific persons, places or things.

Examples:

person — Ms. Steiner, Judge Jones, Lt. Raydon
place — Crestview School, California, China
thing — Declaration of Independence, Encyclopedia Britannica

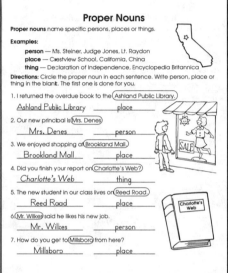

Directions: Circle the proper noun in each sentence. Write person, place or thing in the blank. The first one is done for you.

1. I returned the overdue book to the (Ashland Public Library.)
   Ashland Public Library   _place_
2. Our new principal is (Mrs. Denes.)
   Mrs. Denes   _person_
3. We enjoyed shopping at (Brookland Mall.)
   Brookland Mall   _place_
4. Did you finish your report on (Charlotte's Web?)
   Charlotte's Web   _thing_
5. The new student in our class lives on (Reed Road.)
   Reed Road   _place_
6. (Mr. Wilkes) said he likes his new job.
   Mr. Wilkes   _person_
7. How do you get to (Millsboro) from here?
   Millsboro   _place_

42

Proper Nouns: Capitalization

Proper nouns always begin with a capital letter.

Examples:

Monday   Mr. Logan
Texas   Hamburger Avenue
Karen   Rover

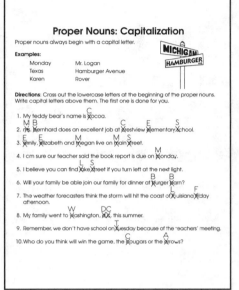

Directions: Cross out the lowercase letters at the beginning of the proper nouns. Write capital letters above them. The first one is done for you.

1. My teddy bear's name is Cocoa.
2. Mrs. Bernhard does an excellent job at Crestview Elementary School.
3. Emily, Elizabeth and Megan live on Main Street.
4. I am sure our teacher said the book report is due on Monday.
5. I believe you can find Like Street if you turn left at the next light.
6. Will your family be able join our family for dinner at Burger Barn?
7. The weather forecasters think the storm will hit the coast of Louisiana Friday afternoon.
8. My family went to Washington, DC, this summer.
9. Remember, we don't have school on Tuesday because of the teachers' meeting.
10. Who do you think will win the game, the Cougars or the Arrows?

43

Pronouns

A **pronoun** is a word that takes the place of a noun in a sentence.

Examples:

I, my, mine, me
we, our, ours, us
you, your, yours
he, his, him
she, her, hers
it, its
they, their, theirs, them

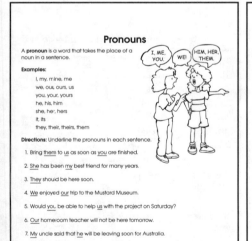

Directions: Underline the pronouns in each sentence.

1. Bring them to us as soon as you are finished.
2. She has been my best friend for many years.
3. They should be here soon.
4. We enjoyed our trip to the Mustard Museum.
5. Would you be able to help us with the project on Saturday?
6. Our homeroom teacher will not be here tomorrow.
7. My uncle said that he will be leaving soon for Australia.
8. Hurry! Could you please open the door for him?
9. She dropped her gloves when she got off the bus.
10. I can't figure out who the mystery writer is today.

44

Nouns and Pronouns

To make a story or report more interesting, pronouns can be substituted for "overused" nouns.

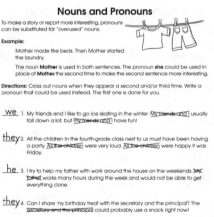

Example:

Mother made the beds. Then Mother started the laundry.
The noun **Mother** is used in both sentences. The pronoun **she** could be used in place of **Mother** the second time to make the second sentence more interesting.

Directions: Cross out nouns when they appear a second and/or third time. Write a pronoun that could be used instead. The first one is done for you.

_we_ 1. My friends and I like to go ice skating in the winter. ~~My friends and I~~ usually fall down a lot, but ~~my friends and I~~ have fun!

they 2. All the children in the fourth-grade class next to us must have been having a party. ~~All the children~~ were very loud. ~~All the children~~ were happy it was Friday.

_he_ 3. I try to help my father with work around the house on the weekends. ~~My father~~ works many hours during the week and would not be able to get everything done.

they 4. Can I share my birthday treat with the secretary and the principal? The ~~secretary and the principal~~ could probably use a snack right now!

him 5. I know Mr. Jones needs a copy of this history report. Please take it to ~~Mr. Jones~~ when you finish.

45

Pronoun Referents

A **pronoun referent** is the noun or nouns a pronoun refers to.

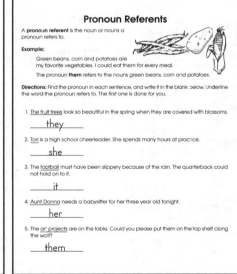

Example:

Green beans, corn and potatoes are my favorite vegetables. I could eat them for every meal.
The pronoun **them** refers to the nouns green beans, corn and potatoes.

Directions: Find the pronoun in each sentence, and write it in the blank below. Underline the word the pronoun refers to. The first one is done for you.

1. The fruit trees look so beautiful in the spring when they are covered with blossoms.
   they
2. Tori is a high school cheerleader. She spends many hours at practice.
   she
3. The football must have been slippery because of the rain. The quarterback could not hold on to it.
   _it_
4. Aunt Donna needs a babysitter for her three year old tonight.
   her
5. The art projects are on the table. Could you please put them on the top shelf along the wall?
   them

46

Answer Key

Pronoun Referents

Directions: Read each sentence carefully. Draw a line to connect each sentence to the correct pronoun.

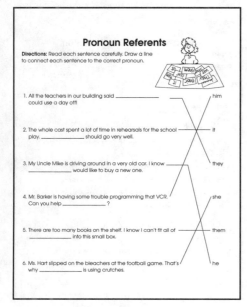

1. All the teachers in our building said _____ could use a day off!

2. The whole cast spent a lot of time in rehearsals for the school play. _____ should go very well.

3. My Uncle Mike is driving around in a very old car. I know _____ would like to buy a new one.

4. Mr. Barker is having some trouble programming that VCR. Can you help _____ ?

5. There are too many books on the shelf. I know I can't fit all of _____ into this small box.

6. Ms. Hart slipped on the bleachers at the football game. That's why _____ is using crutches.

him
it
they
she
them
he

47

Irregular Verbs: Past Tense

Irregular verbs change completely in the past tense. Unlike regular verbs, past-tense forms of irregular verbs are not formed by adding **ed**.

Example: The past tense of **go** is **went**.

Other verbs change some letters to form the past tense.
Example: The past tense of **break** is **broke**.

A **helping verb** helps to tell about the past. **Has**, **have** and **had** are helping verbs used with action verbs to show the action occurred in the past. The past-tense form of the irregular verb sometimes changes when a helping verb is added.

Present-Tense Irregular Verb	Past-Tense Irregular Verb	Past-Tense Irregular Verb With Helper
go	went	have/has/had gone
see	saw	have/has/had seen
do	did	have/has/had done
bring	brought	have/has/had brought
sing	sang	have/has/had sung
drive	drove	have/has/had driven
swim	swam	have/has/had swum
sleep	slept	have/has/had slept

Directions: Choose four words from the chart. Write one sentence using the past-tense form of the verb without a helping verb. Write another sentence using the past-tense form with a helping verb.

1. _____
2. _____
3. _____   *Answers will vary.*
4. _____

48

The Irregular Verb "Be"

Be is an irregular verb. The present-tense forms of **be** are **be, am, is** and **are**. The past-tense forms of **be** are **was** and **were**.

Directions: Write the correct form of **be** in the blanks. The first one has been done for you.

1. I ___am___ so happy for you!

2. Jared ___was___ unfriendly yesterday.

3. English can ___be___ a lot of fun to learn.

4. They ___are___ among the nicest people I know.

5. They ___were___ late yesterday.

6. She promises she ___is___ going to arrive on time.

7. I ___am___ nervous right now about the test.

8. If you ___are___ satisfied now, so am I.

9. He ___was___ as nice to me last week as I had hoped.

10. He can ___be___ very gracious.

11. Would you ___be___ offended if I moved your desk?

12. He ___was___ watching at the window for me yesterday.

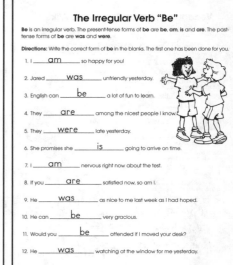

49

Verbs: "Was" and "Were"

Singular	Plural
I was	we were
you were	you were
he, she, it was	they were

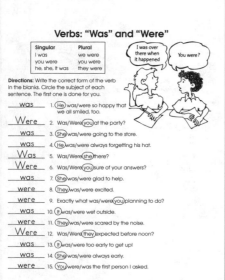

Directions: Write the correct form of the verb in the blanks. Circle the subject of each sentence. The first one is done for you.

1. ___was___ (He) was/were so happy that we all smiled, too.
2. ___Were___ Was/Were (you) at the party?
3. ___was___ (She) was/were going to the store.
4. ___was___ (He) was/were always forgetting his hat.
5. ___Was___ Was/Were (she) there?
6. ___Were___ Was/Were (you) sure of your answers?
7. ___was___ (She) was/were glad to help.
8. ___were___ (They) was/were excited.
9. ___was___ Exactly what was/were (you) planning to do?
10. ___was___ (It) was/were wet outside.
11. ___were___ (They) was/were scared by the noise.
12. ___Were___ Was/Were (they) expected before noon?
13. ___was___ (It) was/were too early to get up!
14. ___was___ (She) was/were always early.
15. ___were___ (You) were/was the first person I asked.

50

Verbs: Present, Past and Future Tense

The **present tense** of a verb tells what is happening now.

Examples:
   I **am** happy.
   I **run** fast.

The **past tense** of a verb tells what has already happened.

Examples:
   I **was** happy.
   I **ran** fast.

The **future tense** of a verb refers to what is going to happen. The word **will** usually comes before the future tense of a verb.

Examples:
   I **will be** happy.
   I **will run** fast.

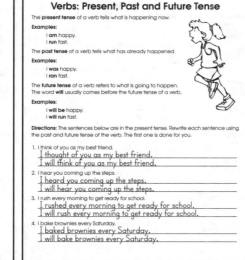

Directions: The sentences below are in the present tense. Rewrite each sentence using the past and future tense of the verb. The first one is done for you.

1. I think of you as my best friend.
   I thought of you as my best friend.
   I will think of you as my best friend.
2. I hear you coming up the steps.
   I heard you coming up the steps.
   I will hear you coming up the steps.
3. I rush every morning to get ready for school.
   I rushed every morning to get ready for school.
   I will rush every morning to get ready for school.
4. I bake brownies every Saturday.
   I baked brownies every Saturday.
   I will bake brownies every Saturday.

51

Verbs: Present, Past and Future Tense

Directions: Read the following sentences. Write **PRES** if the sentence is in present tense. Write **PAST** if the sentence is in past tense. Write **FUT** if the sentence is in future tense. The first one is done for you.

FUT 1. I will be thrilled to accept the award.

FUT 2. Will you go with me to the dentist?

PAST 3. I thought he looked familiar!

PAST 4. They ate every single slice of pizza.

PRES 5. I run myself ragged sometimes.

PRES 6. Do you think this project is worthwhile?

PAST 7. No one has been able to repair the broken plate.

PRES 8. Thoughtful gifts are always appreciated.

PAST 9. I like the way he sang!

FUT 10. With a voice like that, he will go a long way.

PRES 11. It's my fondest hope that they visit soon.

PAST 12. I wanted that coat very much.

FUT 13. She'll be happy to take your place.

PRES 14. Everyone thinks the test will be a breeze.

PRES 15. Collecting stamps is her favorite hobby.

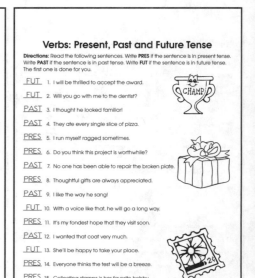

52

Answer Key

Adding "ed" to Make Verbs Past Tense

To make many verbs past tense, add **ed**.

Examples:

cook + ed = cooked   wish + ed = wished   play + ed = played

When a verb ends in a **silent e**, drop the **e** and add **ed**.

Examples:

hops + ed = hoped   hate + ed = hated

When a verb ends in **y** after a consonant, change the **y** to **i** and add **ed**.

Examples:

hurry + ed = hurried   marry + ed = married

When a verb ends in a single consonant after a single short vowel, double the final consonant before adding **ed**.

Examples:

stop + ed = stopped   hop + ed = hopped

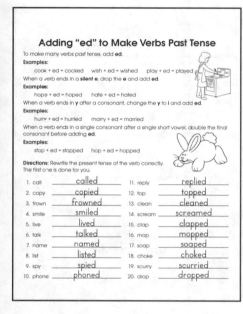

Directions: Rewrite the present tense of the verb correctly. The first one is done for you.

1. call	called	11. reply	replied
2. copy	copied	12. top	topped
3. frown	frowned	13. clean	cleaned
4. smile	smiled	14. scream	screamed
5. live	lived	15. clap	clapped
6. talk	talked	16. mop	mopped
7. name	named	17. soap	soaped
8. list	listed	18. choke	choked
9. spy	spied	19. scurry	scurried
10. phone	phoned	20. drop	dropped

53

Adjectives That Add "er"

The suffix **er** is often added to adjectives to compare two things.

Example:

My feet are **large**.

Your feet are **larger** than my feet.

When a one-syllable adjective ends in a single consonant and the vowel is short, double the final consonant before adding **er**. When a word ends in two or more consonants, add **er**.

Examples:

big — bigger (single consonant)

bold — bolder (two consonants)

When an adjective ends in **y**, change the **y** to **i** before adding **er**.

Examples:

easy — easier

greasy — greasier

breezy — breezier

Directions: Use the correct rule to add **er** to the words below. The first one is done for you.

1. fast	faster	11. skinny	skinnier
2. thin	thinner	12. fat	fatter
3. long	longer	13. poor	poorer
4. few	fewer	14. juicy	juicier
5. ugly	uglier	15. early	earlier
6. silly	sillier	16. clean	cleaner
7. busy	busier	17. thick	thicker
8. grand	grander	18. creamy	creamier
9. lean	leaner	19. deep	deeper
10. young	younger	20. lazy	lazier

54

Adjectives That Add "est"

The suffix **est** is often added to adjectives to compare more than two things.

Example:

My glass is **full**.

Your glass is **fuller**.

His glass is **fullest**.

When a one-syllable adjective ends in a single consonant and the vowel sound is short, you usually double the final consonant before adding **est**.

Examples:

big — biggest (short vowel)

steep — steepest (long vowel)

When an adjective ends in **y**, change the **y** to **i** before adding **est**.

Example:

easy — easiest

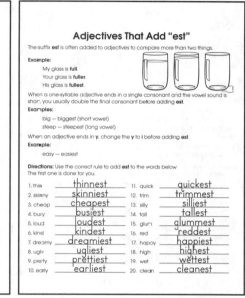

Directions: Use the correct rule to add **est** to the words below. The first one is done for you.

1. thin	thinnest	11. quick	quickest
2. skinny	skinniest	12. trim	trimmest
3. cheap	cheapest	13. silly	silliest
4. busy	busiest	14. tall	tallest
5. loud	loudest	15. glum	glummest
6. kind	kindest	16. red	reddest
7. dreamy	dreamiest	17. happy	happiest
8. ugly	ugliest	18. high	highest
9. pretty	prettiest	19. wet	wettest
10. early	earliest	20. clean	cleanest

55

Adding "er" and "est" to Adjectives

Directions: Circle the correct adjective for each sentence. The first one is done for you.

1. Of all the students in the gym, her voice was (louder, (loudest)).

2. "I can tell you are ((busier), busiest) than I am," he said to the librarian.

3. If you and Carl stand back to back, I can see which one is ((taller), tallest).

4. She is the (kinder, (kindest)) teacher in the whole building.

5. Wow! That is the (bigger, (biggest)) pumpkin I have ever seen!

6. I believe your flashlight is ((brighter), brightest) than mine.

7. "This is the (cleaner, (cleanest)) your room has been in a long time," Mother said.

8. The leaves on that plant are ((prettier), prettiest) than the ones on the window sill.

56

Adjectives Preceded by "More"

Most adjectives of two or more syllables are preceded by the word **more** as a way to show comparison between two things.

Examples:

Correct: intelligent, more intelligent

Incorrect: intelligenter

Correct: famous, more famous

Incorrect: famouser

Directions: Write **more** before the adjectives that fit the rule. Draw an **X** in the blanks of the adjectives that do not fit the rule. To test yourself, say the words aloud using **more** and adding **er** to hear which way sounds correct. The first two have been done for you.

X	1. cheap	more	11. awful
more	2. beautiful	more	12. delicious
X	3. quick	more	13. embarrassing
more	4. terrible	X	14. nice
more	5. difficult	more	15. often
more	6. interesting	X	16. hard
more	7. polite	more	17. valuable
X	8. cute	X	18. close
X	9. dark	X	19. fast
X	10. sad	more	20. important

57

Adjectives Preceded by "Most"

Most adjectives of two or more syllables are preceded by the word **most** as a way to show comparison between more than two things.

Examples:

Correct: intelligent, most intelligent

Incorrect: intelligentest

Correct: famous, most famous

Incorrect: famousest

Directions: Read the following groups of sentences. In the last sentence for each group, write the adjective preceded by **most**. The first one is done for you.

1. My uncle is intelligent.
My aunt is more intelligent.
My cousin is the ___most intelligent___

2. I am thankful.
My brother is more thankful.
My parents are the ___most thankful___

3. Your sister is polite.
Your brother is more polite.
You are the ___most polite___

4. The house was expensive.
The sweater was more expensive.
The coat was the ___most expensive___

5. The class was fortunate.
The teacher was more fortunate.
The principal was the ___most fortunate___

6. The cookies were delicious.
The cake was even more delicious.
The brownies were the ___most delicious___

7. The painting is elaborate.
The sculpture is more elaborate.
The finger painting is the ___most elaborate___

58

Answer Key

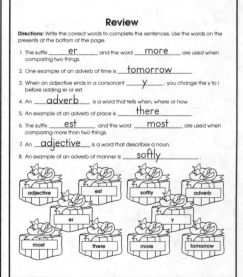

Answer Key

Review

Directions: For the bold word in each sentence, write **N** for noun, **V** for verb, **ADJ** for adjective or **ADV** for adverb.

<u>ADJ</u> 1. She is the **tallest** one outside.

<u>N</u> 2. **She** is the tallest one outside.

<u>V</u> 3. She **is** the tallest one outside.

<u>ADV</u> 4. She is the tallest one **outside**.

Directions: For the bold word in each sentence, write **P** for adverb of place, **T** for adverb of time or **M** for adverb of manner.

<u>P</u> 5. Your shoes are **downstairs**.

<u>M</u> 6. His response was **speedy**.

<u>P</u> 7. **Here** is my homework.

<u>T</u> 8. The present will be mailed **tomorrow**.

Directions: Add **er** and **est** or **more** and **most** to the words below to show comparison.

9. fat — fatter — fattest

10. grateful — more grateful — most grateful

11. serious — more serious — most serious

12. easy — easier — easiest

Directions: For the bold word in each sentence, write **ADV** for adverb or **ADJ** for adjective.

<u>ADJ</u> 13. **Grumpy** people are not pleasant.

<u>ADV</u> 14. Put the package **there**, please.

<u>ADV</u> 15. **Upstairs** is where I sleep.

<u>ADJ</u> 16. **Warm** blankets feel toasty on cold nights.

65

Conjunctions

Directions: Choose the best conjunction from the box to combine the pairs of sentences. Then rewrite the sentences.

and	but	or	because	when	after	so

Answers may vary:

1. I like Leah. I like Ben.
I like Leah and Ben.

2. Should I eat the orange? Should I eat the apple?
Should I eat the orange or the apple?

3. You will get a reward. You turned in the lost item.
You will get a reward when you turn in the lost item.

4. I really mean what I say! You had better listen!
I really mean what I say, so you had better listen!

5. I like you. You're nice, friendly, helpful and kind.
I like you because you're nice, friendly, helpful and kind.

6. You can have dessert. You ate all your peas.
You can have dessert because you ate all your peas.

7. I like your shirt better. You should decide for yourself.
I like your shirt better, but you should decide for yourself.

8. We walked out of the building. We heard the fire alarm.
We walked out of the building after we heard the fire alarm.

9. I like to sing folk songs. I like to play the guitar.
I like to sing folk songs, and I like to play the guitar.

66

Conjunctions

Words that join sentences or combine ideas like **and**, **but**, **or**, **because**, **when**, **after** and **so** are called **conjunctions**.

Examples:

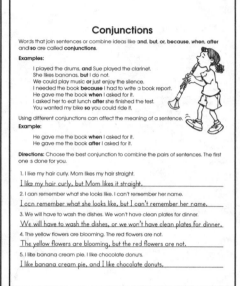

I played the drums, **and** Sue played the clarinet.
She likes bananas, **but** I do not.
We could play music **or** just enjoy the silence.
I needed the book **because** I had to write a book report.
He gave me the book **when** I asked for it.
I asked her to eat lunch **after** she finished the test.
You wanted my bike **so** you could ride it.

Using different conjunctions can affect the meaning of a sentence.

Example:

He gave me the book **when** I asked for it.
He gave me the book **after** I asked for it.

Directions: Choose the best conjunction to combine the pairs of sentences. The first one is done for you.

1. I like my hair curly. Mom likes my hair straight.
I like my hair curly, but Mom likes it straight.

2. I can remember what she looks like. I can't remember her name.
I can remember what she looks like, but I can't remember her name.

3. We will have to wash the dishes. We won't have clean plates for dinner.
We will have to wash the dishes, or we won't have clean plates for dinner.

4. The yellow flowers are blooming. The red flowers are not.
The yellow flowers are blooming, but the red flowers are not.

5. I like banana cream pie. I like chocolate donuts.
I like banana cream pie, and I like chocolate donuts.

67

Run-On Sentences

A **run-on sentence** occurs when two or more sentences are joined together without punctuation.

Examples:

Run-on sentence: I lost my way once did you?
Two sentences with correct punctuation: I lost my way once. Did you?
Run-on sentence: I found the recipe it was not hard to follow.
Two sentences with correct punctuation: I found the recipe. It was not hard to follow.

Directions: Rewrite the run-on sentences correctly with periods, exclamation points and question marks. The first one is done for you.

1. Did you take my umbrella I can't find it anywhere!
Did you take my umbrella? I can't find it anywhere!

2. How can you stand that noise I can't!
How can you stand that noise? I can't!

3. The cookies are gone I see only crumbs.
The cookies are gone. I see only crumbs.

4. The dogs were barking they were hungry.
The dogs were barking. They were hungry.

5. She is quite ill please call a doctor immediately!
She is quite ill. Please call a doctor immediately!

6. The clouds came up we knew the storm would hit soon.
The clouds came up. We knew the storm would hit soon.

7. You weren't home he stopped by this morning.
You weren't home. He stopped by this morning.

68

Combining Sentences

Some simple sentences can be easily combined into one sentence.

Examples:

Simple sentences: The bird sang. The bird was tiny. The bird was in the tree.
Combined sentence: The tiny bird sang in the tree.

Directions: Combine each set of simple sentences into one sentence. The first one is done for you.

1. The big girls laughed. They were friendly. They helped the little girls.
The big, friendly girls laughed as they helped the little girls.

2. The dog was hungry. The dog whimpered. The dog looked at its bowl.

3. Be quiet now. I want you to listen. You listen to my joke!

4. I lost my p— Answers may vary.

5. I see my mother. My mother is walking. My mother is walking down the street.

6. Do you like ice cream? Do you like hot dogs? Do you like mustard?

7. Tell me you'll do it! Tell me you will! Tell me right now!

69

Combining Sentences in Paragraph Form

A **paragraph** is a group of sentences that share the same idea.

Directions: Rewrite the paragraph by combining the simple sentences into larger sentences.

Jason awoke early. He threw off his covers. He ran to his window. He looked outside. He saw snow. It was white and fluffy. Jason thought of something. He thought of his sled. His sled was in the garage. He quickly ate breakfast. He dressed warmly. He got his sled. He went outside. He went to play in the snow.

Jason awoke early and threw off his covers. He ran to his window and looked outside. He saw white and fluffy snow. Jason thought of his sled in the garage. He quickly ate breakfast and dressed warmly. He got his sled and went outside to play in the snow.

Answer may vary.

70

Answer Key

Identifying the Parts of a Sentence

The **subject** tells who or what the sentence is about. The subject is always a noun or pronoun. A **noun** is a word that names a person, place or thing. A **pronoun** is a word that takes the place of a noun.

Example:
The handsome **boy** danced yesterday.
Boy is the subject. The sentence is about the boy.

A **verb** tells what something does or that something exists.

Example:
The handsome boy **danced** yesterday.
Danced is the verb. It shows action.

An **adverb** tells when, where or how something happened.

Example:
The handsome boy danced **yesterday**.
Yesterday is an adverb. It tells when the boy danced.

An **adjective** describes a noun.

Example:
The **handsome** boy danced yesterday.
Handsome is an adjective. It describes the noun **boy**.

Directions: Write **N** for noun, **V** for verb, **ADJ** for adjective or **ADV** for adverb for the bold word in each sentence.

ADJ 1. She is an **excellent** singer.
N 2. The huge black **horse** easily won the race.
ADJ 3. The **red-haired** girl was shy.
ADV 4. Joshua **quickly** finished his homework and went out to play.
N 5. **Carrots** are my least favorite vegetable.
N 6. Why should **I** always have to take out the trash?
V 7. That girl **ran** like the wind!
V 8. Elizabeth **told** her sister to pick him up at noon.
ADJ 9. He was glad he had a **warm** coat to wear.
ADV 10. I live **nearby**.

71

Review

Directions: Circle the subjects.

1. (Everyone) felt the day had been a great success.
2. (Christina and Andrea) were both happy to take the day off.
3. (No one) really understood why he was crying.
4. (Mr. Winston, Ms. Fuller and Ms. Landers) took us on a field trip.

Directions: Underline the predicates.

5. Who can tell what will happen tomorrow?
6. Mark was a carpenter by trade and a talented painter, too.
7. The animals yelped and whined in their cages.
8. Airplane rides made her feel sick to her stomach.

Directions: Combine the sentences to make one sentence with a compound subject.

9. Elizabeth ate everything in sight. George ate everything in sight.
Elizabeth and George ate everything in sight.

10. Wishing something will happen won't make it so. Dreaming something will happen won't make it so.
Wishing and dreaming something will happen won't make it so.

Directions: Combine the sentences to make one sentence with a compound predicate.

11. I jumped for joy. I hugged all my friends.
I jumped for joy and hugged all my friends.

12. She ran around the track before the race. She warmed up before the race.
She ran around the track and warmed up before the race.

72

Direct Objects

A **direct object** is the word or words that come after a verb to complete its meaning. The direct object answers the question **whom** or **what**.

Examples:
Aaron wrote a **letter**.
Letter is the direct object. It tells what Aaron wrote.
We heard **Tom**.
Tom is the direct object. It tells whom we heard.

Directions: Identify the direct object in each sentence. Write it in the blank.

me 1. My mother called me.
it 2. The baby dropped it.
mayor 3. I met the mayor.
you 4. I like you!
them 5. No one visited them.
cat 6. We all heard the cat.
stars 7. Jessica saw the stars.
nap 8. She needs a nap.
bone 9. The dog chewed the bone.
doll 10. He hugged the doll.
radio 11. I sold the radio.
banana 12. Douglas ate the banana.
house 13. We finally found the house.

73

Indirect Objects

An **indirect object** is the word or words that come between the verb and the direct object. Indirect objects tells **to whom** or **what** or **for whom** or **what** something is done.

Examples:
He read **me** a funny story.
Me is the indirect object. It tells to whom something (reading a story) was done.
She told her **mother** the truth.
Mother is the indirect object. It tells to whom something (telling the truth) was done.

Directions: Identify the indirect object in each sentence. Write it in the blank.

1. The coach gave Bill a trophy. — Bill
2. He cooked me a wonderful meal. — me
3. She told Maria her secret. — Maria
4. Someone gave my mother a gift. — mother
5. The class gave the principal a new flag for the cafeteria. — principal
6. The restaurant pays the waiter a good salary. — waiter
7. You should tell your dad the truth. — dad
8. She sent her son a plane ticket. — son
9. The waiter served the patron a salad. — patron
10. Grandma gave the baby a kiss. — baby
11. I sold Steve some cookies. — Steve
12. He told us six jokes. — us
13. She brought the boy a sucker. — boy

74

Direct and Indirect Objects

Example: Sharon told Jennifer a funny (story.)

Jennifer is the indirect object. It tells **to whom** Sharon told the story. Story is the direct object. It tells **what** Sharon told.

Directions: Circle the direct object in each sentence. Underline the indirect object.

1. The teacher gave the class a (test.)
2. Josh brought Elizabeth the (book.)
3. Someone left the cat a (present.)
4. The poet read David all his (poems.)
5. My big brother handed me the (ticket.)
6. Luke told everyone the (secret.)
7. Jason handed his dad the (newspaper.)
8. Mother bought Jack a (suitcase.)
9. They cooked us an excellent (dinner.)
10. I loaned Jonathan my (bike.)
11. She threw him a curve (ball.)
12. You tell Dad the (truth!)

75

Punctuation: Commas

Use a comma to separate words in a series. A comma is used after each word in a series but is not needed before the last word. Both ways are correct. In your own writing, be consistent about which style you use.

Examples:
We ate apples, oranges, and pears.
We ate apples, oranges and pears.

Always use a comma between the name of a city and a state.

Example:
She lives in Fresno, California.
He lives in Wilmington, Delaware.

Directions: Write **C** if the sentence is punctuated correctly. Draw an **X** if the sentence is not punctuated correctly. The first one is done for you.

X 1. She ordered shoes, dresses and shirts to be sent to her home in Oakland California.
C 2. No one knew her pets' names were Fido, Spot and Tiger.
X 3. He likes green beans lima beans, and corn on the cob.
C 4. Typing paper, pens and pencils are all needed for school.
C 5. Send your letters to her in College Park, Maryland.
C 6. Send your letter to her in Reno, Nevada.
X 7. Before he lived in New York, City he lived in San Diego, California.
X 8. She mailed postcards, and letters to him in Lexington, Kentucky.
C 9. Teacups, saucers, napkins, and silverware were piled high.
C 10. Can someone give me a ride to Indianapolis, Indiana?

76

Answer Key

Punctuation: Commas (77)

Use a comma to separate the number of the day of a month and the year. Do not use a comma to separate the month and year if no day is given.

Examples:

June 14, 1999

June 1999

Use a comma after **yes** or **no** when it is the first word in a sentence.

Examples:

Yes, I will do it right now.

No, I don't want any.

Directions: Write **C** if the sentence is punctuated correctly. Draw an **X** if the sentence is not punctuated correctly. The first one is done for you.

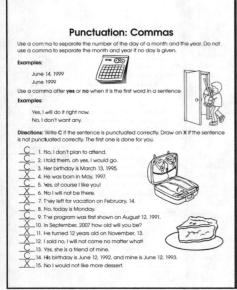

- C 1. No, I don't plan to attend.
- C 2. I told them, oh yes, I would go.
- C 3. Her birthday is March 13, 1995.
- X 4. He was born in May, 1997.
- X 5. Yes, of course I like you!
- X 6. No I will not be there.
- X 7. They left for vacation on February, 14.
- C 8. No, today is Monday.
- C 9. The program was first shown on August 12, 1991.
- X 10. In September, 2007 how old will you be?
- X 11. He turned 12 years old on November, 13.
- C 12. I said no, I will not come no matter what!
- C 13. Yes, she is a friend of mine.
- C 14. His birthday is June 12, 1992, and mine is June 12, 1993.
- X 15. No I would not like more dessert.

"Good" and "Well" (78)

Use the word **good** to describe a noun. Good is an adjective.

Example: She is a **good** teacher.

Use the word **well** to tell or ask how something is done or to describe someone's health. Well is an adverb.

Example: She is not feeling **well**.

Directions: Write **good** or **well** in the blanks to complete the sentences correctly. The first one is done for you.

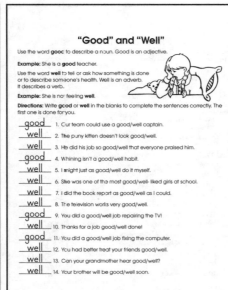

- good 1. Our team could use a good/well captain.
- well 2. The puny kitten doesn't look good/well.
- well 3. He did his job so good/well that everyone praised him.
- good 4. Whining isn't a good/well habit.
- well 5. I might just as good/well do it myself.
- well 6. She was one of the most good/well- liked girls at school.
- well 7. I did the book report as good/well as I could.
- well 8. The television works very good/well.
- good 9. You did a good/well job repairing the TV!
- good 10. Thanks for a job good/well done!
- good 11. You did a good/well job fixing the computer.
- well 12. You had better treat your friends good/well.
- well 13. Can your grandmother hear good/well?
- well 14. Your brother will be good/well soon.

"Your" and "You're" (79)

The word **your** shows possession.

Examples:

Is that **your** book?

I visited **your** class.

The word **you're** is a contraction for **you are**. A **contraction** is two words joined together as one. An apostrophe shows where letters have been left out.

Examples:

You're doing well on that painting.

If **you're** going to pass the test, you should study.

Directions: Write **your** or **you're** on the blanks to complete the sentences correctly. The first one is done for you.

- You're 1. Your/You're the best friend I have!
- You're 2. Your/You're going to drop that!
- Your 3. Your/You're brother came to see me.
- your 4. Is that your/you're cat?
- you're 5. If your/you're going, you'd better hurry!
- your 6. Why are your/you're fingers so red?
- your 7. It's none of your/you're business!
- Your 8. Your/You're bike's front tire is low.
- You're 9. Your/You're kidding!
- your 10. Have it your/you're way.
- your 11. I thought your/you're report was great!
- you're 12. He thinks your/you're wonderful!
- your 13. What is your/you're first choice?
- your 14. What's your/you're opinion?
- you're 15. If your/you're going, so am I!
- You're 16. Your/You're welcome.

"Its" and "It's" (80)

The word **its** shows ownership.

Examples:

Its leaves have all turned green.

Its paw was injured.

The word **it's** is a contraction for **it is**.

Examples:

It's better to be early than late.

It's not fair!

Directions: Write **its** or **it's** to complete the sentences correctly. The first one is done for you.

- It's 1. Its/It's never too late for ice cream!
- Its 2. Its/It's eyes are already open.
- It's 3. Its/It's your turn to wash the dishes!
- Its 4. Its/It's cage was left open.
- Its 5. Its/It's engine was beyond repair.
- Its 6. Its/It's teeth were long and pointed.
- its 7. Did you see its/it's hind legs?
- it's 8. Why do you think its/it's mine?
- it's 9. Do you think its/it's the right color?
- its 10. Don't pet its/it's fur too hard!
- It's 11. Its/It's from my Uncle Harry.
- it's 12. Can you tell its/it's a surprise?
- its 13. Is its/it's stall always this clean?
- It's 14. Its/It's not time to eat yet.
- it's 15. She says its/it's working now.

"Can" and "May" (81)

The word **can** means **am able to** or **to be able to.**

Examples:

I **can** do that for you.

Can you do that for me?

The word **may** means be **allowed to** or **permitted to.** May is used to ask or give permission. **May** can also mean **might** or **perhaps.**

Examples:

May I be excused?

You **may** sit here.

Directions: Write **can** or **may** on the blanks to complete the sentences correctly. The first one is done for you.

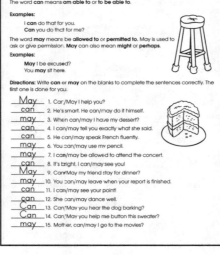

- May 1. Can/May I help you?
- can 2. He's smart. He can/may do it himself.
- may 3. When can/may I have my dessert?
- can 4. I can/may tell you exactly what she said.
- can 5. He can/may speak French fluently.
- may 6. You can/may use my pencil.
- may 7. I can/may be allowed to attend the concert.
- can 8. It's bright. I can/may see you!
- May 9. Can/May my friend stay for dinner?
- may 10. You can/may leave when your report is finished.
- can 11. I can/may see your point!
- can 12. She can/may dance well.
- Can 13. Can/May you hear the dog barking?
- Can 14. Can/May you help me button this sweater?
- may 15. Mother, can/may I go to the movies?

"Sit" and "Set" (82)

The word **sit** means **to rest.**

Examples:

Please **sit** here!

Will you **sit** by me?

The word **set** means **to put** or **place something.**

Examples:

Set your purse there.

Set the dishes on the table.

Directions: Write **sit** or **set** to complete the sentences correctly. The first one is done for you.

- sit 1. Would you please sit/set down here?
- set 2. You can sit/set the groceries there.
- set 3. She sit/set her suitcase in the closet.
- set 4. He sit/set his watch for half past three.
- sit 5. She's a person who can't sit/set still
- Set 6. Sit/Set the baby on the couch beside me.
- set 7. Where did you sit/set your new shoes?
- sit 8. They decided to sit/set together during the movie.
- set 9. Let me sit/set you straight on that!
- sit 10. Instead of swimming, he decided to sit/set in the water.
- sit 11. He sit/set the greasy pan in the sink.
- set 12. She sit/set the file folder on her desk.
- sit 13. Don't ever sit/set on the refrigerator
- set 14. She sit/set the candles on the cake.
- set 15. Get ready! Get sit/set! Go!

Answer Key

"They're," "Their," "There" (83)

The word **they're** is a contraction for **they are**.

Examples:
> They're our very best friends!
> Ask them if **they're** coming over tomorrow.

The word **their** shows ownership.

Examples:
> **Their** dog is friendly.
> It's **their** bicycle.

The word **there** shows place or direction.

Examples:
> Look over **there**.
> **There** it is.

Directions: Write **they're, their** or **there** to complete the sentences correctly. The first one is done for you.

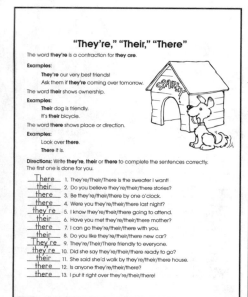

1. **There** They're/Their/There is the sweater I want!
2. **their** Do you believe they're/their/there stories?
3. **there** Be they're/their/there by one o'clock.
4. **there** Were you they're/their/there last night?
5. **they're** I know they're/their/there going to attend.
6. **their** Have you met they're/their/there mother?
7. **there** I can go they're/their/there with you.
8. **their** Do you like they're/their/there new car?
9. **They're** They're/Their/There friendly to everyone.
10. **they're** Did she say they're/their/there ready to go?
11. **their** She said she'd walk by they're/their/there house.
12. **there** Is anyone they're/their/there?
13. **there** I put it right over they're/their/there!

"This" and "These" (84)

The word **this** is an adjective that refers to things that are near. **This** always describes a singular noun. Singular means one.

Example:
> I'll buy **this** coat.
> (Coat is singular.)

The word **these** is also an adjective that refers to things that are near. **These** always describes a plural noun. A plural refers to more than one thing.

Example:
> I will buy **these** flowers.
> (Flowers is a plural noun.)

Directions: Write **this** or **these** to complete the sentences correctly. The first one is done for you.

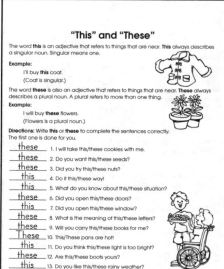

1. **these** I will take this/these cookies with me.
2. **these** Do you want this/these seeds?
3. **these** Did you try this/these nuts?
4. **this** Do it this/these way!
5. **this** What do you know about this/these situation?
6. **these** Did you open this/these doors?
7. **this** Did you open this/these window?
8. **these** What is the meaning of this/these letters?
9. **these** Will you carry this/these books for me?
10. **These** This/These pans are hot!
11. **this** Do you think this/these light is too bright?
12. **these** Are this/these boots yours?
13. **this** Do you like this/these rainy weather?

Review (85)

Directions: Complete the sentences by writing the correct words in the blanks.

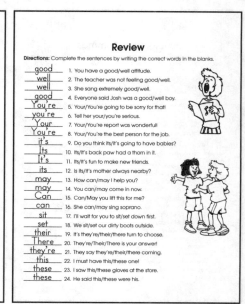

1. **good** You have a good/well attitude.
2. **well** The teacher was not feeling good/well.
3. **well** She sang extremely good/well.
4. **good** Everyone said Josh was a good/well boy.
5. **You're** Your/You're going to be sorry for that!
6. **you're** Tell her your/you're serious.
7. **Your** Your/You're report was wonderful!
8. **You're** Your/You're the best person for the job.
9. **it's** Do you think its/it's going to have babies?
10. **Its** Its/It's back paw had a thorn in it.
11. **It's** Its/It's fun to make new friends.
12. **its** Its is/it's mother always nearby?
13. **may** How can/may I help you?
14. **may** You can/may come in now.
15. **Can** Can/May you lift this for me?
16. **can** She can/may sing soprano.
17. **sit** I'll wait for you to sit/set down first.
18. **set** We sit/set our dirty boots outside.
19. **their** It's they're/their/there turn to choose.
20. **There** They're/Their/There is your answer!
21. **they're** They say they're/their/there coming.
22. **this** I must have this/these one!
23. **these** I saw this/these gloves at the store.
24. **these** He said this/these were his.

Review (86)

Directions: Write the correct answers in the blanks using the words in the box.

good	well	your	you're	its
it's	can	may	sit	set
they're	there	their	this	these

1. **This** is an adjective that refers to a particular thing.
2. Use **well** to tell or ask how something is done or to describe someone's health.
3. **It's** is a contraction for it is.
4. **These** describes a plural noun and refers to particular things.
5. **Sit** means to rest.
6. **Can** means am able to or to be able to.
7. **They're** is a contraction for they are.
8. **Your**, **its** and **their** show ownership or possession.
9. Use **may** to ask politely to be permitted to do something.
10. **You're** is a contraction for you are.
11. **Set** means to place or put.
12. **Good** describes a noun.
13. Use **there** to show direction or placement.

Poetry: Cinquains (88)

A **cinquain** is a type of poetry. The form is:

> Noun
> Adjective, adjective
> Verb + ing, verb + ing, verb + ing
> Four-word phrase
> Synonym for noun in line 1.

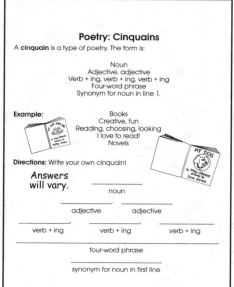

Example:
> Books
> Creative, fun
> Reading, choosing, looking
> I love to read!
> Novels

Directions: Write your own cinquain!

Answers will vary.

_____
noun

_____ _____
adjective   adjective

_____ _____ _____
verb + ing verb + ing verb + ing

_____
four-word phrase

_____
synonym for noun in first line

Idioms (89)

Idioms are a colorful way of saying something ordinary. The words in idioms do not mean exactly what they say.

Directions: Read the idioms listed below. Draw a picture of the literal meaning. Then match the idiom to its correct meaning.

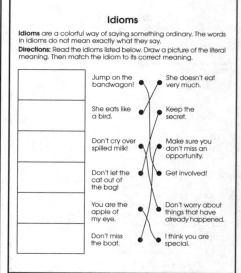

Jump on the bandwagon! — Get involved!

She eats like a bird. — She doesn't eat very much.

Don't cry over spilled milk! — Don't worry about things that have already happened.

Don't let the cat out of the bag! — Keep the secret.

You are the apple of my eye. — I think you are special.

Don't miss the boat. — Make sure you don't miss an opportunity.

Answer Key

Sequencing

When words are in a certain order, they are in sequence.

Directions: Complete each sequence using a word from the box. There are extra words in the box. The first one is done for you.

below	three	fifteen	December	twenty	above
after	go	third	hour	March	yard

1. January, February, __March__

2. before, during, __after__

3. over, on, __above__

4. come, stay, __go__

5. second, minute, __hour__

6. first, second, __third__

7. five, ten, __fifteen__

8. inch, foot, __yard__

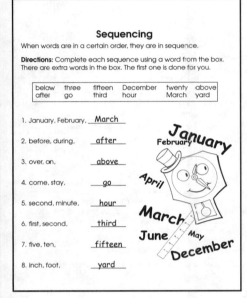

90

Sequencing

Directions: Fill in the blank spaces with what comes next in the series. The first one is done for you.

year	Wednesday	day	sixth	large
twenty	February	night	seventeen	mile
paragraph	winter	ocean		

1. Sunday, Monday, Tuesday, __Wednesday__

2. third, fourth, fifth, __sixth__

3. November, December, January, __February__

4. tiny, small, medium, __large__

5. fourteen, fifteen, sixteen, __seventeen__

6. morning, afternoon, evening, __night__

7. inch, foot, yard, __mile__

8. day, week, month, __year__

9. spring, summer, autumn, __winter__

10. five, ten, fifteen, __twenty__

11. letter, word, sentence, __paragraph__

12. second, minute, hour, __day__

13. stream, lake, river, __ocean__

91

Sequencing

Directions: Read each story. Circle the sentence that tells what might happen next.

1. Sam and Judy picked up their books and left the house. They walked to the bus stop. They got on a big yellow bus.
   What will Sam and Judy do next?
   (They will go to school.)
   They will visit their grandmother.
   They will go to the store.

2. Maggie and Matt were playing in the snow. They made a snowman with a black hat and a red scarf. Then the sun came out.
   What might happen next?
   It will snow again.
   They will play in the sandbox.
   (The snowman will melt.)

3. Megan put on a big floppy hat and funny clothes. She put green make-up on her face.
   What will Megan do next?
   She will go to school.
   (She will go to a costume party.)
   She will go to bed.

4. Mike was eating a hot dog. Suddenly, he smelled smoke. He turned and saw a fire on the stove
   What will Mike do next?
   He will watch the fire.
   (He will call for help.)
   He will finish his hot dog.

92

Sequencing

Directions: Number these sentences from 1 to 8 to show the correct order of the story.

__4__ Jack's father called the family doctor.

__8__ Jack felt much better as his parents drove him home.

__1__ Jack woke up in the middle of the night with a terrible pain in his stomach.

__5__ The doctor told Jack's father to take Jack to the hospital.

__2__ Jack called his parents to come help him.

__7__ At the hospital, the doctors examined Jack. They said the problem was not serious. They told Jack's parents that he could go home.

__3__ Jack's mother took his temperature. He had a fever of 103 degrees.

__6__ On the way to the hospital, Jack rested in the backseat. He was worried.

93

Sequencing

Directions: Read each story. Circle the phrase that tells what happened before.

1. Beth is very happy now that she has someone to play with. She hopes that her new sister will grow up quickly!
   A few days ago . . .
   Beth was sick.
   (Beth's mother had a baby.)
   Beth got a new puppy.

2. Sara tried to mend the tear. She used a needle and thread to sew up the hole.
   While playing, Sara had . . .
   broken her bicycle.
   lost her watch.
   (torn her shirt.)

3. The movers took John's bike off the truck and put it in the garage. Next, they moved his bed into his new bedroom.
   John's family . . .
   (bought a new house.)
   went on vacation.
   bought a new truck.

4. Katie picked out a book about dinosaurs. Jim, who likes sports, chose two books about baseball.
   Katie and Jim . . .
   (went to the library.)
   went to the playground.
   went to the grocery store.

94

Following Directions

Directions: Learning to follow directions is very important. Use the map to find your way to different houses.

green ←
blue ←
→ yellow

1. Color the start house yellow.
2. Go north 2 houses, and east two houses.
3. Go north 2 houses, and west 4 houses.
4. Color the house green.

5. Start at the yellow house.
6. Go east 1 house, and north 3 houses.
7. Go west 3 houses, and south 3 houses.
8. Color the house blue.

North
West ← → East
South

95

Answer Key

Following Directions

Directions: Read each sentence and do what it says to do.

1. Count the syllables in each word. Write the number on the line by the word.
2. Draw a line between the two words in each compound word.
3. Draw a circle around each name of a month.
4. Draw a box around each food word.
5. Draw an **X** on each noise word.
6. Draw a line under each day of the week.
7. Write the three words from the list you did not use. Draw a picture of each of those words.

2	April	4	vegetable
1	bang	1	June
2	sidewalk	3	Saturday
3	astronaut	1	March
1	moon	2	cardboard
2	Friday	1	fruit

3	tablecloth
1	meat
1	crash
2	jingle
2	rocket
2	Monday

moon   astronaut   rocket

96

Following Directions

Directions: Look at the calendar page. Read each sentence and do what it says to do.

February

Sunday	Monday	Tuesday	Wednesday	Thursday	Friday	Saturday
1	2 brown	3	4	5	6	7
8	9	10	11	12	13 red	14
15	16	17	18	19	20	21
22 red	23	24	25	26	27	28

1. Guess the month. It is a winter month, and it is the month with the fewest days. Write the missing letters in the name on the top line.
2. Write the missing numbers for the dates.
3. Write the name of the missing day where it belongs.
4. Write the missing letters in the names of two days.
5. Circle the dates that will be Saturdays.
6. The 2nd is Groundhog Day. Draw a brown **X** in that square.
7. The 12th is Abraham Lincoln's birthday. Draw a black top hat in that square.
8. The 14th is Valentine's Day. Draw a red heart in that square.
9. George Washington's birthday is on the 22nd. Draw a red cherry in that square.

97

Classification

Classification is grouping similar things into one category.

A title can tell a lot about a book. Read the following book titles.

Directions: Write each title in the correct category below. One title does not fit into any of the categories.

The Case of the Missing Key	*How Raccoon Got His Mask*	*Your Heart*
Guide to Computers	*Haunted House Tale*	*Where's Susie?*
The Brain: Nerve Central	*Turtle's Trip*	*The Hidden Passage*
Nutrition Network	*No Bones About It*	*Reptiles of the Desert*
Tommy, the Seeing-Eye Dog	*The Secret Letter*	*The Amazing Body*

Health
The Brain: Nerve Central
Nutrition Network
No Bones About It
Your Heart
The Amazing Body

Animals
Tommy, the Seeing-Eye Dog
How Raccoon Got His Mask
Turtle's Trip
Reptiles of the Desert

Mysteries
The Case of the Missing Key
Haunted House Tale
The Secret Letter
Where's Susie?
The Hidden Passage

Which title is left? **Guide to Computers**

In what section of the library might it be **Nonfiction or Reference**

98

Webs

Webs are another way to classify information. Look at the groups below.

Directions: Add more words in each group.

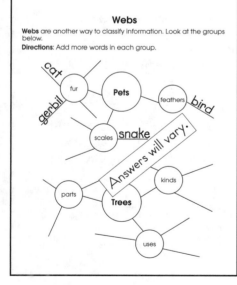

Answers will vary.

99

Completing Analogies

Directions: Complete each analogy using a word from the box. The first one is done for you.

rabbit	fish	cup	left	south	cat
light	bear	small	arm	zoo	evening

1. **Hive** is to **bee** as burrow is to **rabbit**.
2. **Up** is to **down** as right is to **left**.
3. **Lamb** is to **sheep** as kitten is to **cat**.
4. **Big** is to **little** as large is to **small**.
5. **Black** is to **white** as dark is to **light**.
6. **Day** is to **night** as morning is to **evening**.
7. **Knee** is to **leg** as elbow is to **arm**.
8. **Chicken** is to **farm** as monkey is to **zoo**.
9. **Fork** is to **spoon** as glass is to **cup**.
10. **Wing** is to **bird** as fin is to **fish**.
11. **Feather** is to **duck** as fur is to **bear**.
12. **East** is to **west** as north is to **south**.

100

Completing Analogies

Directions: Complete each analogy using a word from the box. The first one is done for you.

finish	less	pony	oven	finger	big
week	hour	cat	weak	under	little

1. **Second** is to **minute** as minute is to **hour**.
2. **Fast** is to **slow** as big is to **little**.
3. **Child** is to **adult** as kitten is to **cat**.
4. **Puppy** is to **kitten** as calf is to **pony**.
5. **Less** is to **more** as little is to **big**.
6. **Freeze** is to **freezer** as bake is to **oven**.
7. **Late** is to **early** as more is to **less**.
8. **First** is to **last** as start is to **finish**.
9. **In** is to **out** as over is to **under**.
10. **Hard** is to **soft** as strong is to **weak**.
11. **Earring** is to **ear** as ring is to **finger**.
12. **Hour** is to **day** as day is to **week**.

101

Answer Key

Main Idea

The **main idea** of a story is what the story is mostly about.

Directions: Read the story. Then answer the questions.

A tree is more than the enormous plant you see growing in your yard. A large part of the tree grows under the ground. This part is called the roots. If the tree is very big and very old, the roots may stretch down 100 feet!

The roots hold the tree in the ground. The roots do another important job for the tree. They gather minerals and water from the soil to feed the tree so it will grow. Most land plants, including trees, could not live without roots to support and feed them.

1. The main idea of this story is:
   The roots of a tree are underground.
   (The roots do important jobs for the tree.)

2. Where are the roots of a tree? __underground__

Circle the correct answer.

3. The roots help to hold the tree up.   (True)   False

4. Name two things the roots collect from the soil for the tree.

   1) __water__   2) __minerals__

102

Parts of a Paragraph

A **paragraph** is a group of sentences that all tell about the same thing. Most paragraphs have three parts: a **beginning**, a **middle** and an **end**.

Directions: Write **beginning**, **middle** or **end** next to each sentence in the scrambled paragraphs below. There can be more than one middle sentence.

Example:

__middle__ — We took the tire off the car.

__beginning__ — On the way to Aunt Louise's, we had a flat tire.

__middle__ — We patched the hole in the tire.

__end__ — We put the tire on and started driving again.

__middle__ — I took all the ingredients out of the cupboard.

__beginning__ — One morning, I decided to bake a pumpkin pie.

__end__ — I forgot to add the pumpkin!

__middle__ — I mixed the ingredients together, but something was missing.

__middle__ — The sun was very hot and our throats were dry.

__end__ — We finally decided to turn back.

__beginning__ — We started our hike very early in the morning.

__middle__ — It kept getting hotter as we walked.

103

Topic Sentences

A **topic sentence** is usually the first sentence in a paragraph. It tells what the story will be about.

Directions: Read the following sentences. Circle the topic sentence that should go first in the paragraph that follows.

(Rainbows have seven colors.)
There's a pot of gold.
I like rainbows.

The colors are red, orange, yellow, green, blue, indigo and violet. Red forms the outer edge, with violet on the inside of the rainbow.

He cut down a cherry tree.
His wife was named Martha.
(George Washington was a good president.)

He helped our country get started. He chose intelligent leaders to help him run the country.

(Mark Twain was a great author.)
Mark Twain was unhappy sometimes.
Mark Twain was born in Missouri.

One of his most famous books is *Huckleberry Finn*. He wrote many other great books.

104

Middle Sentences

Middle sentences support the topic sentence. They tell more about it.

Directions: Underline the middle sentences that support each topic sentence below.

Topic Sentence:
Penguins are birds that cannot fly.

Pelicans can spear fish with their sharp bills.
Many penguins waddle or hop about on land.
Even though they cannot fly, they are excellent swimmers.
Pelicans keep their food in a pouch.

Topic Sentence:
Volleyball is a team sport in which the players hit the ball over the net.

There are two teams with six players on each team.
My friend John would rather play tennis with Lisa.
Players can use their heads or their hands.
I broke my hand once playing handball.

Topic Sentence:
Pikes Peak is the most famous of all the Rocky Mountains.

Some mountains have more trees than other mountains.
Many people like to climb to the top.
Many people like to ski and camp there, too.
The weather is colder at the top of most mountains.

105

Ending Sentences

Ending sentences are sentences that tie the story together.

Directions: Choose the correct ending sentence for each story from the sentences below. Write it at the end of the paragraph.

A new pair of shoes!
All the corn on the cob I could eat!
A new eraser!

Corn on the Cob

Corn on the cob used to be my favorite food. That is, until I lost my four front teeth. For one whole year, I had to sit and watch everyone else eat my favorite food without me. Mom gave me creamed corn, but it just wasn't the same. When my teeth finally came in, Dad said he had a surprise for me. I thought I was going to get a bike or a new C.D. player or something. I was just as happy to get what I did.

__All the corn on the cob I could eat!__

I would like to take a train ride every year.
Trains move faster than I thought they would.
She had brought her new gerbil along for the ride.

A Train Ride

When our family took its first train ride, my sister brought along a big box. She would not tell anyone what she had in it. In the middle of the trip, we heard a sound coming from the box. "Okay, Jan, now you have to open the box," said Mom. When she opened the box, we were surprised.

__She had brought her new gerbil along for the ride.__

106

Review

Directions: Write your own story with a topic sentence, at least three middle sentences and an ending sentence. Use your own idea or use one of these ideas for a story title:

The Best Day I Ever Had   If I Could Do Anything
My First Pet   My Best Friend
I Was So Unhappy I Cried   Why I Like Myself

Title:
_____

Topic Sentence:
_____

Middle Sentences:
_____

Answers will vary.

Ending Sentence:
_____

107

Answer Key

Cause and Effect

A **cause** is the reason for an event. An **effect** is what happens as a result of a cause.

Directions: Circle the cause and underline the effect in each sentence. They may be in any order. The first one is done for you.

1. (The truck hit an icy patch) and skidded off the road.

2. (When the door slammed shut) the baby woke up crying.

3. Our soccer game was cancelled (when it began to storm.)

4. Dad and Mom are adding a room onto the house (since our family is growing.)

5. (Our car ran out of gas on the way to town) so we had to walk.

6. (The home run in the ninth inning) helped our team win the game.

7. We had to climb the stairs (because the elevator was broken.)

8. We were late to school (because the bus had a flat tire.)

108

Cause and Effect

Directions: Draw a line to match each phrase to form a logical cause and effect sentence.

1. Dad gets paid today, so — we're going out for dinner.
2. When the electricity went out, — we grabbed the flashlights.
3. Courtney can't spend the night — because she is sick.
4. Our front window shattered — when the baseball hit it.
5. Sophie got $10.00 for her birthday, — so she bought a new sweater.

Directions: Read each sentence beginning. Choose an ending from the box that makes sense. Write the correct letter on the line.

1. Her arm was in a cast, because __D__

2. They are building a new house on our street, so __A__

3. Since I'd always wanted a puppy, __E__

4. I had to renew my library book, __C__

5. My parents' anniversary is tomorrow, __B__

> A. we all went down to watch.
> B. so my sister and I bought them some flowers.
> C. since I hadn't finished it.
> D. she fell when she was skating.
> E. Mom gave me one for my birthday.

109

Noting Details

Directions: Read the story. Then answer the questions.

Thomas Edison was one of America's greatest inventors. An **inventor** thinks up new machines and new ways of doing things. Edison was born in Milan, Ohio in 1847. He went to school for only three months. His teacher thought he was not very smart because he asked so many questions.

Edison liked to experiment. He had many wonderful ideas. He invented the light bulb and the phonograph (record player).

Thomas Edison died in 1931, but we still use many of his inventions today.

1. What is an inventor?

   A person who thinks up new machines and new ways of doing things.

2. Where was Thomas Edison born?

   Milan, Ohio

3. How long did he go to school?

   three months

4. What are two of Edison's inventions?

   the light bulb and the phonograph

110

Reading Comprehension

Directions: Read the story. Then answer the questions.

Have you ever seen a tree that has been cut down? If so, you may have seen many circles in the trunk. These are called the **annual rings.** You can tell how old a tree is by counting these rings.

Trees have these rings because they grow a new layer of wood every year. The new layer grows right below the bark. In a year when there is a lot of rain and sunlight, the tree grows faster; the annual ring that year will be thick. When there is not much rain or sunlight, the tree grows slower and the ring is thin.

Circle the correct answer.

1. The annual ring of a tree tells how big the tree is.
   True   (False)

2. Each year, a new layer of wood grows on top of the bark.
   True   (False)

3. In a year with lots of rain and sunlight, the annual ring will be thick.
   (True)   False

4. Trees grow faster when there is more rain and sunlight.
   (True)   False

5. How old was the tree on this page? __16 years old__

111

Comprehension: Mary Lou Retton

Mary Lou Retton became the first U.S. woman to win Olympic gold in gymnastics. She accomplished this at the 1984 Olympics held in Los Angeles, when she was 16 years old. "Small but mighty" would certainly describe this gymnast.

She was the youngest of five children—all good athletes. She grew up in Fairmont, West Virginia, and began her gymnastic training at the age of 7.

Most women gymnasts are graceful, but Mary Lou helped open up the field of gymnastics to strong, athletic women. Mary Lou was 4 feet 10 inches tall and weighed a mere 95 pounds!

Directions: Answer these questions about Mary Lou Retton.

1. Circle the main idea:
   Mary Lou loved performing.
   (Mary Lou is a famous Olympic gymnast.)

2. She was born in __Fairmont, West Virginia__.

3. At what age did she begin her gymnastics training?
   __7 years old__

4. Mary Lou won a gold medal when she was __16__ years old.

112

Reading Comprehension

Directions: Read the story. Then answer the questions.

What is a **robot**? Does a robot do any of your work for you?

A robot is any machine that can do work without a person being needed to run it all the time. A dishwasher is a kind of robot. A clock radio is a robot, too. They may not look like the robots you see on television or read about in books, but they are.

Robots are controlled by computers. There are robots to do many useful jobs, such as flying airplanes and building cars. Many factories use robots to do simple jobs, such as picking up objects and putting them in place. These are jobs that people find boring. A robot can do them over and over without becoming tired or bored.

1. What is a robot? __Any machine that can do work without a person running it all the time__

2. Name two uses for robots.

   1) __flying airplanes__   2) __building cars__

3. What controls a robot? __computers__

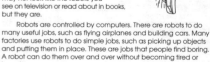

113

Answer Key

Types of Books

A **fiction** book is a book about things that are made up or not true. Fantasy books are fiction. A **nonfiction** book is about things that have really happened. Books can be classified into more types:

Mystery — books that have clues that lead to solving a problem or mystery

Biography — book about a real person's life

Poetry — a collection of poems, which may or may not rhyme

Fantasy — books about things that cannot really happen

Sports — books about different sports or sport figures

Travel — books about going to other places

Directions: Write mystery, biography, poetry, fantasy, sports or travel next to each title.

The Life of Helen Keller	biography
Let's Go to Mexico!	travel
The Case of the Missing Doll	mystery
How to Play Golf	sports
Turtle Soup and Other Poems	poety
Fred's Flying Saucer	fantasy

114

Reading for Information: Dictionaries

Dictionaries contain meanings and pronunciations of words. The words in a dictionary are listed in alphabetical order. Guide words appear at the top of each dictionary page. They help us know at a glance what words are on each page.

Directions: Place the words in alphabetical order.

APPLE	CRAB	CRIB	FROG
apple	cake	crib	ear
atlas	coat	dog	egg
book	crab	drip	frog

apple	dog	crab	ear
book	atlas	cake	frog
egg	drip	coat	crib

115

Dictionary Skills: Entry Words

Words in a dictionary are called **entries**. Some entries have more than one meaning. Dictionaries number each meaning.

Directions: Read the entry word below and its different meanings. Then answer the questions.

fan 1. An instrument shaped like a semicircle that is waved by hand. 2. An instrument with rotating blades that stirs the air. 3. To cause air to blow. 4. A person with a special interest.

1. How many meanings are listed for **fan**? ___4___

2. Write the meaning listed that describes a baseball **fan**.
   a person with a special interest

3. What is the first meaning of **fan** listed?
   An instrument shaped like a semicircle that is waved by hand.

4. Read this sentence: She will **fan** herself because she is hot. What is the meaning of **fan** as it is used in this sentence?
   To cause air to blow.

5. Read the second meaning of **fan**. Write a sentence using that meaning of **fan**.
   Sentences will vary.

116

Reading for Information: The Food Pyramid

Eating foods that are good for you is very important for you to stay healthy.

Directions: List different foods or draw pictures to go in each group.

Food Pyramid (per day)

Food names and/or pictures will vary.

milk and milk-equivalent foods (2 to 3 cups)

beans and meat (3 to 5 ounces)

grains (4 to 6 ounces) vegetables (1 ½ to 2 ½ cups) fruits (1 to 1 ½ cups) oils (use sparingly; 4 to 5 teaspoons)

Circle the correct answers.

1. You should eat as many sweets as possible. True (False)

2. You should eat 4-6 ounces of the grain group per day. (True) False

3. You should eat more than 5 ounces of meat per day. True (False)

4. What is your favorite food? Answer will vary.

117

Reading for Information

Telephone books contain information about people's addresses and phone numbers. They also list business addresses and phone numbers. The information in a telephone book is listed in alphabetical order.

Directions: Use your telephone book to find the following places in your area. Ask your mom or dad for help if you need it.

Can you find . . .

	Name	Phone number
. . . a pizza place?	Answers will vary.	
. . . a bicycle store?		
. . . a pet shop?		
. . . a toy store?		
. . . a water park?		

What other telephone numbers would you like to have?

118

Reading for Information: Newspapers

A newspaper has many parts. Some of the parts of a newspaper are:

- banner — the name of the paper
- lead story — the top news item
- caption — sentences under the picture which give information about the picture
- sports — scores and information on current sports events
- comics — drawings that tell funny stories
- editorial — an article by the editor expressing an opinion about something
- ads — paid advertisements
- weather — information about the weather
- advice column — letters from readers asking for help with a problem
- movie guides — a list of movies and movie times
- obituary — information about people who have died

Directions: Match the newspaper sections below with their definitions.

banner — the name of the paper
lead story — the top news item
caption — sentences under pictures
editorial — an article by the editor
movies — movies and movie times
obituary — information about people who have died

119

Answer Key

Newspaper Writing

Directions: Use the front page below to create a newspaper story about Cinderella. **Answers will vary.**

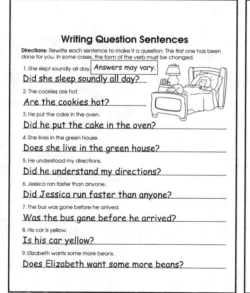

(banner)

Glass Slipper Found!
(lead story)

Draw a picture

(caption)

Evil Stepmothers: What do you think?
(editorial)

Classified Ads: Wanted!

Advice:
Dear Fairy Godmother,
I want to go to the ball, and my stepmother won't let me go. What should I do?

Today's Weather:

120

Newspaper Writing

A good news story gives us important information. It answers the questions:

WHO?   **WHY?**   **WHAT?**

WHERE?   **HOW?**   **WHEN?**

Directions: Think about the story "Little Red Riding Hood." Answer the following questions about the story.

Who are the characters? _Little Red Riding Hood, Grandma, the wolf and the hunter_

What is the story about? _a girl who visits her sick grandmother_

Why does Red go to Granny's house? _to bring food to her sick grandmother_

Where does the story take place? _in the woods, at Grandma's house_

When did she go to Granny's house? _in the afternoon_

Where did the Wolf greet Red? _He met her in the woods._

121

Letter Writing

Directions: Write a friendly letter below. Be sure to include a heading, greeting, body, closing and signature.

(heading)

(greeting)

(body)

Answers will vary.

, (closing)

(signature)

123

Writing Question Sentences

Directions: Rewrite each sentence to make it a question. The first one has been done for you. In some cases, the form of the verb must be changed. **Answers may vary.**

1. She slept soundly all day.
Did she sleep soundly all day?

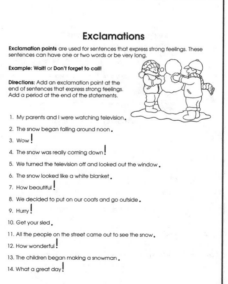

2. The cookies are hot.
Are the cookies hot?

3. He put the cake in the oven.
Did he put the cake in the oven?

4. She lives in the green house.
Does she live in the green house?

5. He understood my directions.
Did he understand my directions?

6. Jessica ran faster than anyone.
Did Jessica run faster than anyone?

7. The bus was gone before he arrived.
Was the bus gone before he arrived?

8. His car is yellow.
Is his car yellow?

9. Elizabeth wants some more beans.
Does Elizabeth want some more beans?

125

Exclamations

Exclamation points are used for sentences that express strong feelings. These sentences can have one or two words or be very long.

Example: Wait! or **Don't forget to call!**

Directions: Add an exclamation point at the end of sentences that express strong feelings. Add a period at the end of the statements.

1. My parents and I were watching television .
2. The snow began falling around noon .
3. Wow !
4. The snow was really coming down !
5. We turned the television off and looked out the window .
6. The snow looked like a white blanket .
7. How beautiful !
8. We decided to put on our coats and go outside .
9. Hurry !
10. Get your sled .
11. All the people on the street came out to see the snow .
12. How wonderful !
13. The children began making a snowman .
14. What a great day !

126

Making Sense of Sentences

A **statement** is a sentence that tells something. It ends with a period (.).

Example: Columbus is the capital of Ohio.

A **question** is a sentence that asks something. It ends with a question mark (?).

Example: Do you like waffles?

An **exclamation** is a sentence that shows strong feeling. It ends with an exclamation mark (!).

Example: You're the best friend in the world!

A **command** is a sentence that orders someone to do something. It ends with a period or exclamation mark.

Example: Shut the door. Watch out for that trunk!

A **request** is a sentence that asks someone to do something. It ends with a period or question mark.

Example: Please shut the door.

Directions: Write **S** if the sentence ___ an exclamation, **C** if it issues a ___ sentence correctly.

Answers may vary but could include:

R 1. Please open your mouth .
Q 2. Will you be going to the party?
E 3. That's hot !
C 4. Give me the car keys right now .
Q 5. Do you think she will run fast?
S 6. It's cold today .
S 7. You're incredible .
E 8. Run for your life !
Q 9. Is today the deadline?
S 10. I turned in my paper early .

C 11. Call the doctor immediately .
C 12. Turn around and touch your toes .
C 13. Be at my house at noon tomorrow .
C 14. Give me a clue .
Q 15. Can you give me a clue?
R 16. Please wipe your face .
S 17. It's time for me to go home .
S 18. No one believed what she said .
Q 19. Are you interested?
S 20. He's badly hurt .

127

Answer Key

Reading Skills: Classifying

Classifying is placing similar things into categories.

Directions: Classify each group by crossing out the word that does not belong.

1. factory   hotel   lodge   ~~pattern~~
2. ~~Thursday~~   September   December   October
3. cottage   hut   ~~carpenter~~   castle
4. cupboard   ~~orchard~~   refrigerator   stove
5. Christmas   Thanksgiving   Easter   ~~spring~~
6. brass   copper   ~~coal~~   tin
7. stomach   ~~breathe~~   liver   brain
8. teacher   mother   dentist   ~~office~~
9. ~~market~~   faucet   bathtub   sink
10. basement   attic   kitchen   ~~neighborhood~~

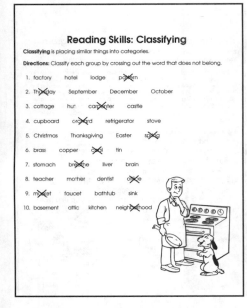

128

Reading Skills: Classifying

Directions: Read the title of each TV show. Write the correct number to tell what kind of show it is.

| 1 — Cooking | 3 — Sports | 5 — Humor |
| 2 — Nature | 4 — Mystery | 6 — Famous People |

- **4** The Secret of the Lost Locket
- **3** Learn Tennis With the Pros
- **2** Birds in the Wild
- **6** The Life of George Washington
- **1** Great Recipes From Around the World
- **5** A Laugh a Minute

Directions: Read the description of each TV show. Write the number of each show above in the blank.

- **6** The years before he became the first president of the United States are examined.
- **2** Featured: eagles and owls
- **4** Clues lead Detective Logan to a cemetery in his search for the missing necklace.
- **3** Famous players give tips on buying a racket.
- **1** Six ways to cook chicken
- **5** Cartoon characters in short stories

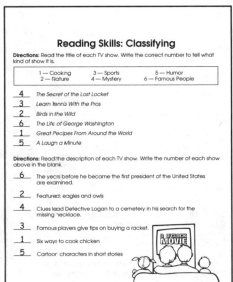

129

Reading Skills: Classifying

Directions: Complete each idea by crossing out the word or phrase that does not belong.

1. If the main idea is **things that are green**, I don't need:
   ~~the sun~~   apples   grass   leaves in summer
2. If the idea is **musical instruments**, I don't need a:
   piano   trombone   ~~baseball~~   tuba
3. If the idea is **months of the year**, I don't need:
   ~~Friday~~   January   July   October
4. If the idea is **colors on the U.S. flag**, I don't need:
   white   blue   ~~black~~   red
5. If the idea is **types of weather**, I don't need:
   sleet   stormy   ~~roses~~   sunny
6. If the idea is **fruits**, I don't need:
   kiwi   orange   ~~spinach~~   banana
7. If the idea is **U.S. presidents**, I don't need:
   Lincoln   ~~Jordan~~   Washington   Adams
8. If the idea is **flowers**, I don't need:
   ~~rose~~   daisy   tulip   daffodil
9. If the idea is **sports**, I don't need:
   ~~pears~~   soccer   wrestling   baseball

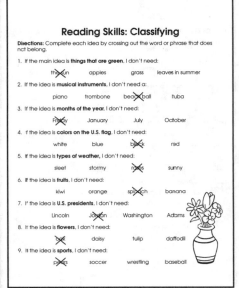

130

Reading Skills: Sequencing

Directions: Read each set of events. Then number them in the correct order.

- **2** Get dressed for school and hurry downstairs for breakfast.
- **1** Roll over, sleepy-eyed, and turn off the alarm clock.
- **3** Meet your friends at the corner to walk to school.

- **3** The fourth-grade class walked quietly to a safe area away from the building.
- **2** The teacher reminded the last student to shut the classroom door.
- **1** The loud clanging of the fire alarm startled everyone in the room.

- **1** Barb's dad watched from the seat of the tractor as the boys and girls climbed into the wagon.
- **3** By the time they returned to the barn, there wasn't much straw left.
- **2** As the wagon bumped along the trail, the boys and girls sang songs they learned in music class.

- **3** The referee blew his whistle and held up the hand of the winner of the match.
- **2** Each wrestler worked hard, trying to out-maneuver his opponent.
- **1** The referee said, "Shake hands, boys, and wrestle a fair match."

131

Reading Skills: Sequencing

Directions: In each group below, one event in the sequence is missing. Write the correct sentence from the box where it belongs.

- Paul put his bait on the hook and cast out into the pond.
- "Sorry," he said, "but the TV repairman can't get here until Friday."
- Everyone pitched in and helped.
- Corey put the ladder up against the trunk of the tree.

1. "All the housework has to be done before anyone goes to the game," said Mom.
2. Everyone pitched in and helped.
3. We all agreed that "many hands make light work."

1. Paul put his bait on the hook and cast out into the pond.
2. It wasn't long until he felt a tug on the line, and we watched the bobber go under.
3. He was the only one to go home with something other than bait!

1. The little girl cried as she stood looking up into the maple tree.
2. Between her tears, she managed to say, "My kitten is up in the tree and can't get down."
3. Corey put the ladder up against the trunk of the tree.

1. Dad hung up the phone and turned to look at us.
2. "Sorry," he said, "but the TV repairman can't get here until Friday."
3. "This would be a good time to get out those old board games in the hall closet," he said.

132

Reading Skills: Sequencing

Directions: Read about how a tadpole becomes a frog. Then number the stages in order below.

Frogs and toads belong to a group of animals called amphibians (am-FIB-ee-ans). This means "living a double life." Frogs and toads live a "double life" because they live part of their lives in water and part on land. They are able to do this because their bodies change as they grow. This series of changes is called metamorphosis (met-a-MORE-fa-sis).

A mother frog lays her eggs in water, then leaves them on their own to grow. The eggs contain cells—the tiny "building blocks" of all living things—that multiply and grow. Soon the cells grow into a swimming tadpole. Tadpoles breathe through gills—small holes in their sides—like fish do. They spend all of their time in the water.

The tadpole changes as it grows. Back legs slowly form. Front legs begin inside the tadpole under the gill holes. They pop out when they are fully developed. At the same time, lungs, which a frog uses to breathe instead of gills, are almost ready to be used.

As the tadpole reaches the last days of its life in the water, its tail disappears. It is ready for life on land. It has become a frog.

- **6** The front legs pop out. The lungs are ready to use for breathing.
- **2** The cells in the egg multiply and grow.
- **8** The tadpole has become a frog.
- **4** Back legs slowly form.
- **3** Soon the cells grow into a swimming tadpole.
- **5** Front legs develop inside the tadpole.
- **7** The tadpole's tail disappears.
- **1** A mother frog lays her eggs in water.

133

Answer Key

Following Directions: A Rocket Launcher

Directions: Read about how to make a rocket launcher. Then number the steps in order below. Have an adult help you.

You can do this in your own backyard. To make this rocket launcher, you need an empty 1-quart soda bottle, cork, paper towel, 1/2 cup water, 1/2 cup vinegar and 1 teaspoon baking soda. You may want to add some streamers.

If you attach tissue paper streamers to the cork or rocket with a thumbtack, this helps you follow the rocket more easily during its flight.

Pour the water and vinegar into the launcher—the bottle. Cut the paper towel into a 4-inch square. Place the baking soda in the middle of the paper towel. Roll up the towel and twist the ends so the baking soda will stay inside.

Outside, you will need plenty of room for the rocket to fly. Drop the paper towel and baking soda into the bottle. Put the cork on as tightly as you can.

When the liquid soaks through the paper towel, the baking soda and vinegar work together to make a gas called carbon dioxide. As the carbon dioxide builds up in the bottle, it will push the cork up into the sky with a loud pop!

3 Pour the vinegar and water into the soda bottle.

2 Attach streamers to the cork so you can follow its flight.

8 Stand back and watch your rocket blast off!

4 Place the baking soda on the paper towel and roll it up.

7 Wait as the vinegar and soda work to make carbon dioxide gas.

5 Drop the paper towel with the baking soda into the bottle.

1 Gather together a bottle, cork, water, vinegar, paper towel and baking soda.

6 Put on the cork as tightly as you can.

134

Compare and Contrast

To **compare** means to discuss how things are similar. To contrast means to discuss how things are different.

Directions: Compare and contrast how people grow gardens. Write at least two answers for each question.

Many people in the country have large gardens. They have a lot of space, so they can plant many kinds of vegetables and flowers. Since the gardens are usually quite large, they use a wheelbarrow to carry the tools they need. Sometimes, they even have to carry water or use a garden hose.

People who live in the city do not always have enough room for a garden. Many people in big cities live in apartment buildings. They can put in a window box or use part of their balcony space to grow things. Most of the time, the only garden tools they need are a hand trowel to loosen the dirt and a watering can to make sure the plant gets enough water.

1. Compare gardening in the country with gardening in the city

Both can plant vegetables and flowers. They both
have to use tools and water.

2. Contrast gardening in the country with gardening in the city

City gardeners usually have smaller gardens and
do not need as many tools as the country gardeners.

135

Compare and Contrast: Venn Diagram

Directions: List the similarities and differences you find below on a chart called a **Venn diagram.** This kind of chart shows comparisons and contrasts.

Butterflies and moths belong to the same group of insects. They both have two pairs of wings. Their wings are covered with tiny scales. Both butterflies and moths undergo metamorphosis, or a change, in their lives. They both begin their lives as caterpillars.

Butterflies and moths are different in some ways. Butterflies usually fly during the day, but moths generally fly at night. Most butterflies have slender, hairless bodies; most moths have plump, furry bodies. When butterflies land, they hold their wings together straight over their bodies. When moths land, they spread their wings out flat.

1. List three ways that butterflies and moths are alike.

Both have two pairs of wings.
Their wings are covered with tiny scales.
Both begin their lives as caterpillars.

2. List three ways that butterflies and moths are different.

Butterflies fly during the day; moths fly at night.
Butterflies' bodies are slender and hairless; moths',
plump and furry. Butterflies land wings up and moths
land wings spread out.

3. Combine your answers from questions 1 and 2 into a Venn diagram. Write the differences in the circle labeled for each insect. Write the similarities in the intersecting part.

Moths — Fly at night, Plump, furry body, Land wings spread out

Butterflies — Fly during the day, Slender, hairless body, Land wings straight up

Both — 2 pairs of wings, Wings have tiny scales, Have been caterpillars

136

Reading Skills: Analogies

An **analogy** is a way of comparing things to show how they are similar.

Directions: Read the sentences below. Determine how the first pair of words is related. Complete the second pair that relates in the same way. The first one is done for you.

cut	carry	ran	arm	listen
paint	lie	children	50	out
puppy	summer	hot	water	egg

1. Pencil is to write as brush is to ___paint___

2. Foot is to leg as hand is to ___arm___

3. Crayons are to draw as scissors are to ___cut___

4. Leg is to walk as arm is to ___carry___

5. Baby is to babies as child is to ___children___

6. Eye is to look as ear is to ___listen___

7. Chair is to sit as bed is to ___lie___

8. 600 is to 300 as 100 is to ___50___

9. White is to black as in is to ___out___

10. Ice skate is to winter as swim is to ___summer___

11. Switch is to light as faucet is to ___water___

12. Fly is to flew as run is to ___ran___

13. Cow is to milk as chicken is to ___egg___

14. Cool is to cold as warm is to ___hot___

15. Cat is to kitten as dog is to ___puppy___

137

Analogies

An **analogy** indicates how different items go together or are similar in some way.

Examples:
Petal is to flower as leaf is to tree.
Book is to library as food is to grocery.

The examples show how the second set of objects is related to the first set. A petal is a part of a flower, and a leaf is a part of a tree. A book can be found in a library, and food can be found in a grocery store.

Directions: Fill in the blanks to complete the analogies. The first one is done for you.

1. Cup is to saucer as glass is to ___coaster___

2. Paris is to France as London is to ___England___

3. Clothes are to hangers as ___shoes___ are to boxes.

4. California is to ___Pacific Ocean___ as Ohio is to Lake Erie.

5. ___Tablecloth___ is to table as blanket is to bed.

6. Pencil is to paper as ___paintbrush___ is to canvas.

7. Cow is to ___barn___ as child is to house.

8. State is to country as ___city___ is to state.

9. Governor is to state as ___president___ is to country.

10. ___Water___ is to ocean as sand is to desert.

11. Engine is to car as hard drive is to ___computer___

12. Beginning is to ___start___ as stop is to end.

Directions: Write three analogies of your own.
Answers will vary.

138

Reading Skills: Main Idea in Sentences

The **main idea** is the most important idea, or main point, in a sentence, paragraph or story.

Directions: Circle the main idea for each sentence.

1. Emily knew she would be late if she watched the end of the TV show.
   a. Emily likes watching TV.
   b. Emily is always running late.
   c. If Emily didn't leave, she would be late.

2. The dog was too strong and pulled Jason across the park on his leash.
   a. The dog is stronger than Jason.
   b. Jason is not very strong.
   c. Jason took the dog for a walk.

3. Jennifer took the book home so she could read it over and over.
   a. Jennifer loves to read.
   b. Jennifer loves the book.
   c. Jennifer is a good reader.

4. Jerome threw the baseball so hard it broke the window.
   a. Jerome throws baseballs very hard.
   b. Jerome was mad at the window.
   c. Jerome can't throw very straight.

5. Lori came home and decided to clean the kitchen for her parents.
   a. Lori is a very nice person.
   b. Lori did a favor for her parents.
   c. Lori likes to cook.

6. It was raining so hard that it was hard to see the road through the windshield.
   a. It always rains hard in April.
   b. The rain blurred our vision.
   c. It's hard to drive in the rain.

139

Answer Key

Main Idea

Directions: Read each main idea sentence on pages 140 and 141. Then read the detail sentences following each main idea. Draw a ✓ on the line in front of each detail that supports the main idea.

Example: Niagara Falls is a favorite vacation spot.

✓ There are so many cars and buses that it is hard to get around.

___ My little brother gets sick when we go camping.

✓ You can see people there from all over the world.

1. Hummingbirds are interesting birds to watch.

✓ They look like tiny helicopters as they move around the flowers.

✓ One second they are "drinking" from the flower; the next, they are gone!

___ It is important to provide birdseed in the winter for our feathered friends.

2. Boys and girls look forward to Valentine's Day parties at school.

✓ For days, children try to choose the perfect valentine for each friend.

___ The school program is next Tuesday night.

✓ Just thinking about frosted, heart-shaped cookies makes me hungry!

140

Main Idea

3. In-line skating has become a very popular activity.

___ Bicycles today are made in many different styles.

✓ It is hard to spend even an hour at a park without seeing children and adults skating.

✓ The stores are full of many kinds and colors of in-line skates.

4. It has been a busy summer!

✓ Dad built a new deck off the back of our house, and everyone helped.

✓ Our next-door neighbor needed my help to watch her three-year-old twins.

___ We will visit my relatives on the East coast for Christmas this year.

141

Main Idea: Snow Fun

The **main idea** of a story or report is a sentence that summarizes the most important point. If a story or report is only one paragraph in length, then the main idea is usually stated in the first sentence (topic sentence). If it is longer than one paragraph, then the main idea is a general sentence including all the important points of the story or report.

Directions: Read the story. Then draw an **X** in the blank for the main idea.

> After a big snowfall, my friends and I enjoy playing in the snow. We bundle up in snow clothes at our homes, then meet with sleds at the hill by my house.
>
> One by one, we take turns sledding down the hill to see who will go the farthest and the fastest. Sometimes we have a contest to see whose sled will reach the fence at the foot of the hill first.
>
> When we tire of sledding, we may build a snowman or snowforts. Sometimes we have a friendly snowball fight.
>
> The end of our snow fun comes too quickly, and we head home to warm houses, dry clothes and hot chocolate.

1. What is the main idea?

✓ Playing in the snow with friends is an enjoyable activity.

___ Sledding in the snow is fast and fun.

The first option is correct. The paragraphs discuss the enjoyable things friends do on a snowy day.

The second option is not correct because the entire story is not about sledding. Only the second paragraph discusses sledding. The other paragraphs discuss the additional ways friends have fun in the snow.

2. Write a paragraph about what you like to do on snowy days. Remember to make the first sentence your main idea.

___ **Paragraphs will vary.** ___

142

Reading Skills: Main Idea in Paragraphs

Directions: Read each paragraph below. Then circle the sentence that tells the main idea.

It looked as if our class field day would have to be cancelled due to the weather. We tried not to show our disappointment, but Mr. Wade knew that it was hard to keep our minds on the math lesson. We noticed that even he had been sneaking glances out the window. All morning the classroom had been buzzing with plans. Each team met to plan team strategies for winning the events. Then, it happened! Clouds began to cover the sky, and soon the thunder and lightning confirmed what we were afraid of—field day cancelled. Mr. Wade explained that we could still keep our same teams. We could put all of our plans into motion, but we would have to get busy and come up with some inside games and competitions. I guess the day would not be a total disaster!

a. Many storms occur in the late afternoon.

ⓑ Our class field day had to be cancelled due to the weather.

c. Each team came up with its own strategies.

Allison and Emma had to work quietly and quickly to get Mom's birthday cake baked before she got home from work. Each of the girls had certain jobs to do—Allison set the oven temperature and got the cake pans prepared, while Emma got out all the ingredients. As they stirred and mixed, the two girls talked about the surprise party Dad had planned for Mom. Even Dad didn't know that the girls were baking this special cake. The cake was delicious. "It shows you what teamwork can do!" said the girls in unison.

a. Dad worked with the girls to bake the cake.

b. Mom's favorite frosting is chocolate cream.

ⓒ Allison and Emma baked a birthday cake for Mom.

143

Main Idea

The **main idea** of a paragraph is the most important point. Often, the first sentence in a paragraph tells the main idea. Most of the other sentences are details that support the main idea.

Directions: One of the sentences in each paragraph below does not belong in the story. Circle the sentence that does not support the main idea.

My family and I went to the zoo last Saturday. It was a beautiful day. The tigers napped in the sun. I guess they liked the warm sunshine as much as we did! Mom and Dad laughed at the baby monkeys. They said the monkeys reminded them of how we act. My sister said the bald eagle reminded her of Dad! I know I'll remember that trip to the zoo for a long time. (My cousin is coming to visit the weekend before school starts.)

Thanksgiving was a special holiday in our classroom. Each child dressed up as either a Pilgrim or a Native American. (My baby sister learned to walk last week.) We prepared food for our "feast" on the last day of school before the holiday. We all helped shake the jar full of cream to make real butter. Our teacher cooked applesauce. It smelled delicious!

144

Reading Skills: Context Clues

When you read, you may confuse words that look alike. You can tell when you read a word incorrectly because it doesn't make sense. You can tell from the **context** (the other words in the sentence or the sentences before or after) what the word should be. These **context clues** can help you figure out the meaning of a word by relating it to other words in the sentence.

Directions: Circle the correct word for each sentence below. Use the context to help you.

1. We knew we were in trouble as soon as we heard the crash. The baseball had gone (through/ thought) the picture window!

2. She was not able to answer my question because her (month/ mouth) was full of pizza.

3. Asia is the largest continent in the (world/ word).

4. I'm not sure I heard the teacher correctly. Did he say what I (through/ though) he said?

5. I was not with them on vacation so I don't know a (think/ thing) about what happened.

6. My favorite (month/ mouth) of the year is July because I love fireworks and parades!

7. You will do better on your book report if you (think/ thing) about what you are going to say.

145

Answer Key

Reading Skills: Context Clues

Directions: In each sentence below, circle the correct meaning for the nonsense word.

1. Be careful when you put that plate back on the shelf—it is **quibbable**.

   flexible   colorful   (breakable)

2. What is your favorite kind of **tonn**, pears or bananas?

   (fruit)   salad   purple

3. The **dinlay** outside this morning was very chilly; I needed my sweater.

   tree   vegetable   (temperature)

4. The whole class enjoyed the **weat**. They wanted to see it again next Friday.

   colorful   plant   (video)

5. Ashley's mother brought in a **zundy** she made by hand.

   temperature   (quilt)   plant

6. "Why don't you sit over here, Ronnie? That **sloey**
   is not very comfortable," said Mr. Gross.

   (chair)   car   cat

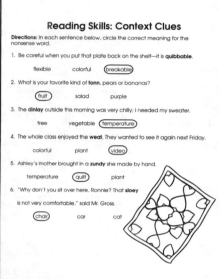

146

Reading Skills: Context Clues

Directions: Use context clues to help you choose the correct word for each sentence below.

selected	match	scarecrow

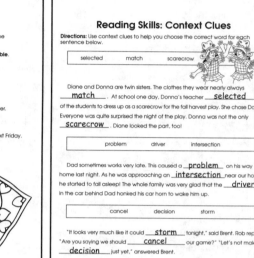

Diane and Donna are twin sisters. The clothes they wear nearly always ___**match**___ . At school one day, Donna's teacher ___**selected**___ one of the students to dress up as a scarecrow for the fall harvest play. She chose Donna. Everyone was quite surprised the night of the play. Donna was not the only ___**scarecrow**___ . Diane looked the part, too!

problem	driver	intersection

Dad sometimes works very late. This caused a ___**problem**___ on his way home last night. As he was approaching an ___**intersection**___ near our home, he started to fall asleep! The whole family was very glad that the ___**driver**___ in the car behind Dad honked his car horn to wake him up.

cancel	decision	storm

"It looks very much like it could ___**storm**___ tonight," said Brent. Rob replied, "Are you saying we should ___**cancel**___ our game?" "Let's not make a ___**decision**___ just yet," answered Brent.

147

Reading Skills: Context Clues

Directions: Read each sentence carefully and circle the word that makes sense.

1. We didn't (except (expect)) you to arrive so early.
2. "I can't hear a ((word) world) you are saying. Wait until I turn down the stereo," said Val.
3. I couldn't sleep last night because of the ((noise) nose) from the apartment below us.
4. Did Peggy say (weather (whether)) or not we needed our binoculars for the game?
5. He broke his (noise (nose)) when he fell off the bicycle.
6. All the students ((except) expect) the four in the front row are excused to leave.
7. The teacher said we should have good (whether (weather)) for our field trip.

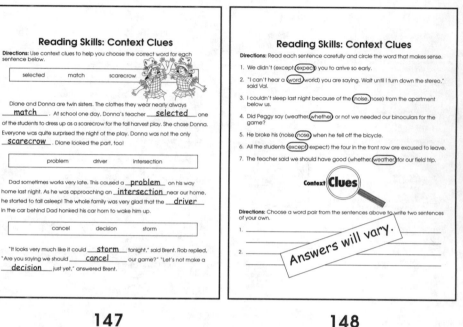

Directions: Choose a word pair from the sentences above to write two sentences of your own.

1. _____

2. _____

Answers will vary.

148

Reading Skills: Context Clues

Directions: Use context clues to figure out the bold word in each sentence below.

1. The teacher wanted all of us to put the names of the students in our class in two **columns**. It was a big help when I saw how she started each list on the board.

2. "I'm glad to see such a **variety** of art projects at the display," said the principal. "I was afraid that many of the projects would be the same."

3. My father used to work for a huge **corporation** in Florida. Since we moved to Virginia, his job is with a smaller company.

4. It would be hard to come up with a **singular** reason for the football team's success. There are so many good things happening that could explain it.

Directions: Draw a line to match the word on the left with its definition on the right.

variety ——— one
corporation ——— a large business
columns ——— vertical listings
singular ——— many different kinds

149

Reading Skills: Context Clues

Directions: Read the story. Match each bold word with its definition below.

Where the northern shores of North America meet the Arctic Ocean, the winters are very long and cold. No plants or crops will grow there. This is the land of the **Eskimo**.

Eskimos have figured out ways to live in the snow and ice. They sometimes live in **igloos**, which are made of snow. It is really very comfortable inside! An oil lamp provides light and warmth.

Often, you will find a big, furry **husky** sleeping in the long tunnel that leads to the igloo. Huskies are very important to Eskimos because they pull their sleds and help with hunting. Eskimos are excellent hunters. Many, many years ago, they learned to make **harpoons** and spears to help them hunt their food.

Eskimos get much of their food from the sea, especially fish, seals and whales. Often, an Eskimo will go out in a **kayak** to fish. Only one Eskimo fits inside, and he drives it with a paddle. The waves may turn the kayak upside down, but the Eskimo does not fall out. He is so skillful with a paddle that he quickly is right side up again.

A ___**husky**___ is a large, strong dog.

An ___**Eskimo**___ is a member of the race of people who live on the Arctic coasts of North America.

___**Igloos**___ are houses made of packed snow.

A ___**kayak**___ is a one-person canoe made of animal skins.

___**Harpoons**___ are spears with a long rope attached. They are used for spearing whales and other large sea animals.

150

Making Deductions

Making a deduction means using reasoning to arrive at a conclusion.

Directions: Read each group of sentences carefully. Then write your deduction.

1. Bob is tall. Jim is taller than Bob. Lee is taller than Jim. Who is the tallest? — ___Lee___

2. Brett was happy. Jenny was happier than Brett. Roger was happier than Jenny. Who was the happiest? — ___Roger___

3. An orange weighs a lot. A grapefruit weighs more than an orange. A watermelon weighs more than a grapefruit. What weighs the most? — ___watermelon___

4. Mark shot many baskets. Ted shot more baskets than Mark. Ed shot fewer than Mark. Who shot the most baskets? — ___Ted___

5. Mandy liked the movie. Teresa liked the movie more than Mandy. Liz liked the movie more than Teresa. Who liked the movie the least? — ___Mandy___

6. Jane danced fast. Duane danced faster than Jane. Luann danced slower than Jane. Who danced the fastest? — ___Duane___

7. The balloon floated high. The bubble went higher than the balloon. The airplane was higher than the bubble. What was the highest? — ___airplane___

8. The kitten was small. The bird was smaller than the kitten. The mouse was smaller than the bird. Which was the largest? — ___kitten___

151

Answer Key

Making Deductions: A Mystery

Ann's dog, Holly, has disappeared. Help Ann and her friends find Holly.

Directions: Look at the picture of Ann's house. Then read the clues. Write the person's name on the line in the room where he/she was.

| Ann's Parents' Room — Holly | Bath-room | Kitchen — mother |
| Ann's Room — Ann | Living Room — father | Outside — Paul |

1. Holly is not under Ann's bed. Ann was in her room, and she did not see Holly go there.
2. Holly is not outside, because Paul was in the yard and did not see her.
3. Ann's mother was in the kitchen. Holly is not there.
4. Ann's father was in a room next to the kitchen. He was not in the bathroom. He did not see Holly either.
5. Holly never goes in the bathroom. She is afraid of the water.
6. Holly cannot leave the yard. There is a fence around it.

Where is Holly? ___Ann's parents' room___

152

Drawing Conclusions

Drawing a conclusion means to use clues to make a final decision about something. To draw a conclusion, you must read carefully.

Directions: Read each story carefully. Use the clues given to draw a conclusion about the story.

The boy and girl took turns pushing the shopping cart. They went up and down the aisles. Each time they stopped the cart, they would look at things on the shelf and decide what they needed. Jody asked her older brother, "Will I need a box of 48 crayons in Mrs. Charles' class?"

"Yes, I think so," he answered. Then he turned to their mother and said, "I need some new notebooks. Can I get some?"

1. Where are they? ___at the store___
2. What are they doing there? ___buying school supplies___
3. How do you know? Write at least two clue words that helped you.
   ___Mrs. Charles's class, notebooks, box of 48 crayons___

Eric and Randy held on tight. They looked around and saw that they were not the only ones holding on. The car moved slowly upward. As they turned and looked over the side, they noticed that the people far below them seemed to be getting smaller and smaller. "Hey, Eric, did I tell you this is my first time on one of these?" asked Randy. As they started down the hill at a frightening speed, Randy screamed, "And it may be my last!"

1. Where are they? ___on a roller coaster___
2. How do you know? Write at least two clue words that helped you.
   ___car moved slowly upward, down at frightening speed___

153

Logic

Logic means to use deductive reasoning to solve a problem.

Maya, Paul, Traci, Kim and Scott went to the park on Saturday. Each child wore a different color t-shirt.

Directions: Read the clues. Fill out the chart to discover who wore what. Use an **X** to mark a "no" and a • to mark a "yes." The first clue is done for you.

1. Maya did not wear a yellow or white t-shirt.
2. Paul wore an orange t-shirt.
3. A boy wore a white t-shirt.
4. The girl who wore the yellow t-shirt was not Kim.
5. Scott did not wear a blue t-shirt.
6. Maya hates the color green.

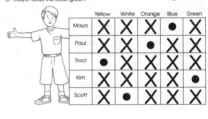

	Yellow	White	Orange	Blue	Green
Maya	X	X	X	•	X
Paul	X	X	•	X	X
Traci	•	X	X	X	X
Kim	X	X	X	X	•
Scott	X	•	X	X	X

154

Comprehension: Kareem Abdul-Jabbar

Kareem Abdul-Jabbar grew up to be more than 7 feet tall. Kareem's father and mother were both very tall. When he was 9 years old, Kareem was already 5 feet 4 inches tall. Kareem was raised in New York City. He went to Power Memorial High School and played basketball on that team. He went to college at UCLA. He played basketball in college, too. At UCLA, Kareem's team lost only two games in 3 years! After college, Kareem made his living playing basketball.

Directions: Answer these questions about Kareem Abdul-Jabbar.

1. Who is the story about?
   ___Kareem Abdul-Jabbar___
2. For what is this athlete famous?
   ___playing basketball___
3. When did Kareem reach the height of 5 feet 4 inches?
   ___when he was 9 years old___
4. Where did Kareem go to college?
   ___UCLA___
5. Why did Kareem grow so tall?
   ___His father and mother were both very tall.___
6. How did Kareem make his living?
   ___playing basketball___

155

Recognizing Details: Using Chopsticks

Directions: Read about chopsticks. Then answer the questions.

Asian people have eaten their food with chopsticks for many years. Chopsticks are two thin pieces of wood that are almost pointed on one end.

Chopsticks were used in China thousands of years ago. Ivory, gold or silver chopsticks were used for special occasions. People who used chopsticks to eat were considered very smart!

Today, some American people like to use chopsticks! But using chopsticks is not easy. Both chopsticks are held in one hand. A person holds one chopstick between the thumb and third finger. This chopstick is not supposed to move. The first and second fingers help move the other chopstick.

Chopsticks are an old custom with people from Asian countries such as China, Japan and Korea, but these people use forks and knives, too!

1. Who used chopsticks first? ___Chinese people___
2. What are chopsticks? ___two thin pieces of wood that are almost pointed on one end___
3. When did the Chinese start using chopsticks? ___thousands of years ago___
4. Where are chopsticks also used today? ___Japan, Korea, China (could include United States)___
5. Why is it hard to use chopsticks? ___because both sticks are held in one hand to pick up food___
6. How do chopsticks work? ___One stick stays still while the other helps pick up food.___
7. What do you think would happen if you tried to eat with chopsticks? ___Answers will vary.___

156

Reading Comprehension: Helen Keller

A B C D E F G H I J K L M
N O P Q R S T U V W X Y Z

When Helen Keller was a child, she often behaved in a wild way. She was very bright and strong, but she could not tell people what she was thinking or feeling. And she didn't know how others thought or felt. Helen was blind and deaf.

Helen was born with normal hearing and sight, but this changed when she was 1 year old. She had a serious illness with a very high fever. After that, Helen was never able to see or hear again.

As a child, Helen was angry and lonely. But when she was 6 years old, her parents got a teacher for her. They brought a young woman named Anne Sullivan to stay at their house and help Helen. After much hard work, Helen began to learn sign language. Anne taught Helen many important things, such as how to behave like other children. Because Helen was so smart, she learned things very quickly. She learned how to read Braille. By the time she was 8 years old, she was becoming very famous. People were amazed at what she could do.

Helen continued to learn. She even learned how to speak. When she was 20 years old, she went to college. Helen did so well in college that a magazine paid her to write the story of her life. After college, she earned money by writing and giving speeches. She traveled all around the world. She worked to get special schools and libraries for the blind and deaf. She wrote many books, including one about her teacher, Anne Sullivan.

Here is how "Helen" is written in Braille:

Directions: Answer these questions about Helen Keller.

1. What caused Helen to be blind and deaf? ___She had a very serious illness with a high fever.___
2. What happy thing happened when Helen was 6 years old? ___Her parents got her a special teacher.___
3. What was her teacher's name? ___Anne Sullivan___

157

Answer Key

Reading Comprehension: Hummingbirds

Hummingbirds are very small birds. This tiny bird is quite an acrobat. Only a few birds, such as kingfishers and sunbirds, can hover, which means to stay in one place in the air. But no other bird can match the flying skills of the hummingbird. The hummingbird can hover, fly backward and fly upside down!

Hummingbirds got their name because their wings move very quickly when they fly. This causes a humming sound. Their wings move so fast that you can't see them at all. This takes a lot of energy. These little birds must have food about every 20 minutes to have enough strength to fly. Their favorite foods are insects and nectar. Nectar is the sweet water deep inside a flower. Hummingbirds use their long, thin bills to drink from flowers. When a hummingbird sips nectar, it hovers in front of a flower. It never touches the flower with its wings or feet.

Besides being the best at flying, the hummingbird is also one of the prettiest birds. Of all the birds in the world, the hummingbird's colors are among the brightest. Some are bright green with red and white markings. Some are purple. One kind of hummingbird can change its color from reddish-brown to purple to red!

The hummingbird's nest is special, too. It looks like a tiny cup. The inside of the nest is very soft. This is because one of the things the mother bird uses to build the nest is the silk from a spider's web.

Directions: Answer these questions about hummingbirds.

1. How did hummingbirds get their name? __because their wings move__ __very quickly when they fly, and it causes a humming sound__
2. What does **hover** mean? __to hang in the air__
3. How often do hummingbirds need to eat? __every 20 minutes__
4. Name two things that hummingbirds eat. __insects and nectar__
5. What is one of the things a mother hummingbird uses to build her nest? __silk from a spider's web__

158

Reading Comprehension: Bats

Bats are the only mammals that can fly. They have wings made of thin skin stretched between long fingers. Bats can fly amazing distances. Some small bats have been known to fly more than 25 miles in one night.

Most bats eat insects or fruit. But some eat only fish, others only blood and still others the nectar and pollen of flowers that bloom at night. Bats are active only at night. They sleep during the day in caves or other dark places. At rest, they always hang with their heads down.

You may have heard the expression "blind as a bat." But bats are not blind. They don't, however, use their eyes to guide their flight or to find the insects they eat. A bat makes a high-pitched squeak, then waits for the echo to return to it. This echo tells it how far away an object is. This is often called the bat's sonar system. Using this system, a bat can fly through a dark cave without bumping into anything. Hundreds of bats can fly about in the dark without ever running into each other. They do not get confused by the squeaks of the other bats. They always recognize their own echoes.

Directions: Answer these questions about bats.

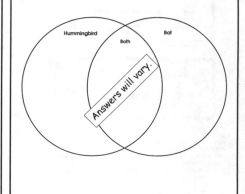

1. Bats are the only mammals that
   ☐ eat insects. ☒ fly. ☐ live in caves.
2. Most bats eat
   ☐ plants. ☐ other animals. ☒ fruits and insects.
3. Bats always sleep
   ☒ with their heads down. ☐ lying down. ☐ during the night.
4. Bats are blind. True (False)
5. Bats use a built-in sonar system to guide them. (True) False
6. Bats are confused by the squeaks of other bats. True (False)

159

Review: Venn Diagram

Directions: Make a Venn diagram comparing hummingbirds (see page 158) and bats (see page 159). Use page 136 to help you. Write at least three characteristics for each section of the diagram.

Hummingbird — Both — Bat

Answers will vary.

160

Reading Skills: Fact and Opinion

A **fact** is a statement that can be proven true. An **opinion** is a statement that tells how someone feels or what he/she thinks about something or someone.

Example:
 Fact: Ms. Davis is the new principal at Hayes Elementary.
 Opinion: Ms. Davis is the nicest principal we ever had.

Directions: Read each pair of sentences below. One is a fact; one is an opinion. Write F for the fact and O before the opinion.

O 1. Soccer is the best sport at our school.
F   More students at our school play soccer than any other sport.
F 2. Grandmother Hall lives in Clarksburg.
O   Grandmother Hall makes the best chocolate-chip cookies!
F 3. The county fair gate opens at 10:00 a.m.
O   We're going to have a great time at the fair.
O 4. The drive along the river is very scenic.
F   It is a 5-mile drive along the river.
O 5. Computers make our work much easier.
F   We have four computers in our classroom.
O 6. *The Cinnamon Lake Mysteries* is a very good series.
F   Our library has several copies of *The Cinnamon Lake Mysteries.*
F 7. Jerry falls asleep in class every day!
O   Jerry is so tired, he can't stay awake.
O 8. That car is too old to make it across the country.
F   That car was built in 1964.

161

Fact and Opinion

Directions: Write F before the facts and O before the opinions.

F 1. Our school football team had a winning season this year.
O 2. Mom's spaghetti is the best in the world!
O 3. Autumn is the nicest season of the year.
F 4. Mrs. Burns took her class on a field trip last Thursday.
F 5. The library always puts 30 books in our classroom book collection.
O 6. They should put only books about horses in the collection.
O 7. Our new art teacher is very strict.
O 8. Everyone should keep take-home papers in a folder so they don't have to look for them when it is time to go home.
F 9. The bus to the mall goes right by her house at 7:45 a.m.
O 10. Our new superintendent, Mr. Willeke, is very nice.

162

Fact and Opinion

Directions: Each fact sentence below has a "partner" opinion sentence in the box. Match "partners" by writing the correct sentences on the lines.

Maps can be very difficult to figure out.	Those brownies tasted awful!
The bridesmaids' dresses turned out beautiful!	Each child in here needs a computer.
You make the best cherry pie.	She is the best artist in the class.
If I can't go to the party, I will be really upset.	That car is so old, it looks like it will fall apart.

1. Paige helped her mother bake brownies last night.
   __Those brownies tasted awful!__
2. Katherine made all the drawings for the book.
   __She is the best artist in the class.__
3. That cherry tree is full of cherries.
   __You make the best cherry pie.__
4. We have four computers in the classroom.
   __Each child in here needs a computer.__
5. Mom made dresses for all of my bridesmaids.
   __The bridesmaids' dresses turned out beautiful!__
6. If I can't go to the party, I won't be able to give her the present.
   __If I can't go to the party, I will be really upset.__
7. The car is old and rusty.
   __That car is so old, it looks like it will fall apart.__
8. However he looked at it, he still couldn't figure out the map.
   __Maps can be very difficult to figure out.__

163

Answer Key

Facts and Opinions (164)

Facts are statements or events that have happened and can be proven to be true.
Example: George Washington was the first president of the United States.
This statement is a fact. It can be proven to be true by researching the history of our country.

Opinions are statements that express how someone thinks or feels.

Example George Washington was the greatest president the United States has ever had.

This statement is an opinion. Many people agree that George Washington was a great president, but not everyone agrees he was the greatest president. In some people's opinion, Abraham Lincoln was our greatest president.

Directions: Read each sentence. Write **F** for fact or **O** for opinion.

F 1. There is three feet of snow on the ground.
O 2. A lot of snow makes the winter enjoyable.
O 3. Chris has a better swing set than Mary.
F 4. Both Chris and Mary have swing sets.
F 5. California is a state.
O 6. California is the best state in the west.

Directions: Write three facts and three opinions.

Facts:
1) ___
2) ___
3) ___
Opinions:
1) ___
2) ___
3) ___

Answers will vary.

Review (165)

Directions: Read the paragraph. Then circle the sentence that tells the main idea.

Justin and Mina did everything together. They rode their bikes to school together, ate their lunches together, did their homework together, and even spent their weekends together playing baseball and video games. Even though Justin and Mina sometimes argued about silly things, they still loved being together. Sometimes the arguments were even fun, because then they got to make up! People often thought they were brother and sister because they sounded alike and even looked alike! Justin and Mina promised they would be friends forever.

(a.) Justin and Mina did everything together.
b. Justin and Mina like riding bikes.
c. Justin and Mina like to argue.

Directions: Write **F** before the facts and **O** before the opinions.

O 1. Justin loved to ride his bike.
F 2. Mina promised they would always be friends.
O 3. Justin and Mina should never argue.
O 4. Justin's dog needed to be washed.
F 5. That car is only big enough for three people!
F 6. The laundry basket is in the corner of the basement.
O 7. That laundry needs to be done today.
O 8. Brownies are my favorite snack.
F 9. She made chocolate cake for Mom's birthday.
F 10. I came all the way from Texas to see you.

Fiction and Nonfiction (166)

Fiction writing is a story that has been invented. The story might be about things that could really happen (realistic) or about things that couldn't possibly happen (fantasy). **Nonfiction** writing is based on facts. It usually gives information about people, places or things. A person can often tell while reading whether a story or book is fiction or nonfiction.

Directions: Read the paragraphs below and on page 167. Determine whether each paragraph is fiction or nonfiction. Circle the letter **F** for fiction or the letter **N** for nonfiction.

"Do not be afraid, little flowers," said the oak. "Close your yellow eyes in sleep and trust in me. You have made me glad many a time with your sweetness. Now, I will take care that the winter shall do you no harm. **F** N

The whole team watched as the ball soared over the outfield fence. The game was over! It was hard to walk off the field and face parents, friends and each other. It had been a long season. Now, they would have to settle for second place. **F** N

Be careful when you remove the dish from the microwave. It will be very hot, so take care not to get burned by the dish or the hot steam. If time permits, leave the dish in the microwave for 2 or 3 minutes to avoid getting burned. It is a good idea to use a potholder, too. F **N**

Fiction and Nonfiction (167)

Megan and Mariah skipped out to the playground. They enjoyed playing together at recess. Today, it was Mariah's turn to choose what they would do first. To Megan's surprise, Mariah asked, "What do you want to do, Megan? I'm going to let you pick since it's your birthday!" **F** N

It is easy to tell an insect from a spider. An insect has three body parts and six legs. A spider has eight legs and no wings. Of course, if you see the creature spinning a web, you will know what it is. An insect wouldn't want to get too close to the web or it would be stuck. It might become dinner! F **N**

My name is Lee Chang, and I live in a country that you call China. My home is on the other side of the world from yours. When the sun is rising in my country, it is setting in yours. When it is day at your home, it is night at mine. F **N**

Henry washed the dog's foot in cold water from the brook. The dog lay very still, for he knew that the boy was trying to help him. **F** N

Reading a Diagram (168)

A **family tree** is a diagram of a person's family and ancestors. Peter made a family tree as part of a school project.

Directions: Look at Peter's family tree, then answer the questions about his family.

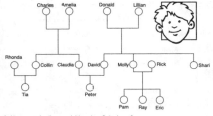

1. How many brothers and sisters does Peter have?
   brothers **0** sisters **0**
2. Is Peter's mother an only child? **No**
3. Who are Peter's uncles? **Collin and Rick**
4. How many cousins does Peter have? **4**
5. Who is Claudia's mother? **Amelia**
6. Who is Claudia's husband? **David**

Reading Skills: Advertisements (169)

Stores pay for advertisements, or ads, to let people know what is being sold. You see ads in newspapers and magazines, and on television and radio.

Directions: Use the following newspaper ad to answer the questions.

Home Cooking Restaurant

Open Easter Sunday 10:30 a.m. to 8:00 p.m.

Special Easter Menu
• Roast Turkey $10.50
• Baked Ham $12.00
• Roast Leg of Lamb $15.50

Many other dishes available, including veal, chicken, seafood and pasta.

Call for reservations 555–6241

Home Cooking Restaurant
1485 City Street

1. The restaurant is advertising special holiday meals. What holiday are they for?
   Easter
2. What is the most expensive meal listed on the menu?
   roast leg of lamb
3. What hours will the restaurant be open on Easter?
   10:30 a.m. to 8:00 p.m.

Answer Key

Reading Skills: Bus Schedules

Schedules are important to our daily lives. Your parents' jobs, school, even watching television—all are based on schedules. When you travel, you probably follow a schedule, too. Most forms of public transportation, such as subways, buses and trains, run on schedules. These "timetables" tell passengers when they will leave each stop or station.

Directions: Use the following city bus schedule to answer the questions.

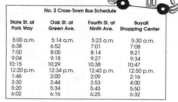

No. 2 Cross-Town Bus Schedule

State St. at Park Way	Oak St. at Green Ave.	Fourth St. at Ninth Ave.	Buyall Shopping Center
5:00 a.m.	5:14 a.m.	5:23 a.m.	5:30 a.m.
6:38	6:52	7:01	7:08
7:50	8:05	8:14	8:21
9:04	9:18	9:27	9:34
10:15	10:29	10:38	10:47
12:20 p.m.	12:34 p.m.	12:43 p.m.	12:50 p.m.
1:46	2:00	2:09	2:16
3:30	3:44	3:53	4:00
5:20	5:34	5:43	5:50
6:02	6:16	6:25	6:32

1. The first bus of the day leaves the State St./Park Way stop at 5 a.m. What time does the last bus of the day leave this stop? __6:02 p.m.__

2. The bus that leaves the Oak St./Green Ave. stop at 8:05 a.m. leaves the Buyall Shopping Center at what time? __8:21 a.m.__

3. What time does the first afternoon bus leave the Fourth St./Ninth Ave. stop? __12:43 p.m.__

4. How many buses each day run between the State St./Park Way stop and the Buyall Shopping Center? __10__

170

Reading Skills: Labels

Directions: It is good to know how to read the label of a medicine bottle. Read the label to answer the questions.

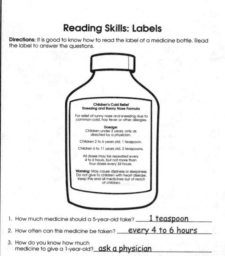

Children's Cold Relief
Sneezing and Runny Nose Formula

For relief of runny nose and sneezing due to common cold, hay fever or other allergies.

Dosage:
Children under 2 years, only as directed by a physician.

Children 2 to 6 years old. 1 teaspoon.

Children 6 to 11 years old. 2 teaspoons.

All doses may be repeated every 4 to 6 hours, but not more than four doses every 24 hours.

Warning: May cause dizziness or sleepiness. Do not give to children with heart disease. Keep this and all medicines out of reach of children.

1. How much medicine should a 5-year-old take? __1 teaspoon__
2. How often can this medicine be taken? __every 4 to 6 hours__
3. How do you know how much medicine to give to a 1-year-old? __ask a physician__
4. Who should not take this medicine? __children with heart disease__

171

Dictionary Skills: Guide Words

Guide words are the first and last words on a dictionary page. They are listed at the top of each page. All words on that page come between those two words.

Directions: Circle the pair of guide words that would appear on the same page as the flower name.

1. rose
   - rain — refuse
   - rock — rode
   - (roar — ruler)

2. tulip
   - tube — tug
   - (track — twin)
   - two — us

3. violet
   - vase — vent
   - (vine — visit)
   - visit — voice

4. daisy
   - bait — bar
   - (dad — deck)
   - dare — delight

5. sunflower
   - slip — space
   - some — sun
   - (such — swim)

6. lily
   - lamb — late
   - light — like
   - (lift — line)

172

Library Skills: Finding Books

Fiction books in a library are filed in alphabetical order using the author's last name.

Example: Ezra Jack Keats would be Keats, Ezra Jack and found under K.

Nonfiction books are grouped by subject. All books about snakes are grouped together, and all books about space are grouped together.

Directions: Practice filing books in alphabetical order. Number the authors' names in alphabetical order.

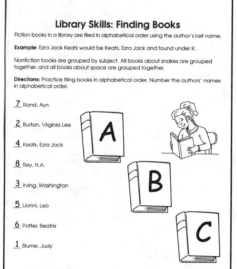

- 7 Rand, Ayn
- 2 Burton, Virginia Lee
- 4 Keats, Ezra Jack
- 8 Rey, H.A.
- 3 Irving, Washington
- 5 Lionni, Leo
- 6 Potter, Beatrix
- 1 Blume, Judy

173

Library Skills: Alphabetical Order

Ms. Ling, the school librarian, needs help shelving books. Fiction titles are arranged in alphabetical order by the author's last name. Ms. Ling has done the first set for you.

- 3 Silverstein, Shel
- 1 Bridwell, Norman
- 2 Farley, Walter

Directions: Number the following groups of authors in alphabetical order.

- 2 Bemelmans, Ludwig
- 4 Stein, R.L.
- 3 Sawyer, Ruth
- 1 Baum, L. Frank
- 4 Perkins, Al
- 2 Dobbs, Rose
- 1 Baldwin, James
- 3 Kipling, Rudyard

The content of some books is also arranged alphabetically.

Directions: Circle the books that are arranged in alphabetical order.

T.V. guide   (dictionary)   (encyclopedia)   novel

almanac   science book   (Yellow Pages)   catalog

Write the books you circled in alphabetical order.

1. dictionary
2. encyclopedia
3. Yellow Pages

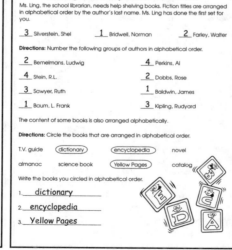

174

Reference Books

Reference books are books that tell basic facts. They usually cannot be checked out from the library. Dictionaries and encyclopedias are reference books. A dictionary tells you about words. Encyclopedias give you other information, such as when the president was born, what the Civil War was and where Eskimos live. Encyclopedias usually come in sets of more than 20 books. Information is listed in alphabetical order, just like words are listed in the dictionary. There are other kinds of reference books, too, like books of maps called atlases. Reference books are not usually read from cover to cover.

Directions: Draw a line from each sentence to the correct type of book. The first one is done for you.

1. I can tell you the definition of **divide**.
2. I can tell you when George Washington was born.
3. I can give you the correct spelling for many words.
4. I can tell you where Native Americans live.
5. I can tell you the names of many butterflies.
6. I can tell you what **modern** means.
7. I can give you the history of dinosaurs.
8. If you have to write a paper about Eskimos, I can help you.

A-D
E-G
H-J
K-M
N-P
Q-S
T-V
W-Y
Z

175

Answer Key

Periodicals

Libraries also have **periodicals** such as magazines and newspapers. They are called **periodicals** because they are printed regularly within a set period of time. There are many kinds of magazines. Some discuss the news. Some cover fitness, cats or other topics of special interest. Almost every city or town has a newspaper. Newspapers usually are printed daily, weekly or even monthly. Newspapers cover what is happening in your town and in the world. They usually include sections on sports and entertainment. They present a lot of information.

Directions: Follow the instructions.

> Answers will vary.

1. Choose an interesting magazine.

What is the name of the magazine? _____

List the titles of three articles in the magazine.

_____

_____

2. Now, look at a newspaper.

What is the name of the newspaper? _____

The title of a newspaper story is called a headline.

What are some of the headlines in your local newspaper?

_____

_____

176

References

Paul and Maria want to learn about the Moon. They go to the library. Where should they look while they are there?

Directions: Answer the questions to help Paul and Maria find information about the Moon.

1. Should they look in the children's section or in the adult's section? — **children's**

2. Should they look for a fiction book or a nonfiction book? — **nonfiction**

3. Who at the library can help them? — **the librarian**

4. What reference books should they look at? — **encyclopedias**

5. Where can they find information that may have been in the news? — **in periodicals**

6. What word would they look up in the encyclopedia to get the information they need? — **moon**

177

Proofreading

Proofreading means searching for and correcting errors by carefully reading and rereading what has been written. Use the proofreading marks below when correcting your writing or someone else's.

To insert a word or a punctuation mark that has been left out, use a caret ⋀.

Example: We ⋀ to the dance together. (went)

To show that a letter should be capitalized, put three lines under it.

Example: Mrs. jones drove us to school.

To show that a capital letter should be a small or lowercase, draw a diagonal line through it.

Example: Mrs. Jones Drove us to school.

To show that a word is spelled incorrectly, draw a horizontal line through it and write the correct spelling above it.

Example: The welres is an amazing animal. (walrus)

Directions: Proofread the two paragraphs using the proofreading marks you learned. The author's last name, Towne, is spelled correctly.

The Modern ark

My book report is on the modern ark by Cecilia Fitzsimmons. The book tells about (about) 80 of worlds endangered animals. The book also an are and animals inside for kids (has ark / the) to put together.

Their House

there house is a great book! The arthur's name is Mary Towne. they're house tells (Their / author's / Their) about a girl name Molly. Molly's family bys an old house from some people named (buys) warren. Then there big problems begin! (their)

178

Proofreading

Directions: Proofread the paragraphs, using the proofreading marks you learned. There are seven capitalization errors, three missing words and eleven errors in spelling or word usage.

Key West

key West has been tropical paradise ever since Ponce de Leon first saw the set of islands called the keys in 1513. Two famus streets in Key West are named duval and whitehead. You will find the city cemetery cemetery on Francis Street. The tombstones are funny!

The message on one is, "I told you I was sick!" On sailor's tombston is this message his widow: "At least I know where to find him now." (a tombstone / message from / least know)

The cemetery is on 21 acres in the midle of town. (acres / middle)

The most famous home in key west is that of the author author, Ernest Hemingway. Hemingway's home was at 907 whitehead Street. He lived their for 30 years. (Hemingway's / there)

179

Proofreading

Directions: Proofread the sentences. Write **C** if the sentence has no errors. Draw an **X** if the sentence contains missing words or other errors. The first one is done for you.

C 1. The new Ship Wreck Museum in Key West is exciting!

X 2. Another thing I liked was the litehouse.

C 3. Do you remember Hemingway's address in Key West?

X 4. The Key West semetery is on 21 acres of ground.

X 5. Ponce de eor discovered Key West.

C 6. The cemetery in Key West is on Francis Street.

X 7. My favorite tombstone was the sailor's.

C 8. His wife wrote the words on it. Remember?

X 9. The words said, "at least I know where to find him now!"

C 10. That sailor must have been away at sea all the time.

X 11. The troley ride around Key West is very interesting.

X 12. Do you why it is called Key West?

C 13. Can you imagine a lighthouse in the middle of your town?

X 14. It's interesting to no that Key West is our southernmost city.

C 15. Besides Harry Truman and Hemingway, did other famous people live there?

180

Review

Directions: Use the correct proofreading marks to show the two capitalization errors in each sentence.

1. Mrs. edwards drove us to edison Elementary School.

2. Who can say what john's real problem was?

3. Did you tell dr. Lynn we would be there at noon?

4. My Aunt Nellie was there and so was aunt susan.

Directions: Use the correct proofreading mark to insert the missing word or letter in each sentence.

5. He promised me he be there on time! ('d)

6. Who tell me the answer to the first problem? (can)

7. What his nickname when he was a baby? (was)

8. Dic he tell you same thing? (the)

Directions: Use the correct proofreading mark, then correct the misspelled or misused word in each sentence.

9. I wondered if the princepal knew what had happened? (principal)

10. I herd her whole family was there! (heard)

11. Our team easley beat the other team. (easily)

12. Don't laugh to hard at those silly jokes! (too)

181

Answer Key

Place Value

The place value of a digit, or numeral, is shown by where it is in the number. For example, in the number 1,234, 1 has the place value of thousands, 2 is hundreds, 3 is tens and 4 is ones.

Hundred Thousands	Ten Thousands	Thousands		Hundreds	Tens	Ones
9	4	3		8	5	2

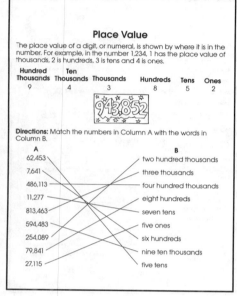

Directions: Match the numbers in Column A with the words in Column B.

A	B
62,453	two hundred thousands
7,641	three thousands
486,113	four hundred thousands
11,277	eight hundreds
813,463	seven tens
594,483	five ones
254,089	six hundreds
79,841	nine ten thousands
27,115	five tens

183

Place Value

Place value is the value of a digit, or numeral, shown by where it is in the number. For example, in 1,234, 1 has the place value of thousands, 2 is hundreds, 3 is tens and 4 is ones.

Directions: Write the numbers in the correct boxes to find how far the car has traveled.

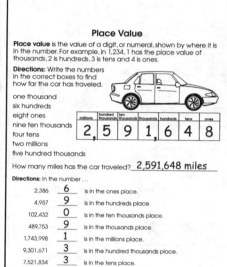

one thousand
six hundreds
eight ones
nine ten thousands
four tens
two millions
five hundred thousands

millions	hundred thousands	ten thousands	thousands	hundreds	tens	ones
2,	5	9	1,	6	4	8

How many miles has the car traveled? __2,591,648 miles__

Directions: In the number . . .

2,386	**6**	is in the ones place.
4,957	**9**	is in the hundreds place.
102,432	**0**	is in the ten thousands place.
489,753	**9**	is in the thousands place.
1,743,998	**1**	is in the millions place.
9,301,671	**3**	is in the hundred thousands place.
7,521,834	**3**	is in the tens place.

184

Addition: Regrouping

Addition means "putting together" or adding two or more numbers to find the sum. For example, 3 + 5 = 8. To regroup is to use ten ones to form one ten, ten tens to form one 100, and so on.

Directions: Add using regrouping.

Example:

Add the ones.	Add the tens with regrouping.
88 +21 / 9	88 +21 / 109

37 +72 / 109	56 +67 / 123	51 +88 / 139	37 +55 / 92	70 +68 / 138

93 +54 / 147	47 +82 / 129	81 +77 / 158	23 +92 / 115	36 +71 / 107

92 + 13 = __105__   73 + 83 = __156__   54 + 61 = __115__

The Blues scored 63 points. The Reds scored 44 points.
How many points were scored in all?   __107__

185

Subtraction: Regrouping

Subtraction means "taking away" or subtracting one number from another to find the difference. For example, 10 - 3 = 7. To regroup is to use one ten to form ten ones, one 100 to form ten tens, and so on.

Directions: Study the example. Subtract using regrouping.

Example:

32 =	2 tens + 12 ones
-13 =	1 ten + 3 ones
19 =	1 ten + 9 ones

33 -28 / 5	86 -59 / 27	92 -37 / 55	71 -48 / 23

63 -47 / 16	45 -18 / 27	31 -22 / 9	55 -39 / 16

82 - 69 = __13__   73 - 36 = __37__

The Yankees won 85 games.
The Cubs won 69 games.
How many more games
did the Yankees win?   __16__

186

Problem Solving: Addition, Subtraction

Directions: Read and solve each problem. The first one is done for you.

The clown started the day with 200 balloons. He gave away 128 of them. Some broke. At the end of the day he had 18 balloons left. How many of the balloons broke?   __54__

On Monday, there were 925 tickets sold to adults and 1,412 tickets sold to children. How many more children attended the fair than adults?   __487__

At one game booth, prizes were given out for scoring 500 points in three attempts. Sally scored 178 points on her first attempt, 149 points on her second attempt and 233 points on her third attempt. Did Sally win a prize?   __yes__

The prize-winning steer weighed 2,348 pounds. The runner-up steer weighed 2,179 pounds. How much more did the prize steer weigh?   __169 pounds__

There were 3,418 people at the fair on Tuesday, and 2,294 people on Wednesday. What was the total number of people there for the two days?   __5,712__

187

Multiples

Directions: Draw a red circle around the numbers that can be divided by 2. We say these are multiples of 2.
Draw a blue **X** on the multiples of 3.
Draw a green square around the multiples of 5.
Draw a yellow triangle around the multiples of 10.

1	2	X	4	5	X	7	8	X	10
11	X	13	14	X	16	17	X	19	20
X	22	23	X	25	26	X	28	29	30
31	32	X	34	35	X	37	38	X	40
41	X	43	44	X	46	47	X	49	50
X	52	53	X	55	56	X	58	59	60
61	62	X	64	65	X	67	68	X	70
71	X	73	74	X	76	77	X	79	80
X	82	83	X	85	86	X	88	89	90
91	92	X	94	95	X	97	98	X	100

Look at your chart. Common multiples are those which are shared. You have marked them in more than one way/color. What numbers are common? __30, 60, 90__

188

Answer Key

Multiplication

Factors are the numbers multiplied together in a multiplication problem. The answer is called the product. If you change the order of the factors, the product stays the same.

Example:
There are 4 groups of fish.
There are 3 fish in each group.
How many fish are there in all?
4 × 3 = 12
factor × factor = product

Directions: Draw 3 groups of 4 fish.

3 × 4 = 12

Compare your drawing and answer with the example. What did you notice? **same**

Directions: Fill in the missing numbers. Multiply.

5 × 4 = <u>20</u>   3 × 6 = <u>18</u>   4 × 2 = <u>8</u>

4 × 5 = <u>20</u>   6 × 3 = <u>18</u>   2 × 4 = <u>8</u>

3	7	2	9	8	4
×7	×3	×9	×2	×4	×8
21	21	18	18	32	32

5	2	6	3	5	6
×2	×5	×3	×6	×6	×5
10	10	18	18	30	30

189

Factor Trees

Factors are the smaller numbers multiplied together to make a larger number. Factor trees are one way to find all the factors of a number.
Directions: Complete each factor tree.

Example:

190

Division

Division is a way to find out how many times one number is contained in another number. The ∏ sign means "divided by." Another way to divide is to use ⌐. The dividend is the larger number that is divided by the smaller number, or divisor. The answer of a division problem is called the quotient.

Directions: Study the example. Divide.
Example:
20 ∏ 4 = 5
dividend divisor quotient

quotient
5
4⌐20
divisor dividend

35 ∏ 7 = <u>5</u>   7⌐35 ⁵   42 ∏ 6 = <u>7</u>   6⌐42 ⁷

2⌐12 ⁶   3⌐18 ⁶   4⌐36 ⁹   5⌐50 ¹⁰

6⌐24 ⁴   7⌐21 ³   8⌐32 ⁴   9⌐27 ³

36 ∏ 6 = <u>6</u>   28 ∏ 4 = <u>7</u>   15 ∏ 5 = <u>3</u>   12 ∏ 2 = <u>6</u>

A tree farm has 36 trees. There are 4 rows of trees.
How many trees are there in each row?   <u>9</u>

191

Division: Zero And One

Directions: Study the rules of division and the examples. Divide, then write the number of the rule you used to solve each problem.

Examples:
Rule 1: 1⌐5 ⁵   Any number divided by 1 is that number.
Rule 2: 5⌐5 ¹   Any number except 0 divided by itself is 1.
Rule 3: 7⌐0 ⁰   Zero divided by any number is zero.
Rule 4: 0⌐7   You cannot divide by zero.

1⌐6 ⁶   Rule <u>1</u>   4 ∏ 1 = <u>4</u>   Rule <u>1</u>

7⌐7 ¹   Rule <u>2</u>   9 ∏ 9 = <u>1</u>   Rule <u>2</u>

9⌐0 ⁰   Rule <u>3</u>   7 ∏ 1 = <u>7</u>   Rule <u>1</u>

1⌐4 ⁴   Rule <u>1</u>   6 ∏ 0 = <u>0</u>   Rule <u>4</u>

ZERO ONE

192

Divisibility Rules

A number is divisible... by 2 if the last digit is 0 or even (2, 4, 6, 8).
by 3 if the sum of all digits is divisible by 3.
by 4 if the last two digits are divisible by 4.
by 5 if the last digit is a 0 or 5.
by 10 if the last digit is 0.

Example: 250 is divisible by <u>2, 5, 10</u>

Directions: Tell what numbers each of these numbers is divisible by.

3,732 <u>2, 3, 4</u>   439 <u>—</u>

50 <u>2, 5, 10</u>   444 <u>2, 3, 4</u>

7,960 <u>2, 4, 5, 10</u>   8,212 <u>2, 4</u>

104,924 <u>2, 4</u>   2,345 <u>5</u>

193

Division: Remainders

Division is a way to find out how many times one number is contained in another number. For example, 28 ∏ 4 = 7 means that there are seven groups of four in 28. The dividend is the larger number that is divided by the smaller number, or divisor. The quotient is the answer in a division problem. The remainder is the amount left over. The remainder is always less than the divisor.

Directions: Study the example. Find each quotient and remainder.
Example:
There are 11 dog biscuits.
Put them in groups of 3.
There are 2 left over.

3⌐11 ³ -9 / 2 remainder   3⌐11 ^{3 r 2}

Remember: The remainder must be less than the **divisor!**

3⌐13 ^{4 r1}   4⌐17 ^{4 r1}   6⌐32 ^{5 r2}   5⌐26 ^{5 r1}

9 ∏ 4 = <u>2 r1</u>   12 ∏ 5 = <u>2 r2</u>   26 ∏ 4 = <u>6 r2</u>   49 ∏ 9 = <u>5 r4</u>

The pet store has 7 cats.
Two cats go in each
cage. How many cats
are left over?   <u>1</u>

194

Answer Key

Problem Solving: Multiplication, Division

Directions: Read and solve each problem.

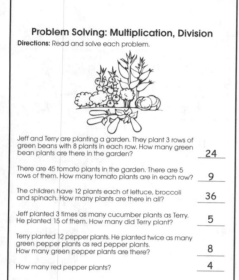

Jeff and Terry are planting a garden. They plant 3 rows of green beans with 8 plants in each row. How many green bean plants are there in the garden? **24**

There are 45 tomato plants in the garden. There are 5 rows of them. How many tomato plants are in each row? **9**

The children have 12 plants each of lettuce, broccoli and spinach. How many plants are there in all? **36**

Jeff planted 3 times as many cucumber plants as Terry. He planted 15 of them. How many did Terry plant? **5**

Terry planted 12 pepper plants. He planted twice as many green pepper plants as red pepper plants. How many green pepper plants are there? **8**

How many red pepper plants? **4**

195

Coordinates

Directions: Locate the points on the grid and color in each box.

What animal did you form? _Answers will vary._

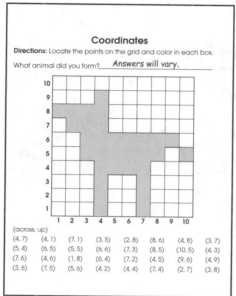

(across, up)

(4, 7)	(4, 1)	(7, 1)	(3, 5)	(2, 8)	(8, 6)	(4, 8)	(3, 7)
(5, 4)	(6, 5)	(5, 5)	(6, 6)	(7, 3)	(8, 5)	(10, 5)	(4, 3)
(7, 6)	(4, 6)	(1, 8)	(6, 4)	(7, 2)	(4, 5)	(9, 6)	(4, 9)
(3, 6)	(7, 5)	(5, 6)	(4, 2)	(4, 4)	(7, 4)	(2, 7)	(3, 8)

196

Fractions

A **fraction** is a number that names part of a whole, such as $\frac{1}{2}$ or $\frac{1}{3}$.

A fraction is made up of two numbers—the **numerator** (top number) and the **denominator** (bottom number). The larger the denominator, the smaller each of the equal parts. $\frac{1}{12}$ is smaller than $\frac{1}{2}$.

Directions: Study the fractions below.

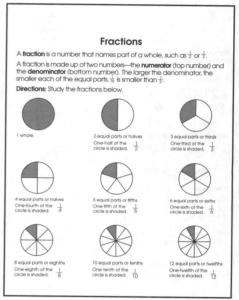

1 whole.

2 equal parts or halves
One-half of the circle is shaded. $\frac{1}{2}$

3 equal parts or thirds
One-third of the circle is shaded. $\frac{1}{3}$

4 equal parts or halves
One-fourth of the circle is shaded. $\frac{1}{4}$

5 equal parts or fifths
One-fifth of the circle is shaded. $\frac{1}{5}$

6 equal parts or sixths
One-sixth of the circle is shaded. $\frac{1}{6}$

8 equal parts or eighths
One-eighth of the circle is shaded. $\frac{1}{8}$

10 equal parts or tenths
One-tenth of the circle is shaded. $\frac{1}{10}$

12 equal parts or twelfths
One-twelfth of the circle is shaded. $\frac{1}{12}$

201

Fractions: Equivalent

Fractions that name the same part of a whole are equivalent fractions.

Example:

$\frac{1}{2} = \frac{2}{4}$

Directions: Fill in the numbers to complete the equivalent fractions.

$\frac{1}{4} = \frac{2}{8}$ $\frac{2}{3} = \frac{4}{6}$

$\frac{1}{6} = \frac{2}{12}$ $\frac{2}{3} = \frac{4}{6}$

$\frac{1}{3} = \frac{4}{12}$ $\frac{1}{5} = \frac{3}{15}$ $\frac{1}{4} = \frac{2}{8}$

$\frac{1}{2} = \frac{3}{6}$ $\frac{2}{3} = \frac{6}{9}$ $\frac{2}{6} = \frac{6}{18}$

202

Fractions: Division

A fraction is a number that names part of an object. It can also name part of a group.

Directions: Study the example. Divide by the bottom number of the fraction to find the answers.

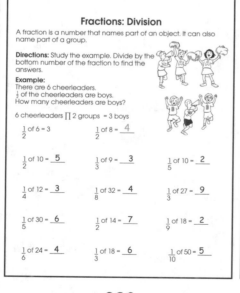

Example:
There are 6 cheerleaders.
$\frac{1}{3}$ of the cheerleaders are boys.
How many cheerleaders are boys?

6 cheerleaders ∏ 2 groups = 3 boys

$\frac{1}{2}$ of 6 = 3 $\frac{1}{2}$ of 8 = **4**

$\frac{1}{2}$ of 10 = **5** $\frac{1}{3}$ of 9 = **3** $\frac{1}{5}$ of 10 = **2**

$\frac{1}{4}$ of 12 = **3** $\frac{1}{8}$ of 32 = **4** $\frac{1}{3}$ of 27 = **9**

$\frac{1}{5}$ of 30 = **6** $\frac{1}{2}$ of 14 = **7** $\frac{1}{9}$ of 18 = **2**

$\frac{1}{6}$ of 24 = **4** $\frac{1}{3}$ of 18 = **6** $\frac{1}{10}$ of 50 = **5**

203

Decimals: Addition and Subtraction

Decimals are added and subtracted in the same way as other numbers. Simply carry down the decimal point to your answer.

Directions: Add or subtract.

Examples:

$\begin{array}{r} 1 \\ 1.3 \\ +2.8 \\ \hline 4.1 \end{array}$ $\begin{array}{r} 4.5 \\ -2.2 \\ \hline 2.3 \end{array}$

$\begin{array}{r} 1.3 \\ +2.2 \\ \hline 3.5 \end{array}$ $\begin{array}{r} 4.6 \\ -3.4 \\ \hline 1.2 \end{array}$ $\begin{array}{r} 5.1 \\ +8.8 \\ \hline 13.9 \end{array}$ $\begin{array}{r} 6.7 \\ -4.3 \\ \hline 2.4 \end{array}$

$\begin{array}{r} 7.9 \\ -3.7 \\ \hline 4.2 \end{array}$ $\begin{array}{r} 6.4 \\ +8.7 \\ \hline 15.1 \end{array}$ $\begin{array}{r} 11.4 \\ -9.5 \\ \hline 1.9 \end{array}$ $\begin{array}{r} 0.5 \\ +3.6 \\ \hline 4.1 \end{array}$

9.3 + 1.2 = **10.5**   2.5 - 0.7 = **1.8**   1.2 + 5.0 = **6.2**

Bob jogs around the school every day. The distance for one time around is 0.7 of a mile. If he jogs around the school two times, how many miles does he jog each day? **1.4 miles**

204

Answer Key

Problem-Solving: Fractions, Decimals

A fraction is a number that names part of a whole, such as $\frac{1}{2}$ or $\frac{1}{3}$.

Directions: Read and solve each problem.

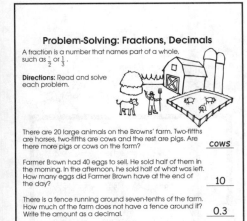

There are 20 large animals on the Browns' farm. Two-fifths are horses, two-fifths are cows and the rest are pigs. Are there more pigs or cows on the farm? **cows**

Farmer Brown had 40 eggs to sell. He sold half of them in the morning. In the afternoon, he sold half of what was left. How many eggs did Farmer Brown have at the end of the day? **10**

There is a fence running around seven-tenths of the farm. How much of the farm does not have a fence around it? Write the amount as a decimal. **0.3**

The Browns have 10 chickens. Two are roosters and the rest are hens. Write a decimal for the number that are roosters and for the number that are hens. **0.2** roosters **0.8** hens

Mrs. Brown spends three-fourths of her day working outside and the rest working inside. Does she spend more time inside or outside? **outside**

205

Percentages

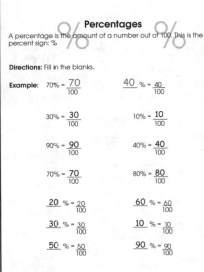

A percentage is the amount of a number out of 100. This is the percent sign: %

Directions: Fill in the blanks.

Example: $70\% = \frac{70}{100}$ $\underline{40}\% = \frac{40}{100}$

$30\% = \frac{30}{100}$ $10\% = \frac{10}{100}$

$90\% = \frac{90}{100}$ $40\% = \frac{40}{100}$

$70\% = \frac{70}{100}$ $80\% = \frac{80}{100}$

$\underline{20}\% = \frac{20}{100}$ $\underline{60}\% = \frac{60}{100}$

$\underline{30}\% = \frac{30}{100}$ $\underline{10}\% = \frac{10}{100}$

$\underline{50}\% = \frac{50}{100}$ $\underline{90}\% = \frac{90}{100}$

206

Place Value: Standard Form

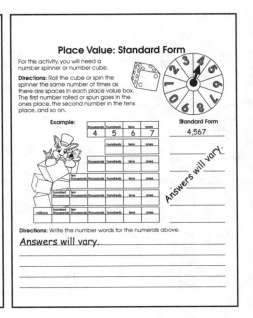

For this activity, you will need a number spinner or number cube.

Directions: Roll the cube or spin the spinner the same number of times as there are spaces in each place value box. The first number rolled or spun goes in the ones place, the second number in the tens place, and so on.

Example:

thousands	hundreds	tens	ones
4	5	6	7

Standard Form
4,567

Answers will vary.

Directions: Write the number words for the numerals above.

Answers will vary.

208

Place Value: Expanded Notation and Standard Form

Directions: Use the number cube or spinner to create numbers for the place value boxes below. Then write the number in expanded notation and standard form.

Example:

thousands	hundreds	tens	ones
8	6	2	4

Standard Form **8,624**
Expanded Notation **8,000 + 600 + 20 + 4**

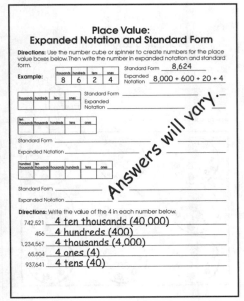

Answers will vary.

Directions: Write the value of the 4 in each number below.

742,521 **4 ten thousands (40,000)**
456 **4 hundreds (400)**
1,234,567 **4 thousands (4,000)**
65,504 **4 ones (4)**
937,641 **4 tens (40)**

209

Computing

Many people use computers on a daily basis at home, work or school. Computers help us to complete many tasks quickly and efficiently.

The Chinese used a computing device more than 4,000 years ago. It was called an abacus. An **abacus** is a wooden frame with four rows of beads representing ones, tens, hundreds and thousands.

The beads on the bottom half of the abacus are worth one unit. The beads on the top half of the unit are worth five units.

The bottom beads are pushed up to the middle bar of the abacus. The top beads are pushed down to the middle bar of the abacus.

Directions: Determine the number shown on each abacus and write it in the blank. The first one is done for you.

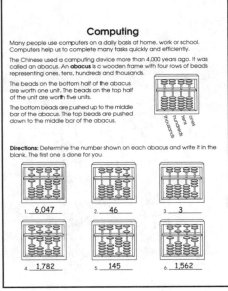

1. 6,047   2. 46   3. 3

4. 1,782   5. 145   6. 1,562

210

Estimating

To **estimate** means to give an approximate rather than an exact answer. To find an estimated sum or difference, round the numbers of the problem, then add or subtract. If the number has 5 ones or more, round up to the nearest ten. If the number has 4 ones or less, round down to the nearest ten.

Directions: Round the numbers to the nearest ten, hundred or thousand. Then add or subtract.

Examples:

Ten	Hundred	Thousand
74 → 70 + 39 → + 40 110	352 → 400 − 164 → − 200 200	7,681 → 8,000 + 4,321 → + 4,000 12,000

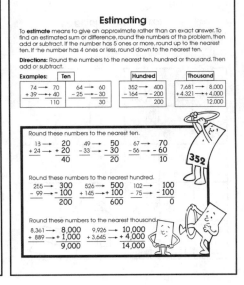

Round these numbers to the nearest ten.

13 → 20   49 → 50   67 → 70
+ 24 → + 20   − 33 → − 30   − 56 → − 60
40   20   10

Round these numbers to the nearest hundred.

255 → 300   526 → 500   102 → 100
− 99 → − 100   + 145 → + 100   − 75 → − 100
200   600   100

Round these numbers to the nearest thousand.

8,361 → 8,000   9,926 → 10,000
+ 889 → + 1,000   + 3,645 → + 4,000
9,000   14,000

211

Answer Key

212

Rounding

Directions: Round these numbers to the nearest ten.

18 **20**   33 **30**   82 **80**   56 **60**
24 **20**   49 **50**   91 **90**   67 **70**

689

Directions: Round these numbers to the nearest hundred.

243 **200**   689 **700**   263 **300**   162 **200**
389 **400**   720 **700**   351 **400**   490 **500**
463 **500**   846 **800**   928 **900**   733 **700**

Directions: Round these numbers to the nearest thousand.

2,638 **3,000**   3,940 **4,000**   8,653 **9,000**
6,238 **6,000**   1,429 **1,000**   5,061 **5,000**
7,289 **7,000**   2,742 **3,000**   9,460 **9,000**
3,109 **3,000**   4,697 **5,000**   8,302 **8,000**

Directions: Round these numbers to the nearest ten thousand.

11,368 **10,000**   38,421 **40,000**
75,302 **80,000**   67,932 **70,000**
14,569 **10,000**   49,926 **50,000**
93,694 **90,000**   81,648 **80,000**
26,784 **30,000**   87,065 **90,000**
57,843 **60,000**   29,399 **30,000**

213

Estimating

Estimating is used for certain mathematical calculations. For example, to figure the cost of several items, round their prices to the nearest dollar, then add up the approximate cost. A store clerk, on the other hand, needs to know the exact prices in order to charge the correct amount. To estimate to the nearest hundred, round up numbers over 50. **Example:** 251 is rounded up to 300. Round down numbers less than 50. **Example:** 128 is rounded down to 100.

Directions: In the following situations, write whether an exact or estimated answer should be used.

Example:
You make a deposit in your bank account. Do you want an estimated total or an exact total?   **Exact**

1. Your family just ate dinner at a restaurant. Your parents are trying to calculate the tip for your server. Should they estimate by rounding or use exact numbers?   **Estimate**

2. You are at the store buying candy, and you want to know if you have enough money to pay for it. Should you estimate or use exact numbers?   **Estimate**

3. Some friends are planning a trip from New York City to Washington, D.C. They need to know about how far they will travel in miles. Should they estimate or use exact numbers?   **Estimate**

4. You plan a trip to the zoo. Beforehand, you call the zoo for the price of admission. Should the person at the zoo tell you an estimated or exact price?   **Exact**

5. The teacher is grading your papers. Should your scores be exact or estimated?   **Exact**

215

Adding Larger Numbers

When adding two-, three- and four-digit numbers, add the ones first, then tens, hundreds, thousands, and so on.

Examples:

Tens	Ones
5	4
+ 2	5
7	9

Tens	Ones
5	4
+ 2	5
7	9

Directions: Add the following numbers.

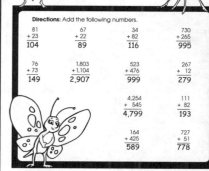

81 + 23 = **104**	67 + 22 = **89**	34 + 82 = **116**	730 + 265 = **995**
76 + 73 = **149**	1,803 + 1,104 = **2,907**	523 + 476 = **999**	267 + 12 = **279**
		4,254 + 545 = **4,799**	111 + 82 = **193**
		164 + 425 = **589**	727 + 51 = **778**

216

Addition: Regrouping

Regrouping uses 10 ones to form one 10, 10 tens to form one hundred, one 10 and 5 ones to form 15, and so on.

Directions: Add using regrouping. Color in all the boxes with a 5 in the answer to help the dog find its way home.

	63 + 22 = **85**	5,268 + 4,910 + 1,683 = **11,861**	248 + 463 = **711**	291 + 543 = **834**	2,934 + 112 = **3,046**
1,736 + 5,367 = **7,103**	2,946 + 7,384 = **10,330**	3,245 + 1,239 + 981 = **5,465**	738 + 692 = **1,430**	896 + 728 = **1,624**	594 + 738 = **1,332**
2,603 + 5,004 = **7,607**	4,507 + 289 = **4,796**	1,483 + 6,753 = **8,236**	1,258 + 6,301 = **7,559**	27 + 469 + 6,002 = **6,498**	4,637 + 7,531 = **12,168**
782 + 65 = **847**	485 + 276 = **761**	3,421 + 8,064 = **11,485**			
48 + 93 + 26 = **167**	90 + 263 + 864 = **1,217**	362 + 453 + 800 = **1,615**			

217

Going in Circles

Directions: Where the circles meet, write the sum of the numbers from the circles on the right and left and above and below. The first one is done for you.

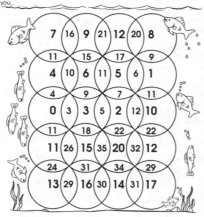

7	16	9	21	12	20	8
11	15	17	9
4	10	6	11	5	6	1
4	9	7	11
0	3	3	5	2	12	10
11	18	22	22
11	26	15	35	20	32	12
24	31	34	29
13	29	16	30	14	31	17

218

Subtracting Larger Numbers

When you subtract larger numbers, subtract the ones first, then the tens, hundreds, thousands, and so on.

Example:

Tens	Ones
9	4
− 2	1
	3

Tens	Ones
9	4
− 2	1
7	3

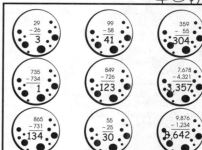

Directions: Solve these subtraction problems.

29 − 26 = **3**	99 − 58 = **41**	359 − 55 = **304**
735 − 734 = **1**	849 − 726 = **123**	7,678 − 4,321 = **3,357**
865 − 731 = **134**	55 − 25 = **30**	9,876 − 1,234 = **8,642**

Answer Key

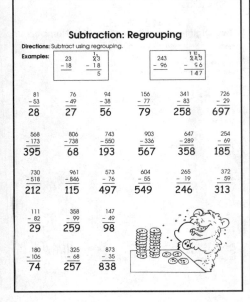

Subtraction: Regrouping

Directions: Subtract using regrouping.

Examples:

23	1	243	1 12
− 18	2̸3̸	− 96	2̸4̸3̸
	− 18		− 96
	5		147

81 − 53 = **28**	76 − 49 = **27**	94 − 38 = **56**	156 − 77 = **79**	341 − 83 = **258**	726 − 29 = **697**

568 − 173 = **395**	806 − 738 = **68**	743 − 550 = **193**	903 − 336 = **567**	647 − 289 = **358**	254 − 69 = **185**

730 − 518 = **212**	961 − 846 = **115**	573 − 76 = **497**	604 − 55 = **549**	265 − 19 = **246**	372 − 59 = **313**

111 − 82 = **29**	358 − 99 = **259**	147 − 49 = **98**

180 − 106 = **74**	325 − 68 = **257**	873 − 35 = **838**

219

Addition and Subtraction

Directions: Add or subtract, using regrouping when needed.

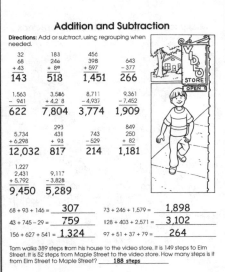

32 + 68 + 43 = **143**	183 + 246 + 89 = **518**	456 + 398 + 597 = **1,451**	643 − 377 = **266**

1,563 − 941 = **622**	3,516 + 4,218 = **7,804**	8,711 − 4,937 = **3,774**	9,361 − 7,452 = **1,909**

5,734 + 6,298 = **12,032**	293 + 431 + 93 = **817**	743 − 529 = **214**	849 + 250 + 82 = **1,181**

1,227 + 2,431 + 5,792 = **9,450**	9,117 − 3,828 = **5,289**

68 + 93 + 146 = **307** 73 + 246 + 1,579 = **1,898**

43 + 745 − 29 = **759** 128 + 403 + 2,571 = **3,102**

156 + 627 + 541 = **1,324** 97 + 51 + 37 + 79 = **264**

Tom walks 389 steps from his house to the video store. It is 149 steps to Elm Street. It is 52 steps from Maple Street to the video store. How many steps is it from Elm Street to Maple Street? **188 steps**

220

Addition and Subtraction

Directions: Add or subtract, using regrouping when needed.

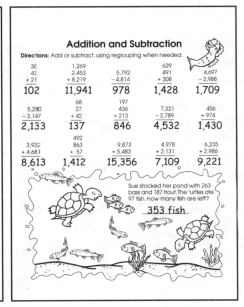

38 + 43 + 21 = **102**	1,269 + 2,453 + 8,219 = **11,941**	5,792 − 4,814 = **978**	629 + 491 + 308 = **1,428**	4,697 − 2,988 = **1,709**

5,280 − 3,147 = **2,133**	68 + 27 + 42 = **137**	197 + 436 + 213 = **846**	7,321 − 2,789 = **4,532**	456 + 974 = **1,430**

3,932 + 4,681 = **8,613**	492 + 863 + 57 = **1,412**	9,873 + 5,483 = **15,356**	4,978 + 2,131 = **7,109**	6,235 + 2,986 = **9,221**

Sue stocked her pond with 263 bass and 187 trout. The turtles ate 97 fish. How many fish are left?

353 fish

221

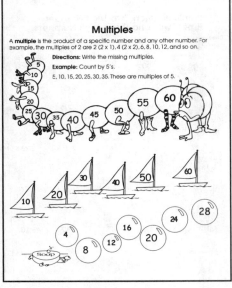

Multiples

A **multiple** is the product of a specific number and any other number. For example, the multiples of 2 are 2 (2 x 1), 4 (2 x 2), 6, 8, 10, 12, and so on.

Directions: Write the missing multiples.

Example: Count by 5's.

5, 10, 15, 20, 25, 30, 35. These are multiples of 5.

222

Multiplication

Multiplication is a short way to find the sum of adding the same number a certain amount of times, such as 7 x 4 = 28 instead of 7 + 7 + 7 + 7 = 28.

Directions: Multiply.

4 ×7 = **28**	7 ×6 = **42**	0 ×8 = **0**	7 ×2 = **14**	9 ×5 = **45**	1 ×5 = **5**	6 ×4 = **24**

8 ×3 = **24**	7 ×1 = **7**	4 ×2 = **8**	9 ×6 = **54**	8 ×5 = **40**	6 ×7 = **42**	9 ×8 = **72**

3 ×5 = **15**	7 ×8 = **56**	3 ×9 = **27**	5 ×6 = **30**	9 ×9 = **81**	7 ×5 = **35**	9 ×4 = **36**

3 ×6 = **18**	2 ×8 = **16**	8 ×6 = **48**	7 ×7 = **49**

0 ×7 = **0**	3 ×3 = **9**	5 ×9 = **45**

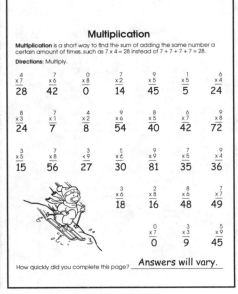

How quickly did you complete this page? **Answers will vary.**

223

Fact Factory

Factors are the numbers multiplied together in a multiplication problem. The **product** is the answer.

Directions: Write the missing factors or products.

x	5		x	9		x	7		x	3		x	1		x	8
1	5		8	72		2	14		7	21		1	1		9	72
5	25		3	27		5	35		4	12		12	12		8	64
4	20		4	36		6	42		6	18		10	10		4	32
6	30		9	81		8	56		1	3		3	3		5	40
3	15		6	54		7	49		3	9		9	9		6	48
2	10		7	63		4	28		2	6		7	7		7	56
7	35		2	18		3	21		5	15		6	6		3	24
9	45		0	0		8	24		4	12		0	0		2	16

x	2		x	4		x	6		x	10		x	11		x	12
12	24		2	8		7	42		2	20		4	44		1	12
1	2		4	16		6	36		3	30		7	77		2	24
11	22		6	24		5	30		4	40		9	99		3	36
2	4		8	32		4	24		5	50		10	110		4	48
10	20		1	4		3	18		6	60		3	33		5	60
3	6		3	12		2	12		7	70		5	55		6	72
9	18		5	20		1	6		8	80		6	66		7	84
4	8		7	28		0	0		9	90		8	88		8	96

224

Answer Key

Multiplication: One-Digit Numbers Times Two-Digit Numbers

Follow the steps for multiplying a one-digit number by a two-digit number using regrouping.

Example: Step 1: Multiply the ones. Regroup.
$\begin{array}{r} 2 \\ 54 \\ \times\ 7 \\ \hline 8 \end{array}$

Step 2: Multiply the tens. Add two tens.
$\begin{array}{r} 2 \\ 54 \\ \times\ 7 \\ \hline 378 \end{array}$

Directions: Multiply.

$\begin{array}{r} 27 \\ \times\ 3 \\ \hline 81 \end{array}$
$\begin{array}{r} 63 \\ \times\ 4 \\ \hline 252 \end{array}$
$\begin{array}{r} 52 \\ \times\ 5 \\ \hline 260 \end{array}$
$\begin{array}{r} 91 \\ \times\ 9 \\ \hline 819 \end{array}$
$\begin{array}{r} 45 \\ \times\ 7 \\ \hline 315 \end{array}$
$\begin{array}{r} 75 \\ \times\ 2 \\ \hline 150 \end{array}$

$\begin{array}{r} 64 \\ \times\ 5 \\ \hline 320 \end{array}$
$\begin{array}{r} 76 \\ \times\ 3 \\ \hline 228 \end{array}$
$\begin{array}{r} 93 \\ \times\ 6 \\ \hline 558 \end{array}$
$\begin{array}{r} 87 \\ \times\ 4 \\ \hline 348 \end{array}$
$\begin{array}{r} 66 \\ \times\ 7 \\ \hline 462 \end{array}$
$\begin{array}{r} 38 \\ \times\ 2 \\ \hline 76 \end{array}$

$\begin{array}{r} 47 \\ \times\ 8 \\ \hline 376 \end{array}$
$\begin{array}{r} 64 \\ \times\ 9 \\ \hline 576 \end{array}$
$\begin{array}{r} 51 \\ \times\ 8 \\ \hline 408 \end{array}$
$\begin{array}{r} 99 \\ \times\ 3 \\ \hline 297 \end{array}$

$\begin{array}{r} 13 \\ \times\ 7 \\ \hline 91 \end{array}$
$\begin{array}{r} 32 \\ \times\ 4 \\ \hline 128 \end{array}$
$\begin{array}{r} 25 \\ \times\ 8 \\ \hline 200 \end{array}$
$\begin{array}{r} 15 \\ \times\ 7 \\ \hline 105 \end{array}$

The chickens on the Smith farm produce 48 dozen eggs each day. How many dozen eggs do they produce in 7 days?

336 dozen

225

Multiplication: Tens, Hundreds, Thousands

When multiplying a number by 10, the answer is the number with a 0 behind it. It is like counting by tens.

Examples:

$\begin{array}{r} 10 \\ \times\ 1 \\ \hline 10 \end{array}$
$\begin{array}{r} 10 \\ \times\ 2 \\ \hline 20 \end{array}$
$\begin{array}{r} 10 \\ \times\ 3 \\ \hline 30 \end{array}$
$\begin{array}{r} 10 \\ \times\ 4 \\ \hline 40 \end{array}$
$\begin{array}{r} 10 \\ \times\ 5 \\ \hline 50 \end{array}$
$\begin{array}{r} 10 \\ \times\ 6 \\ \hline 60 \end{array}$

When multiplying a number by 100, the answer is the number with two 0's. When multiplying by 1,000, the answer is the number with three 0's.

Examples:

$\begin{array}{r} 100 \\ \times\ 1 \\ \hline 100 \end{array}$
$\begin{array}{r} 100 \\ \times\ 2 \\ \hline 200 \end{array}$
$\begin{array}{r} 100 \\ \times\ 3 \\ \hline 300 \end{array}$
$\begin{array}{r} 1,000 \\ \times\ 1 \\ \hline 1,000 \end{array}$
$\begin{array}{r} 1,000 \\ \times\ 2 \\ \hline 2,000 \end{array}$
$\begin{array}{r} 1,000 \\ \times\ 3 \\ \hline 3,000 \end{array}$

$\begin{array}{r} 4 \\ \times\ 2 \\ \hline 8 \end{array}$
$\begin{array}{r} 400 \\ \times\ 2 \\ \hline 800 \end{array}$
$\begin{array}{r} 8 \\ \times\ 3 \\ \hline 24 \end{array}$
$\begin{array}{r} 800 \\ \times\ 3 \\ \hline 2,400 \end{array}$
$\begin{array}{r} 7 \\ \times\ 5 \\ \hline 35 \end{array}$
$\begin{array}{r} 700 \\ \times\ 5 \\ \hline 3,500 \end{array}$

Directions: Multiply.

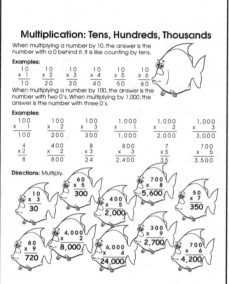

$\begin{array}{r} 10 \\ \times\ 3 \\ \hline 30 \end{array}$
$\begin{array}{r} 60 \\ \times\ 5 \\ \hline 300 \end{array}$
$\begin{array}{r} 400 \\ \times\ 5 \\ \hline 2,000 \end{array}$
$\begin{array}{r} 700 \\ \times\ 8 \\ \hline 5,600 \end{array}$
$\begin{array}{r} 50 \\ \times\ 7 \\ \hline 350 \end{array}$

$\begin{array}{r} 80 \\ \times\ 9 \\ \hline 720 \end{array}$
$\begin{array}{r} 4,000 \\ \times\ 2 \\ \hline 8,000 \end{array}$
$\begin{array}{r} 6,000 \\ \times\ 4 \\ \hline 24,000 \end{array}$
$\begin{array}{r} 300 \\ \times\ 9 \\ \hline 2,700 \end{array}$
$\begin{array}{r} 700 \\ \times\ 6 \\ \hline 4,200 \end{array}$

226

Multiplication: Two-Digit Numbers Times Two-Digit Numbers

Follow the steps for multiplying a two-digit number by a two-digit number using regrouping.

Example:

Step 1: Multiply the ones. Regroup.
$\begin{array}{r} 2 \\ 63 \\ \times\ 68 \\ \hline 504 \end{array}$

Step 2: Multiply the tens. Regroup. Add.
$\begin{array}{r} 1 \\ 63 \\ \times\ 68 \\ \hline 504 \\ +3,780 \\ \hline 4,284 \end{array}$
$\begin{array}{r} 63 \\ \times\ 68 \\ \hline 3,780 \end{array}$

Directions: Multiply.

$\begin{array}{r} 12 \\ \times 55 \\ \hline 660 \end{array}$
$\begin{array}{r} 27 \\ \times 15 \\ \hline 405 \end{array}$
$\begin{array}{r} 65 \\ \times 27 \\ \hline 1,755 \end{array}$
$\begin{array}{r} 19 \\ \times 39 \\ \hline 741 \end{array}$
$\begin{array}{r} 99 \\ \times 13 \\ \hline 1,287 \end{array}$
$\begin{array}{r} 35 \\ \times 14 \\ \hline 490 \end{array}$

$\begin{array}{r} 43 \\ \times 26 \\ \hline 1,118 \end{array}$
$\begin{array}{r} 38 \\ \times 17 \\ \hline 646 \end{array}$
$\begin{array}{r} 53 \\ \times 86 \\ \hline 4,558 \end{array}$
$\begin{array}{r} 47 \\ \times 72 \\ \hline 3,384 \end{array}$
$\begin{array}{r} 57 \\ \times 62 \\ \hline 3,534 \end{array}$
$\begin{array}{r} 48 \\ \times 33 \\ \hline 1,584 \end{array}$

$\begin{array}{r} 27 \\ \times 54 \\ \hline 1,458 \end{array}$
$\begin{array}{r} 93 \\ \times 45 \\ \hline 4,185 \end{array}$
$\begin{array}{r} 64 \\ \times 16 \\ \hline 1,024 \end{array}$
$\begin{array}{r} 53 \\ \times 23 \\ \hline 1,219 \end{array}$

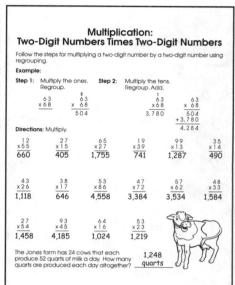

The Jones farm has 24 cows that each produce 52 quarts of milk a day. How many quarts are produced each day altogether?

1,248 quarts

227

Multiplication: Two-Digit Numbers Times Three-Digit Numbers

Follow the steps for multiplying a two-digit number by a three-digit number using regrouping.

Example: Step 1: Multiply the ones. Regroup.
$\begin{array}{r} 22 \\ 287 \\ \times\ 43 \\ \hline 861 \end{array}$

Step 2: Multiply the tens. Regroup. Add.
$\begin{array}{r} 287 \\ \times\ 43 \\ \hline 11,480 \end{array}$
$\begin{array}{r} 287 \\ \times\ 43 \\ \hline 861 \\ +11,480 \\ \hline 12,341 \end{array}$

Directions: Multiply.

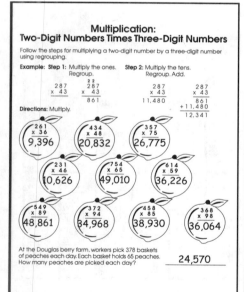

$\begin{array}{r} 261 \\ \times\ 36 \\ \hline 9,396 \end{array}$
$\begin{array}{r} 434 \\ \times\ 48 \\ \hline 20,832 \end{array}$
$\begin{array}{r} 357 \\ \times\ 75 \\ \hline 26,775 \end{array}$

$\begin{array}{r} 231 \\ \times\ 46 \\ \hline 10,626 \end{array}$
$\begin{array}{r} 754 \\ \times\ 65 \\ \hline 49,010 \end{array}$
$\begin{array}{r} 614 \\ \times\ 59 \\ \hline 36,226 \end{array}$

$\begin{array}{r} 549 \\ \times\ 89 \\ \hline 48,861 \end{array}$
$\begin{array}{r} 372 \\ \times\ 94 \\ \hline 34,968 \end{array}$
$\begin{array}{r} 458 \\ \times\ 85 \\ \hline 38,930 \end{array}$
$\begin{array}{r} 368 \\ \times\ 98 \\ \hline 36,064 \end{array}$

At the Douglas berry farm, workers pick 378 baskets of peaches each day. Each basket holds 65 peaches. How many peaches are picked each day?

24,570

228

Multiplication Drill

Directions: Multiply.

$\begin{array}{r} 134 \\ \times\ 22 \\ \hline 2,948 \end{array}$
$\begin{array}{r} 48 \\ \times 66 \\ \hline 3,168 \end{array}$
$\begin{array}{r} 876 \\ \times\ 13 \\ \hline 11,388 \end{array}$
$\begin{array}{r} 432 \\ \times\ 64 \\ \hline 27,648 \end{array}$

$\begin{array}{r} 68 \\ \times 11 \\ \hline 748 \end{array}$
$\begin{array}{r} 5,478 \\ \times\ 8 \\ \hline 43,824 \end{array}$
$\begin{array}{r} 248 \\ \times\ 61 \\ \hline 15,128 \end{array}$
$\begin{array}{r} 6,897 \\ \times\ 6 \\ \hline 41,382 \end{array}$

$\begin{array}{r} 82 \\ \times\ 4 \\ \hline 328 \end{array}$
$\begin{array}{r} 6,798 \\ \times\ 5 \\ \hline 33,990 \end{array}$
$\begin{array}{r} 79 \\ \times 86 \\ \hline 6,794 \end{array}$
$\begin{array}{r} 694 \\ \times\ 38 \\ \hline 26,372 \end{array}$

Directions: Color the picture by matching each number with its paintbrush.

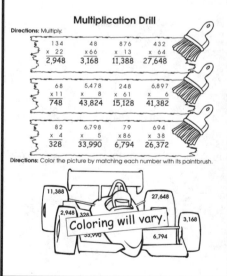

Coloring will vary.

229

Multiplication: Two-Digit Numbers Times Two- and Three-Digit Numbers

Directions: Multiply.

$\begin{array}{r} 25 \\ \times 72 \\ \hline 1,800 \end{array}$
$\begin{array}{r} 70 \\ \times 66 \\ \hline 4,620 \end{array}$
$\begin{array}{r} 844 \\ \times\ 24 \\ \hline 20,256 \end{array}$
$\begin{array}{r} 124 \\ \times\ 15 \\ \hline 1,860 \end{array}$

$\begin{array}{r} 45 \\ \times 41 \\ \hline 1,845 \end{array}$
$\begin{array}{r} 76 \\ \times 78 \\ \hline 5,928 \end{array}$
$\begin{array}{r} 74 \\ \times 69 \\ \hline 5,106 \end{array}$
$\begin{array}{r} 261 \\ \times\ 88 \\ \hline 22,968 \end{array}$

$\begin{array}{r} 48 \\ \times 36 \\ \hline 1,728 \end{array}$
$\begin{array}{r} 263 \\ \times\ 57 \\ \hline 14,991 \end{array}$
$\begin{array}{r} 37 \\ \times 64 \\ \hline 2,368 \end{array}$
$\begin{array}{r} 52 \\ \times 43 \\ \hline 2,236 \end{array}$

$\begin{array}{r} 321 \\ \times\ 78 \\ \hline 25,038 \end{array}$
$\begin{array}{r} 544 \\ \times\ 58 \\ \hline 31,552 \end{array}$
$\begin{array}{r} 797 \\ \times\ 24 \\ \hline 19,128 \end{array}$
$\begin{array}{r} 998 \\ \times\ 37 \\ \hline 36,926 \end{array}$

$\begin{array}{r} 249 \\ \times\ 33 \\ \hline 8,217 \end{array}$
$\begin{array}{r} 24 \\ \times 19 \\ \hline 456 \end{array}$
$\begin{array}{r} 48 \\ \times 20 \\ \hline 960 \end{array}$
$\begin{array}{r} 817 \\ \times\ 59 \\ \hline 48,203 \end{array}$

230

Panel 231

Multiplication:
Three-Digit Numbers Times Three-Digit Numbers

Directions: Multiply. Regroup when needed.

Example:
```
   563
  x248
 4,504
22,520
+112,600
139,624
```

Hint: When multiplying by the tens, start writing the number in the tens place. When multiplying by the hundreds, start in the hundreds place.

```
  842       932       759       531
 x167      x272      x468      x556
140,614   253,504   355,212   295,236
```

```
  383       523       229       738
 x476      x349      x189      x513
182,308   182,527    43,281   378,594
```

James grows pumpkins on his farm. He has 362 rows of pumpkins. There are 593 pumpkins in each row. How many pumpkins does James grow?   **214,666 pumpkins**

231

Panel 232

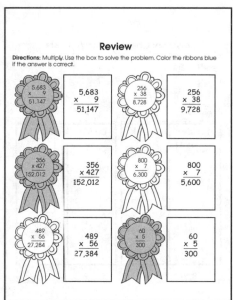

Review

Directions: Multiply. Use the box to solve the problem. Color the ribbons blue if the answer is correct.

```
 5,683         256
x    9        x 38
51,147        9,728
```

```
  356          800
x 427         x  7
152,012       5,600
```

```
  489           60
x  56         x   5
27,384         300
```

232

Panel 233

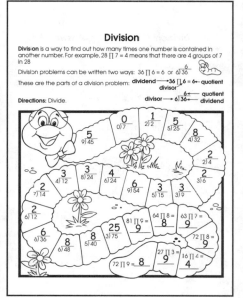

Division

Division is a way to find out how many times one number is contained in another number. For example, 28 ÷ 7 = 4 means that there are 4 groups of 7 in 28

Division problems can be written two ways: 36 ÷ 6 = 6 or 6)36

These are the parts of a division problem: dividend → 36 ÷ 6 = 6 ← quotient, divisor
divisor → 6)36 ← quotient, dividend

Directions: Divide.

233

Panel 234

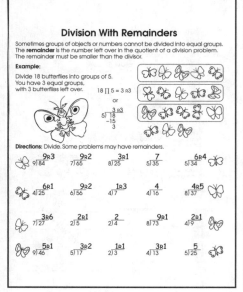

Division With Remainders

Sometimes groups of objects or numbers cannot be divided into equal groups. The **remainder** is the number left over in the quotient of a division problem. The remainder must be smaller than the divisor.

Example:
Divide 18 into groups of 5. You have 3 equal groups, with 3 butterflies left over.

18 ÷ 5 = 3 R3

or
```
  3 R3
5)18
 -15
   3
```

Directions: Divide. Some problems may have remainders.

```
   9R3      9R2      3R1       7      6R4
 9)84     7)65     8)25     5)35    5)34
```

```
   6R1      9R2      1R3       4      4R5
 4)25     6)56     4)7      4)16    8)37
```

```
   3R6      2R1       2       9R1     2R1
 7)27     2)5      2)4      8)73    4)9
```

```
   5R1      3R2      1R1      3R1      5
 9)46     5)17     2)3      4)13    5)25
```

234

Panel 235

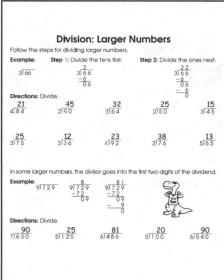

Division: Larger Numbers

Follow the steps for dividing larger numbers.

Example: **Step 1:** Divide the tens first.   **Step 2:** Divide the ones next.
```
 3)66          2              22
             3)66           3)66
             -6             -6
              06             06
                            - 6
                             0
```

Directions: Divide.
```
   21       45       32       25       15
 4)84     2)90     2)64     2)50     3)45
```

```
   25       12       23       38       13
 3)75     3)36     4)92     2)76     5)65
```

In some larger numbers, the divisor goes into the first two digits of the dividend.

Example:
```
 9)729      8          81
          9)729      9)729
          -72        -72
            09         09
                      - 9
                       0
```

Directions: Divide.
```
   90       25       81       20       90
 7)630    5)125    6)486    5)100    6)540
```

235

Panel 236

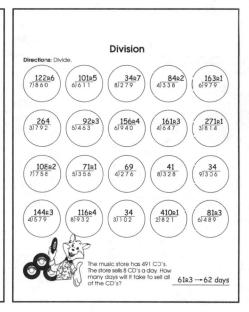

Division

Directions: Divide.

```
122R6     101R5     34R7      84R2      163R1
7)860     6)611     8)279     3)338     6)979
```

```
 264      92R3      156R4     161R3     271R1
3)792     5)463     6)940     4)647     3)814
```

```
108R2      71R1       69        41        34
7)758     5)356     4)276     8)328     9)306
```

```
144R3     116R4      34       410R1     81R3
4)579     8)932     3)102     2)821     6)489
```

The music store has 491 CD's. The store sells 8 CD's a day. How many days will it take to sell all of the CD's?   61R3 → **62 days**

236

Answer Key

Division: Checking the Answers

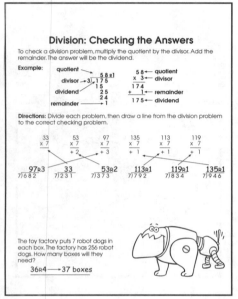

To check a division problem, multiply the quotient by the divisor. Add the remainder. The answer will be the dividend.

Example:

```
quotient →    5 8 R1        5 8 ← quotient
divisor → 3⟌ 1 7 5        x  3 ← divisor
              1 5          1 7 4
dividend      2 5        +   1 ← remainder
remainder      2 4        1 7 5 ← dividend
                1
```

Directions: Divide each problem, then draw a line from the division problem to the correct checking problem.

```
  33        53        97       135       113       119
x  7      x  7      x  7      x  7      x  7      x  7
+  2      + 3      + 1      + 1      + 1      + 1
```

```
  97R3       33       53R2      113R1     119R1     135R1
7⟌6 8 2   7⟌2 3 1   7⟌3 7 3   7⟌7 9 2   7⟌8 3 4   7⟌9 4 6
```

The toy factory puts 7 robot dogs in each box. The factory has 256 robot dogs. How many boxes will they need?

36R4 → 37 boxes

237

Division: Checking the Answers

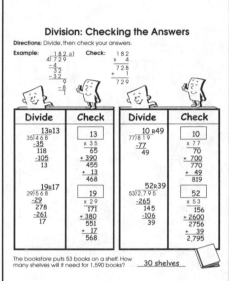

Directions: Divide, then check your answers.

Example:
```
    1 8 2 R1        Check:   1 8 2
4⟌ 7 2 9                  x    4
  - 4                      7 2 8
  - 3 2                  +    1
      9                    7 2 9
    - 8
      1
```

Divide	Check	Divide	Check
13R13 35⟌4 6 8 -35 118 -105 13	13 x 3 5 65 + 390 455 + 13 468	10 R49 77⟌8 1 9 -77 49	10 x 7 7 70 + 700 770 + 49 819
19R17 29⟌5 6 8 -29 278 -261 17	19 x 2 9 171 + 380 551 + 17 568	52R39 53⟌2 7 9 5 -265 145 -106 39	52 x 5 3 156 + 2600 2756 + 39 2,795

The bookstore puts 53 books on a shelf. How many shelves will it need for 1,590 books?

30 shelves

238

Division: Two-Digit Divisors

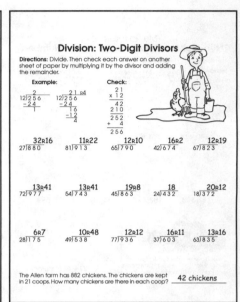

Directions: Divide. Then check each answer on another sheet of paper by multiplying it by the divisor and adding the remainder.

Example:
```
       2            21 R4              21
12⟌2 5 6       12⟌2 5 6          x  1 2
 -2 4           -2 4                 42
   1              16               2 1 0
                 -1 2              2 5 2
                    4            +    4
                                  2 5 6
```

```
  32R16       11R22      12R10     16R2      12R19
27⟌8 8 0   81⟌9 1 3   65⟌7 9 0  42⟌6 7 4  67⟌8 2 3
```

```
  13R41       13R41      19R8       18        20R12
72⟌9 7 7   54⟌7 4 3   45⟌8 6 3  24⟌4 3 2  18⟌3 7 2
```

```
   6R7        10R48      12R12     16R11     13R16
28⟌1 7 5   49⟌5 3 8   77⟌9 3 6  37⟌6 0 3  63⟌8 3 5
```

The Allen farm has 882 chickens. The chickens are kept in 21 coops. How many chickens are there in each coop?   42 chickens

239

Averaging

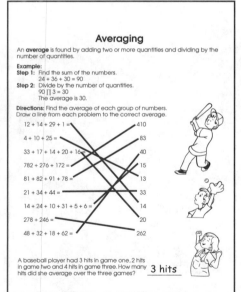

An **average** is found by adding two or more quantities and dividing by the number of quantities.

Example:
Step 1: Find the sum of the numbers.
24 + 36 + 30 = 90
Step 2: Divide by the number of quantities.
90 ⟌ 3 = 30
The average is 30.

Directions: Find the average of each group of numbers. Draw a line from each problem to the correct average.

```
12 + 14 + 29 + 1 =                    410
4 + 10 + 25 =                         83
33 + 17 + 14 + 20 + 16 =              40
782 + 276 + 172 =                     15
81 + 82 + 91 + 78 =                   13
21 + 34 + 44 =                        33
14 + 24 + 10 + 31 + 5 + 6 =           14
278 + 246 =                           20
48 + 32 + 18 + 62 =                   262
```

A baseball player had 3 hits in game one, 2 hits in game two and 4 hits in game three. How many hits did she average over the three games?   3 hits

240

Averaging

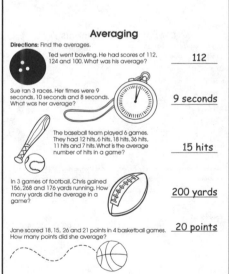

Directions: Find the averages.

Ted went bowling. He had scores of 112, 124 and 100. What was his average?   112

Sue ran 3 races. Her times were 9 seconds, 10 seconds and 8 seconds. What was her average?   9 seconds

The baseball team played 6 games. They had 12 hits, 6 hits, 18 hits, 36 hits, 11 hits and 7 hits. What is the average number of hits in a game?   15 hits

In 3 games of football, Chris gained 156, 268 and 176 yards running. How many yards did he average in a game?   200 yards

Jane scored 18, 15, 26 and 21 points in 4 basketball games. How many points did she average?   20 points

241

Averaging

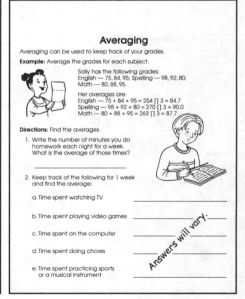

Averaging can be used to keep track of your grades.

Example: Average the grades for each subject.

Sally has the following grades:
English — 75, 84, 95; Spelling — 98, 92, 80; Math — 80, 88, 95.

Her averages are:
English — 75 + 84 + 95 = 254 ⟌ 3 = 84.7
Spelling — 98 + 92 + 80 = 270 ⟌ 3 = 90.0
Math — 80 + 88 + 95 = 263 ⟌ 3 = 87.7

Directions: Find the averages.

1. Write the number of minutes you do homework each night for a week. What is the average of those times?

2. Keep track of the following for 1 week and find the average:

   a. Time spent watching TV

   b. Time spent playing video games

   c. Time spent on the computer

   d. Time spent doing chores

   e. Time spent practicing sports or a musical instrument

Answers will vary.

242

Answer Key

Graphing

A **graph** is a drawing that shows information about changes in numbers.

Directions: Answer the questions by reading the graphs.

Bar Graph

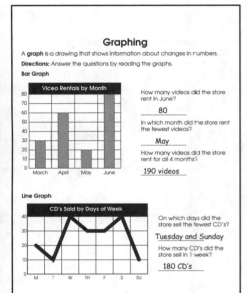

How many videos did the store rent in June?

80

In which month did the store rent the fewest videos?

May

How many videos did the store rent for all 4 months?

190 videos

Line Graph

On which days did the store sell the fewest CD's?

Tuesday and Sunday

How many CD's did the store sell in 1 week?

180 CD's

243

Ordered Pairs

An **ordered pair** is a pair of numbers used to locate a point.

Example: (8, 3)

Step 1: Count across to line 8 on the graph.
Step 2: Count up to line 3 on the graph.
Step 3: Draw a dot to mark the spot.

Directions: Map the following spots on the grid using ordered pairs.

(4, 7) (9, 10) (2, 1) (5, 5) (2, 2) (1, 5) (7, 4) (3, 8)

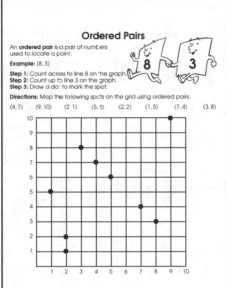

244

Graphing: Finding Ordered Pairs

Graphs or grids are sometimes used to find the location of objects.

Example: The ice-cream cone is located at point (5, 6) on the graph. To find the ice cream's location, follow the line to the bottom of the grid to get the first number — 5. Then go back to the ice cream and follow the grid line to the left for the second number — 6.

Directions: Write the ordered pair for the following objects. The first one is done for you.

book **(4, 8)** bike **(8, 6)** suitcase **(1, 4)** house **(8, 3)**
globe **(4, 4)** cup **(9, 9)** triangle **(7, 2)** airplane **(7, 8)**

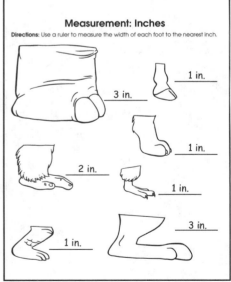

Directions: Identify the objects located at the following points. The first one is done for you.

(9, 1) **trophy**
(3, 5) **star**
(2, 2) **elephant**
(6, 4) **pear**
(1, 2) **flower**
(5, 1) **bird**
(1, 7) **bear**

245

Geometry: Polygons

A **polygon** is a closed figure with three or more sides.

Examples:

triangle 3 sides square 4 equal sides rectangle 4 sides pentagon 5 sides hexagon 6 sides octagon 8 sides

Directions: Identify the polygons.

octagon   **rectangle**

square   **hexagon**

pentagon   **triangle**

246

Measurement: Inches

An **inch** is a unit of length in the standard system equal to $\frac{1}{12}$ of a foot. A ruler is used to measure inches.

This illustration shows a ruler measuring a 4-inch pencil, which can be written as 4" or 4 in.

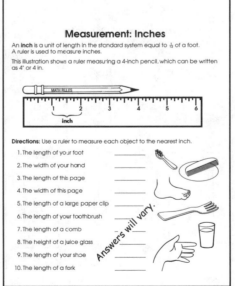

Directions: Use a ruler to measure each object to the nearest inch.

1. The length of your foot _____
2. The width of your hand _____
3. The length of this page _____
4. The width of this page _____
5. The length of a large paper clip _____
6. The length of your toothbrush _____
7. The length of a comb _____
8. The height of a juice glass _____
9. The length of your shoe _____
10. The length of a fork _____

Answers will vary.

247

Measurement: Inches

Directions: Use a ruler to measure the width of each foot to the nearest inch.

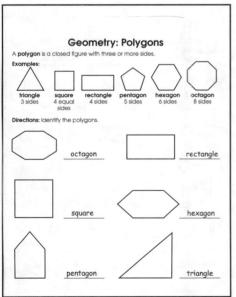

3 in.

1 in.

2 in.

1 in.

1 in.

3 in.

248

Answer Key

Measurement: Fractions of an Inch

An inch is divided into smaller units, or fractions of an inch.

Example: This stick of gum is 2¾ inches long.

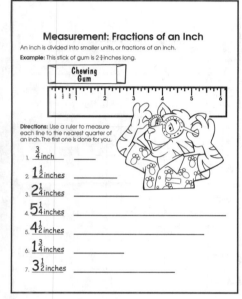

Directions: Use a ruler to measure each line to the nearest quarter of an inch. The first one is done for you.

1. $\frac{3}{4}$ inch _____
2. $1\frac{1}{2}$ inches _____
3. $2\frac{1}{4}$ inches _____
4. $5\frac{1}{4}$ inches _____
5. $4\frac{1}{2}$ inches _____
6. $1\frac{3}{4}$ inches _____
7. $3\frac{1}{2}$ inches _____

249

Measurement: Fractions of an Inch

Directions: Use a ruler to measure to the nearest quarter of an inch.

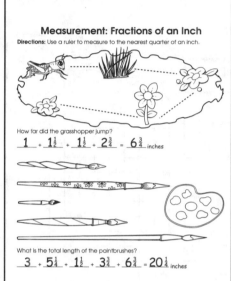

How far did the grasshopper jump?

$1 + 1\frac{1}{2} + 1\frac{1}{2} + 2\frac{3}{4} = 6\frac{3}{4}$ inches

What is the total length of the paintbrushes?

$3 + 5\frac{1}{4} + 1\frac{1}{2} + 3\frac{3}{4} + 6\frac{3}{4} = 20\frac{1}{4}$ inches

250

Measurement: Foot, Yard, Mile

Directions: Choose the measure of distance you would use for each object.

1 foot = 12 inches
1 yard = 3 feet
1 mile = 1,760 yards or 5,280 feet

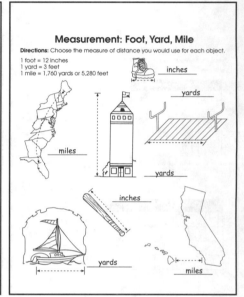

inches

yards

miles

yards

inches

yards

miles

251

Geometry: Perimeter

The **perimeter** is the distance around an object. Find the perimeter by adding the lengths of all the sides.

Directions: Find the perimeter for each object (ft. = feet).

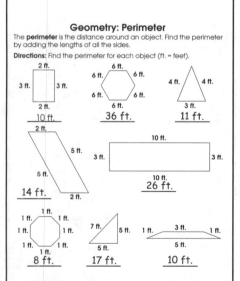

2 ft. rectangle: **10 ft.**
6 ft. hexagon: **36 ft.**
4 ft. triangle: **11 ft.**
parallelogram: **14 ft.**
10 ft. rectangle: **26 ft.**
octagon: **8 ft.**
triangle: **17 ft.**
10 ft.

252

Measurement: Perimeter

Directions: Find the perimeter of the following figures.

Examples:

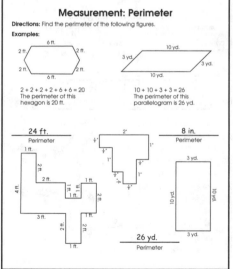

$2 + 2 + 2 + 2 + 6 + 6 = 20$
The perimeter of this hexagon is 20 ft.

$10 + 10 + 3 + 3 = 26$
The perimeter of this parallelogram is 26 yd.

24 ft. Perimeter

8 in. Perimeter

26 yd. Perimeter

253

Measurement: Perimeter and Area

Perimeter is the distance around a figure. It is found by adding the lengths of the sides. **Area** is the number of square units needed to cover a region. The area is found by adding the number of square units. A unit can be any unit of measure. Most often, inches, feet or yards are used.

Directions: Find the perimeter and area for each figure. The first one is done for you. ☐ = 1 square unit

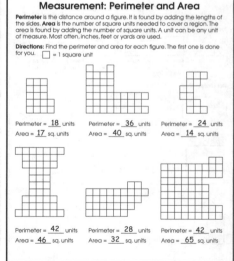

Perimeter = **18** units
Area = **17** sq. units

Perimeter = **36** units
Area = **40** sq. units

Perimeter = **24** units
Area = **14** sq. units

Perimeter = **42** units
Area = **46** sq. units

Perimeter = **28** units
Area = **32** sq. units

Perimeter = **42** units
Area = **65** sq. units

254

Answer Key

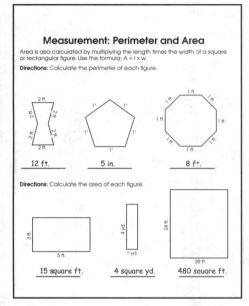

Measurement: Perimeter and Area

Area is also calculated by multiplying the length times the width of a square or rectangular figure. Use the formula: A = l x w.

Directions: Calculate the perimeter of each figure.

12 ft.   5 in.   8 ft.

Directions: Calculate the area of each figure.

15 square ft.   4 square yd.   480 square ft.

255

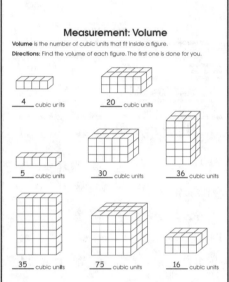

Measurement: Volume

Volume is the number of cubic units that fit inside a figure.

Directions: Find the volume of each figure. The first one is done for you.

4 cubic units   20 cubic units

5 cubic units   30 cubic units   36 cubic units

35 cubic units   75 cubic units   16 cubic units

256

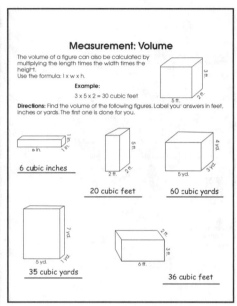

Measurement: Volume

The volume of a figure can also be calculated by multiplying the length times the width times the height.
Use the formula: l x w x h.

Example:
3 x 5 x 2 = 30 cubic feet

Directions: Find the volume of the following figures. Label your answers in feet, inches or yards. The first one is done for you.

6 cubic inches

20 cubic feet   60 cubic yards

35 cubic yards

36 cubic feet

257

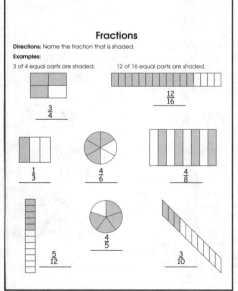

Fractions

Directions: Name the fraction that is shaded.

Examples:

3 of 4 equal parts are shaded.   12 of 16 equal parts are shaded.

$\frac{12}{16}$

$\frac{3}{4}$

$\frac{1}{3}$ $\frac{4}{6}$ $\frac{4}{8}$

$\frac{5}{12}$ $\frac{4}{5}$ $\frac{3}{10}$

258

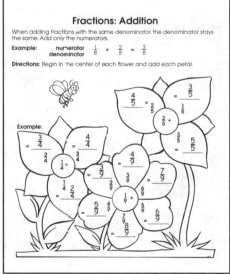

Fractions: Addition

When adding fractions with the same denominator, the denominator stays the same. Add only the numerators.

Example: numerator $\frac{1}{8}$ + $\frac{2}{8}$ = $\frac{3}{8}$ denominator

Directions: Begin in the center of each flower and add each petal.

259

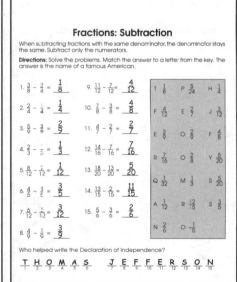

Fractions: Subtraction

When subtracting fractions with the same denominator, the denominator stays the same. Subtract only the numerators.

Directions: Solve the problems. Match the answer to a letter from the key. The answer is the name of a famous American.

1. $\frac{3}{8} - \frac{2}{8} = \frac{1}{8}$ 9. $\frac{11}{12} - \frac{7}{12} = \frac{4}{12}$

2. $\frac{2}{4} - \frac{1}{4} = \frac{1}{4}$ 10. $\frac{7}{8} - \frac{3}{8} = \frac{4}{8}$

3. $\frac{5}{9} - \frac{3}{9} = \frac{2}{9}$ 11. $\frac{4}{7} - \frac{2}{7} = \frac{2}{7}$

4. $\frac{2}{3} - \frac{1}{3} = \frac{1}{3}$ 12. $\frac{14}{16} - \frac{7}{16} = \frac{7}{16}$

5. $\frac{8}{12} - \frac{7}{12} = \frac{1}{12}$ 13. $\frac{18}{20} - \frac{13}{20} = \frac{5}{20}$

6. $\frac{4}{9} - \frac{1}{9} = \frac{3}{9}$ 14. $\frac{15}{15} - \frac{4}{15} = \frac{11}{15}$

7. $\frac{6}{12} - \frac{3}{12} = \frac{3}{12}$ 15. $\frac{5}{6} - \frac{3}{6} = \frac{2}{6}$

8. $\frac{4}{9} - \frac{1}{9} = \frac{3}{9}$

T $\frac{1}{8}$	P $\frac{5}{24}$	H $\frac{1}{4}$
F $\frac{4}{12}$	E $\frac{2}{7}$	J $\frac{3}{12}$
E $\frac{5}{9}$	O $\frac{2}{9}$	F $\frac{4}{8}$
R $\frac{7}{16}$	O $\frac{3}{9}$	Y $\frac{8}{20}$
Q $\frac{1}{32}$	M $\frac{1}{3}$	S $\frac{5}{20}$
A $\frac{1}{12}$	R $\frac{4}{5}$	S $\frac{3}{6}$
N $\frac{2}{7}$	O $\frac{1}{8}$	

Who helped write the Declaration of Independence?

T H O M A S   J E F F E R S O N
1 2 3 4 5 6   7 8 9 10 11 12 13 14 15

260

Answer Key

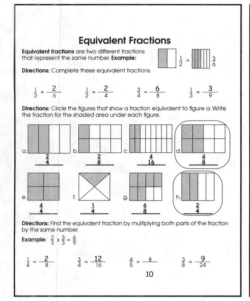

Equivalent Fractions

Equivalent fractions are two different fractions that represent the same number. **Example:** $\frac{1}{2} = \frac{3}{6}$

Directions: Complete these equivalent fractions.

$\frac{1}{3} = \frac{2}{6}$ $\frac{1}{2} = \frac{2}{4}$ $\frac{3}{4} = \frac{6}{8}$ $\frac{1}{3} = \frac{3}{9}$

Directions: Circle the figures that show a fraction equivalent to figure a. Write the fraction for the shaded area under each figure.

a. $\frac{2}{4}$ b. $\frac{2}{8}$ c. $\frac{4}{16}$ d. $\frac{4}{8}$

e. $\frac{4}{4}$ f. $\frac{1}{4}$ g. $\frac{6}{8}$ h. $\frac{2}{4}$

Directions: Find the equivalent fraction by multiplying both parts of the fraction by the same number.

Example: $\frac{2}{3} \times \frac{3}{3} = \frac{6}{9}$

$\frac{1}{4} = \frac{2}{8}$ $\frac{3}{4} = \frac{12}{16}$ $\frac{4}{5} = \frac{8}{10}$ $\frac{3}{8} = \frac{9}{24}$

261

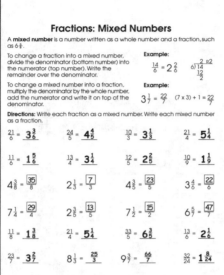

Fractions: Mixed Numbers

A **mixed number** is a number written as a whole number and a fraction, such as $6\frac{1}{4}$.

To change a fraction into a mixed number, divide the denominator (bottom number) into the numerator (top number). Write the remainder over the denominator.

Example: $\frac{14}{6} = 2\frac{2}{6}$

To change a mixed number into a fraction, multiply the denominator by the whole number, add the numerator and write it on top of the denominator.

Example: $3\frac{1}{7} = \frac{22}{7}$ $(7 \times 3) + 1 = \frac{22}{7}$

Directions: Write each fraction as a mixed number. Write each mixed number as a fraction.

$\frac{21}{6} = 3\frac{3}{6}$ $\frac{24}{5} = 4\frac{4}{5}$ $\frac{10}{3} = 3\frac{1}{3}$ $\frac{21}{4} = 5\frac{1}{4}$

$\frac{11}{6} = 1\frac{5}{6}$ $\frac{13}{4} = 3\frac{1}{4}$ $\frac{12}{5} = 2\frac{2}{5}$ $\frac{10}{9} = 1\frac{1}{9}$

$4\frac{3}{8} = \frac{35}{8}$ $2\frac{1}{3} = \frac{7}{3}$ $4\frac{3}{5} = \frac{23}{5}$ $3\frac{4}{6} = \frac{22}{6}$

$7\frac{1}{4} = \frac{29}{4}$ $2\frac{3}{5} = \frac{13}{5}$ $7\frac{1}{2} = \frac{15}{2}$ $6\frac{5}{7} = \frac{47}{7}$

$\frac{11}{8} = 1\frac{3}{8}$ $\frac{21}{4} = 5\frac{1}{4}$ $\frac{33}{5} = 6\frac{3}{5}$ $\frac{13}{6} = 2\frac{1}{6}$

$\frac{23}{7} = 3\frac{2}{7}$ $8\frac{1}{3} = \frac{25}{3}$ $9\frac{3}{7} = \frac{66}{7}$ $\frac{32}{24} = 1\frac{8}{24}$

262

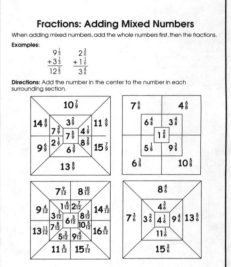

Fractions: Adding Mixed Numbers

When adding mixed numbers, add the whole numbers first, then the fractions.

Examples:

$\begin{array}{r} 9\frac{1}{8} \\ +3\frac{1}{8} \\ \hline 12\frac{2}{8} \end{array}$ $\begin{array}{r} 2\frac{2}{8} \\ +1\frac{1}{8} \\ \hline 3\frac{3}{8} \end{array}$

Directions: Add the number in the center to the number in each surrounding section.

263

Fractions: Subtracting Mixed Numbers

When subtracting mixed numbers, subtract the fractions first, then the whole numbers.

Directions: Subtract the mixed numbers. The first one is done for you.

$\begin{array}{r} 7\frac{3}{8} \\ -4\frac{2}{8} \\ \hline 3\frac{1}{8} \end{array}$ $\begin{array}{r} 4\frac{5}{6} \\ -3\frac{1}{6} \\ \hline 1\frac{4}{6} \end{array}$ $\begin{array}{r} 4\frac{1}{2} \\ -3 \\ \hline 1\frac{1}{2} \end{array}$ $\begin{array}{r} 7\frac{3}{8} \\ -6\frac{1}{8} \\ \hline 1\frac{2}{8} \end{array}$ $\begin{array}{r} 6\frac{6}{8} \\ -1\frac{1}{8} \\ \hline 5\frac{5}{8} \end{array}$ $\begin{array}{r} 5\frac{3}{4} \\ -1\frac{1}{4} \\ \hline 4\frac{2}{4} \end{array}$

$\begin{array}{r} 5\frac{2}{3} \\ -3\frac{1}{3} \\ \hline 2\frac{1}{3} \end{array}$ $\begin{array}{r} 4\frac{6}{10} \\ -3\frac{1}{10} \\ \hline 1\frac{5}{10} \end{array}$ $\begin{array}{r} 9\frac{8}{9} \\ -4\frac{3}{9} \\ \hline 5\frac{5}{9} \end{array}$ $\begin{array}{r} 7\frac{2}{3} \\ -6\frac{1}{3} \\ \hline 1\frac{1}{3} \end{array}$ $\begin{array}{r} 7\frac{3}{8} \\ -5 \\ \hline 2\frac{3}{8} \end{array}$ $\begin{array}{r} 9\frac{8}{10} \\ -6\frac{3}{10} \\ \hline 3\frac{5}{10} \end{array}$

$\begin{array}{r} 4\frac{6}{9} \\ -2 \\ \hline 2\frac{7}{9} \end{array}$ $\begin{array}{r} 6\frac{8}{8} \\ -5\frac{4}{8} \\ \hline 1\frac{4}{8} \end{array}$ $\begin{array}{r} 6\frac{3}{4} \\ -3\frac{1}{4} \\ \hline 3\frac{2}{4} \end{array}$ $\begin{array}{r} 5\frac{9}{7} \\ -2\frac{7}{7} \\ \hline 2\frac{5}{7} \end{array}$ $\begin{array}{r} 7\frac{9}{8} \\ -2\frac{7}{8} \\ \hline 5\frac{2}{8} \end{array}$

Sally needs $1\frac{1}{8}$ yards of cloth to make a dress. She has $4\frac{4}{8}$ yards. How much cloth will be left over? $3\frac{3}{8}$

264

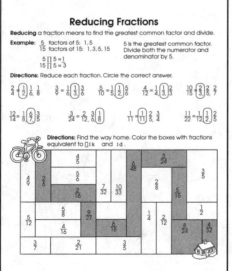

Reducing Fractions

Reducing a fraction means to find the greatest common factor and divide.

Example: factors of 5: 1, 5
factors of 15: 1, 3, 5, 15
5 is the greatest common factor.
Divide both the numerator and denominator by 5.

$\frac{5}{15} \div 5 = 1$
$\frac{5}{15} \div 5 = 3$

Directions: Reduce each fraction. Circle the correct answer.

Directions: Find the way home. Color the boxes with fractions equivalent to $\frac{1}{1k}$ and $\frac{1}{d}$.

265

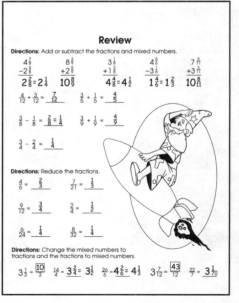

Review

Directions: Add or subtract the fractions and mixed numbers.

$\begin{array}{r} 4\frac{7}{8} \\ -2\frac{6}{8} \\ \hline 2\frac{2}{8}=2\frac{1}{4} \end{array}$ $\begin{array}{r} 8\frac{3}{8} \\ +2\frac{5}{8} \\ \hline 10\frac{8}{8} \end{array}$ $\begin{array}{r} 3\frac{1}{6} \\ +1\frac{3}{6} \\ \hline 4\frac{4}{6}=4\frac{2}{3} \end{array}$ $\begin{array}{r} 4\frac{5}{6} \\ -3\frac{1}{6} \\ \hline 1\frac{4}{6}=1\frac{2}{3} \end{array}$ $\begin{array}{r} 7\frac{11}{11} \\ +3\frac{11}{11} \\ \hline 10\frac{8}{11} \end{array}$

$\frac{4}{12} + \frac{3}{12} = \frac{7}{12}$ $\frac{3}{5} + \frac{1}{5} = \frac{4}{5}$

$\frac{3}{8} - \frac{1}{8} = \frac{2}{8} = \frac{1}{4}$ $\frac{3}{9} + \frac{1}{9} = \frac{4}{9}$

$\frac{3}{4} - \frac{2}{4} = \frac{1}{4}$

Directions: Reduce the fractions.

$\frac{4}{6} = \frac{2}{3}$ $\frac{7}{21} = \frac{1}{3}$

$\frac{9}{12} = \frac{3}{4}$ $\frac{2}{4} = \frac{1}{2}$

$\frac{6}{24} = \frac{1}{4}$ $\frac{8}{32} = \frac{1}{4}$

Directions: Change the mixed numbers to fractions and the fractions to mixed numbers.

$3\frac{1}{3} = \frac{10}{3}$ $\frac{14}{4} = 3\frac{2}{4} = 3\frac{1}{2}$ $\frac{26}{6} = 4\frac{2}{6} = 4\frac{1}{3}$ $3\frac{7}{12} = \frac{43}{12}$ $\frac{22}{7} = 3\frac{1}{7}$

266

Answer Key

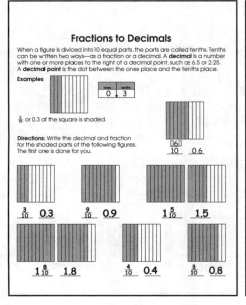

Fractions to Decimals

When a figure is divided into 10 equal parts, the parts are called tenths. Tenths can be written two ways—as a fraction or a decimal. A **decimal** is a number with one or more places to the right of a decimal point, such as 6.5 or 2.25. A **decimal point** is the dot between the ones place and the tenths place.

Examples:

ones	tenths
0	3

$\frac{3}{10}$ or 0.3 of the square is shaded.

Directions: Write the decimal and fraction for the shaded parts of the following figures. The first one is done for you.

$\frac{6}{10}$ 0.6

$\frac{3}{10}$ 0.3 $\frac{9}{10}$ 0.9 $1\frac{5}{10}$ 1.5

$1\frac{8}{10}$ 1.8 $\frac{4}{10}$ 0.4 $\frac{3}{10}$ 0.8

267

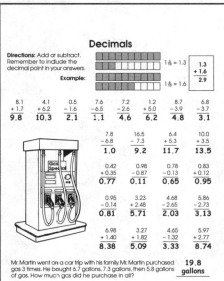

Decimals

Directions: Add or subtract. Remember to include the decimal point in your answers.

Example:

$1\frac{3}{10} = 1.3$

$1\frac{6}{10} = 1.6$

$\begin{array}{r} 1.3 \\ +1.6 \\ \hline 2.9 \end{array}$

| $\begin{array}{r}8.1\\+1.7\\\hline9.8\end{array}$ | $\begin{array}{r}4.1\\+6.2\\\hline10.3\end{array}$ | $\begin{array}{r}0.5\\-1.6\\\hline2.1\end{array}$ | $\begin{array}{r}7.6\\-6.5\\\hline1.1\end{array}$ | $\begin{array}{r}7.2\\-2.6\\\hline4.6\end{array}$ | $\begin{array}{r}1.2\\+5.0\\\hline6.2\end{array}$ | $\begin{array}{r}8.7\\-3.9\\\hline4.8\end{array}$ | $\begin{array}{r}6.8\\-3.7\\\hline3.1\end{array}$ |

| $\begin{array}{r}7.8\\-6.8\\\hline1.0\end{array}$ | $\begin{array}{r}16.5\\-7.3\\\hline9.2\end{array}$ | $\begin{array}{r}6.4\\+5.3\\\hline11.7\end{array}$ | $\begin{array}{r}10.0\\+3.5\\\hline13.5\end{array}$ |

| $\begin{array}{r}0.42\\+0.35\\\hline0.77\end{array}$ | $\begin{array}{r}0.98\\-0.87\\\hline0.11\end{array}$ | $\begin{array}{r}0.78\\-0.13\\\hline0.65\end{array}$ | $\begin{array}{r}0.83\\+0.12\\\hline0.95\end{array}$ |

| $\begin{array}{r}0.95\\-0.14\\\hline0.81\end{array}$ | $\begin{array}{r}3.23\\+2.48\\\hline5.71\end{array}$ | $\begin{array}{r}4.68\\-2.65\\\hline2.03\end{array}$ | $\begin{array}{r}5.86\\-2.73\\\hline3.13\end{array}$ |

| $\begin{array}{r}6.98\\+1.40\\\hline8.38\end{array}$ | $\begin{array}{r}3.27\\+1.82\\\hline5.09\end{array}$ | $\begin{array}{r}4.65\\-1.32\\\hline3.33\end{array}$ | $\begin{array}{r}5.97\\+2.77\\\hline8.74\end{array}$ |

Mr. Martin went on a car trip with his family. Mr. Martin purchased gas 3 times. He bought 6.7 gallons, 7.3 gallons, then 5.8 gallons of gas. How much gas did he purchase in all?   **19.8 gallons**

268

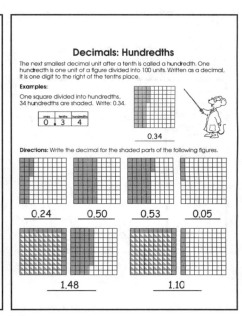

Decimals: Hundredths

The next smallest decimal unit after a tenth is called a hundredth. One hundredth is one unit of a figure divided into 100 units. Written as a decimal, it is one digit to the right of the tenths place.

Examples:

One square divided into hundredths, 34 hundredths are shaded. Write: 0.34.

ones	tenths	hundredths
0	3	4

0.34

Directions: Write the decimal for the shaded parts of the following figures.

0.24   0.50   0.53   0.05

1.48   1.10

269

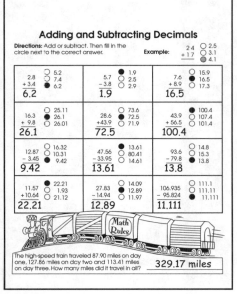

Adding and Subtracting Decimals

Directions: Add or subtract. Then fill in the circle next to the correct answer.

Example:
$\begin{array}{r}24\\+17\\\hline\end{array}$ ○ 2.5 ○ 3.1 ● 4.1

$\begin{array}{r}2.8\\+3.4\\\hline6.2\end{array}$ ○5.2 ○7.4 ●6.2	$\begin{array}{r}5.7\\-3.8\\\hline1.9\end{array}$ ●1.9 ○2.5 ○2.9	$\begin{array}{r}7.6\\+8.9\\\hline16.5\end{array}$ ○15.9 ●16.5 ○17.3
$\begin{array}{r}16.3\\+9.8\\\hline26.1\end{array}$ ○25.11 ●26.1 ○26.01	$\begin{array}{r}28.6\\+43.9\\\hline72.5\end{array}$ ○73.6 ●72.5 ○71.9	$\begin{array}{r}43.9\\+56.5\\\hline100.4\end{array}$ ●100.4 ○107.4 ○101.4
$\begin{array}{r}12.87\\-3.45\\\hline9.42\end{array}$ ○16.32 ○10.31 ●9.42	$\begin{array}{r}47.56\\-33.95\\\hline13.61\end{array}$ ●13.61 ○80.41 ○14.61	$\begin{array}{r}93.6\\-79.8\\\hline13.8\end{array}$ ○14.8 ○15.3 ●13.8
$\begin{array}{r}11.57\\+10.64\\\hline22.21\end{array}$ ●22.21 ○1.93 ○21.12	$\begin{array}{r}27.83\\-14.94\\\hline12.89\end{array}$ ○14.09 ●12.89 ○11.97	$\begin{array}{r}106.935\\-95.824\\\hline11.111\end{array}$ ○111.1 ○111.11 ●11.111

The high-speed train traveled 87.90 miles on day one, 127.86 miles on day two and 113.41 miles on day three. How many miles did it travel in all?   **329.17 miles**

270

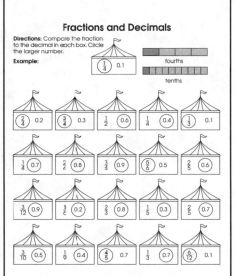

Fractions and Decimals

Directions: Compare the fraction to the decimal in each box. Circle the larger number.

Example:

$\frac{1}{4}$ 0.1

fourths

tenths

$\frac{2}{4}$ ⊙0.2	$\frac{3}{4}$ ⊙0.3	$\frac{1}{2}$ ⊙0.6	$\frac{1}{4}$ ⊙0.4	$\frac{1}{3}$ ⊙0.1
$\frac{1}{4}$ ⊙0.7	$\frac{1}{2}$ ⊙0.8	$\frac{3}{4}$ ⊙0.9	$\frac{5}{9}$ ⊙0.5	$\frac{2}{9}$ ⊙0.6
$\frac{3}{12}$ ⊙0.9	$\frac{1}{5}$ ⊙0.5	$\frac{2}{3}$ ⊙0.5	$\frac{1}{5}$ ⊙0.5	$\frac{2}{5}$ ⊙0.7
$\frac{3}{10}$ ⊙0.5	$\frac{1}{9}$ ⊙0.4	$\frac{4}{5}$ ⊙0.7	$\frac{1}{3}$ ⊙0.7	$\frac{6}{12}$ ⊙0.1

271

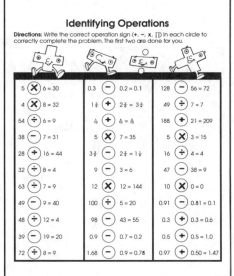

Identifying Operations

Directions: Write the correct operation sign (+, −, x, ÷) in each circle to correctly complete the problem. The first two are done for you.

5 Ⓧ 6 = 30	0.3 ⊖ 0.2 = 0.1	128 ⊖ 56 = 72
4 Ⓧ 8 = 32	$1\frac{1}{9}$ ⊕ $2\frac{2}{9}$ = $3\frac{3}{9}$	49 ⊕ 7 = 7
54 ÷ 6 = 9	$\frac{1}{16}$ ⊕ $\frac{7}{16}$ = $\frac{8}{16}$	188 ⊕ 21 = 209
38 ⊖ 7 = 31	5 Ⓧ 7 = 35	5 Ⓧ 3 = 15
28 ⊕ 16 = 44	$3\frac{3}{4}$ ⊖ $2\frac{2}{4}$ = $1\frac{1}{4}$	16 ÷ 4 = 4
32 ÷ 8 = 4	9 ⊖ 3 = 6	47 ⊖ 38 = 9
63 ÷ 7 = 9	12 Ⓧ 12 = 144	10 Ⓧ 0 = 0
49 ⊖ 9 = 40	100 ÷ 5 = 20	0.91 ⊖ 0.81 = 0.1
48 ÷ 12 = 4	98 ⊖ 43 = 55	0.3 ⊕ 0.3 = 0.6
39 ⊖ 19 = 20	0.9 ⊖ 0.7 = 0.2	0.5 ⊕ 0.5 = 1.0
72 ÷ 8 = 9	1.68 ⊖ 0.9 = 0.78	0.97 ⊕ 0.50 = 1.47

272

Identifying Operations

Directions: Solve the problems. Circle the letter with the correct answer. Write the letters in order to read the message.

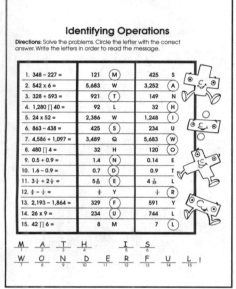

1. 348 − 227 =	121	(M)	425	S
2. 542 × 6 =	5,683	W	3,252	(A)
3. 328 + 593 =	921	(T)	149	N
4. 1,280 ∏ 40 =	92	L	32	(H)
5. 24 × 52 =	2,386	W	1,248	(I)
6. 863 − 438 =	425	(S)	234	U
7. 4,586 + 1,097 =	3,489	Q	5,683	(W)
8. 480 ∏ 4 =	32	H	120	(O)
9. 0.5 + 0.9 =	1.4	(N)	0.14	E
10. 1.6 − 0.9 =	0.7	(D)	0.9	T
11. $3\frac{1}{7} + 2\frac{1}{7}$ =	$5\frac{2}{7}$	(E)	$4\frac{7}{10}$	L
12. $\frac{5}{7} - \frac{1}{7}$ =	$\frac{4}{7}$	Y	$\frac{6}{7}$	(R)
13. 2,193 − 1,864 =	329	(F)	591	Y
14. 26 × 9 =	234	(U)	744	L
15. 42 ∏ 6 =	8	M	7	(L)

M A T H I S
1 2 3 4 5 6

W O N D E R F U L !
7 8 9 10 11 12 13 14 15

273

Review

Directions: Add or subtract to find the answers.

Bill jumped 28.5 feet. Jim jumped 27.3 feet. How much farther did Bill jump than Jim? — **1.2 feet**

Sue threw the discus 86.4 feet. Julie threw the discus 93.8 feet. How much farther did Julie throw the discus than Sue? — **7.4 feet**

Kim, Monica and Kelly swam on the same team in the butterfly relay race. Their individual times were 32.8 seconds, 29.9 seconds and 31.7 seconds. The winning team's time was 93.5 seconds. Did Kim, Monica and Kelly swim the fastest race? — **yes**

Jake's times for the 100-meter dash were 10.1 seconds, 12.5 seconds and 11.8 seconds. What was his total time? — **34.4**

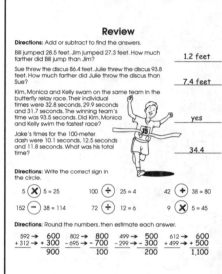

Directions: Write the correct sign in the circle.

5 (✗) 5 = 25   100 (÷) 25 = 4   42 (+) 38 = 80

152 (−) 38 = 114   72 (÷) 12 = 6   9 (✗) 5 = 45

Directions: Round the numbers, then estimate each answer.

592 → 600	802 → 800	499 → 500	612 → 600
+ 312 → + 300	− 695 → − 700	− 299 → − 300	+ 499 → + 500
900	100	200	1,100

274

Magic Squares

Directions: Some of the number squares below are "magic" and some are not. Squares that add up to the same number horizontally, vertically and diagonally are "magic." Add the numbers in each square to discover which ones are "magic."

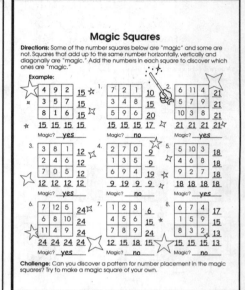

Example:

4	9	2	**15**
3	5	7	**15**
8	1	6	**15**
15	**15**	**15**	**15**

Magic? **yes**

1.
7	2	1	**10**
3	4	8	**15**
5	9	6	**20**
15	**15**	**15**	**17**

Magic? **no**

2.
6	11	4	**21**
5	7	9	**21**
10	3	8	**21**
21	**21**	**21**	**21**

Magic? **yes**

3.
3	8	1	**12**
2	4	6	**12**
7	0	5	**12**
12	**12**	**12**	**12**

Magic? **yes**

4.
2	7	0	**9**
1	3	5	**9**
6	4	9	**19**
9	**19**	**9**	**9**

Magic? **no**

5.
5	10	3	**18**
4	6	8	**18**
9	2	7	**18**
18	**18**	**18**	**18**

Magic? **yes**

6.
7	12	5	**24**
6	8	10	**24**
11	4	9	**24**
24	**24**	**24**	**24**

Magic? **yes**

7.
1	2	3	**6**
4	5	6	**15**
7	8	9	**24**
12	**15**	**18**	**15**

Magic? **no**

8.
6	7	4	**17**
1	5	9	**15**
8	3	2	**13**
15	**15**	**15**	**15**

Magic? **no**

Challenge: Can you discover a pattern for number placement in the magic squares? Try to make a magic square of your own.

275

Geometric Coloring

Directions: Color the geometric shapes in the box below.

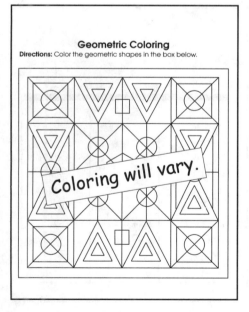

Coloring will vary.

276